Other books by Charles Cuno Lehrmann:

**The Jewish Element in French Literature**
**Heinrich Heine, Kaempfer und Dichter**
**Bergsonisme et Judaïsme**
**Stacheldraht um Jacobs Zelte**
**La Communauté Juive de Luxembourg** (with
Preface by Prime Minister Pierre Frieden)
**L'Ame luxembourgeoise** (with Preface by the
Minister of Education)

# Jewish Influences
## on
## European Thought

### *Charles C. Lehrmann*

Translated from the French by GEORGE KLIN
and from the German by VICTOR CARPENTER

Rutherford • Madison • Teaneck
FAIRLEIGH DICKINSON UNIVERSITY PRESS
London: ASSOCIATED UNIVERSITY PRESSES

© 1976 by Associated University Presses, Inc.

Associated University Presses, Inc.
Cranbury, New Jersey 08512

Associated University Presses
108 New Bond Street
London W1Y OQX, England

**Library of Congress Cataloging in Publication Data**

Lehrmann, Chanan.
    Jewish influences on European thought.
    1. Civilization—Jewish influences. 2. Jews in literature 3. Jewish
literature—History and criticism. I. Title.
DS113.L37                914'.03                72-3264
ISBN 0-8386-7908-0

# Dedication

To my parents, who were deported and disappeared
somewhere in Poland.

They were very simple people, not to say humble people, without
social ambitions, without any other earthly pretensions than to lead
an honorable life, according to the letter and the spirit of the Ten
Commandments, and to teach these principles to their children. My
father, as the name indicates, came from a long line of scholars and
masters of the Talmud. But he did not think it proper to exploit his
knowledge and earned his living and that of his large family as a
small businessman, always satisfied with what the day brought him,
because he observed the words of the Psalmist: "Praised be the
Lord, day unto day." His major concern was to be able to set aside
a few hours every day for the study of the Law, and to teach it personally to his children. Didn't the Bible say: "You will teach it to
thy children"? Yourself, not by hiring a teacher. This was his ideal
and his character. His touching sincerity went hand in hand with a
profound kindness and an irrepressible sense of humor that never
abandoned him, even during the darkest moments of his life.

Furthermore, he could lean on a wife whose vitality, courage, in-
genuity in daily life, selflessness, and devotion were proverbial. The

life of this woman, small in size, and of delicate health, but alert and endowed with inexhaustible energy, has been enshrined in the hearts of all those who knew her. Raising her nine children, one more complex than the other, was nothing. Supporting them during the First World War after their father was drafted was not the whole story.

She still found time to help her neighbors, succor the sick, console the poor, and not merely with words. She translated her charity into deeds that she readily deprecated with an amusing comment. When she was confronted on Friday eve, with an unexpected guest, or even several, she greeted them with a smile and a soothing remark: "Another guest? It's just one more spoonful of water in the soup." Her faith was of the kind that moves mountains, going as far as what we intellectuals disdainfully call fanaticism. Was it not fanaticism to refuse to stop lighting a candle in the middle of the First World War for each of her children on the eve of the Sabbath? She always managed to find these candles that had become extremely rare. Each time, at the end of the symbolic ceremony, her heart was solaced by the renewed alliance with God over the fate of her family. This woman was a torrent of love whose source was God. This torrent became irresistible when the life of one of her children was at stake, even to the head of a concentration camp. For when a son was imprisoned, she managed to free him, without money, without connections, through her tears alone. When the two old people were deported to Poland together with their youngest daughter, they succeeded in getting her out of the vast cemetery that wretched land had become. God respected the alliance concluded over the Sabbath candles.

My parents were able to accomplish the task of blessing their children by teaching them moral values and sending them to a safe haven, although scattered to the four corners of the earth. That was the ultimate consolation of their tragic destiny. At the end they remained alone, cast away in the basement of a factory, subsisting on a few potatoes and an occasional package, perhaps one out of five that were sent to them from the other side of the world. They were kept alive only by the hope of one day being reunited with their family.

Their sufferings continued. The winter of 1941-42, the last before the great massacre, reduced them to a desperate plight, without clothes, without heat, without food. Once, out of the depth of their prostration, they cried out with Job-like despair. But this was only a momentary weakness. It cast a light on their true situation, which they ordinarily concealed with reassuring words. Their last card, dated July 1942, briefly stated in a trembling handwriting that they had been deported to another place, that they had for the moment no personal address, but that we were not to worry about their fate. Since then, their cards have stopped coming; their tribulations have ceased. Like thousands of others, they have been freed from a long martyrdom under conditions that are now coming to light.

Their fate is only that of millions of others, and I apologize for having imposed on your patience for a private, and today, banal case. Our imagination, however, is incapable of grasping the horror represented by enormous numbers and reacts only to specific situations. By your indulgence in allowing me to honor the memory of my parents, you have honored the deportees of all nations.

A pious custom of the Jewish tradition dictates that on the anniversary of the death of a relative the Kaddish be recited, a majestic prayer praising the divine will. A candle is lit, symbolizing the effort transmitted from father to son to spread the spiritual light that will establish peace on earth. I will probably never know the date of this anniversary. But may today's lesson on the relationship of faith and reason be received in the spirit of that tradition, as a humble contribution to the collective enlightenment, thanks to the spark that my parents have deposited in me.

This text is drawn from the public lecture given November 9, 1944, at the University of Lausanne, inaugurating the course on Jewish Thought in the History of Philosophy.

# Contents

# Foreword

Although Mr. Lehrmann has already gained recognition through numerous publications, I am delighted to introduce the present (French) volume to the reader, as I have had the pleasure of being Mr. Lehrmann's teacher and of observing his spiritual development.

Mr. Charles Lehrmann was born in Poland, and his early childhood was spent in a strictly Jewish milieu, which did not prevent him from attending elementary school in Poland, and then graduating from secondary school and higher institutions in Germany and Switzerland. As for his parents, he has paid them a tribute that one cannot read without genuine emotion. "My parents," says he, "had no other ambition than to lead an honorable life, according to the letter and the spirit of the Ten Commandments, and to teach these principles to their children." The spiritual influence of such parents inevitably left an indelible mark on the children.

When he arrived in Lausanne as a student and emigré, Charles Lehrmann had to overcome many difficulties, both in surviving materially and in adjusting to his new environment. Among others, he had the problem of mastering the French language. No obstacle discouraged him. After his graduation, he held for several years the post of *privat-docent* in French-Jewish literature at the University of Lausanne. Recently he has been appointed *chargé de cours* for the teaching of Jewish thought at the same university. This appointment is thoroughly deserved. Mr. Lehrmann combines the gifts of

11

philosopher, poet, and apostle, and is, therefore, eminently qualified to fulfill the demands of his position.

As a philosopher, and as his first book *(Bergsonisme et judaïsme)* indicates, Mr. Lehrmann treats the questions that he tackles with a sure hand. For any given period he strives to distinguish and to classify the intellectual currents that characterize it, to outline their major traits, and to relate them to the circumstances that either favored or retarded their development. Finally, he attempts to bring out their significance, however controversial.

His panorama, for instance, of Arabic philosophy in the eleventh and twelfth centuries is lively and informative. The essential problems of the era (reason and faith, revelation, etc.) are lucidly expounded. The great philosophical orientations (Neoplatonism, Aristotelianism, ethical voluntarism, without forgetting the Kabbalah) are also clearly indicated. Furthermore, the influence of individual temperaments on philosophical solutions are rightly brought out, for a thinker's vision of reality differs according to whether he is an empiricist, a logician, or a mystic.

Besides his aptitude for speculative thinking, Mr. Lehrmann has an unquestionable poetical sense. It is noticeable in his essay entitled: "The Golden Age of Jewish Poetry." The quotations are aptly chosen. A good example is the analysis of the works of André Spire, in which the following lines are remarkably evocative: "For they live only of fever, my two ancient protectors, my anxiety and my sadness," and elsewhere, "But could my sated heart still live if you had castrated it of its splendid dream: this eternal Tomorrow that walks ahead of me."

Such quotations do not diminish the strength of the reasoning. On the contrary, they emphasize and reinforce it. Just as music, it seems to me, intensifies the meaning of the lines when a poem is sung, so does poetry elucidate and concretize the vigor of reasoning.

What is particularly striking in the present work is its apologetic character. Let us be clear about this point, however. While from the beginning of his career Mr. Lehrmann has felt entrusted with a mission, he never wanted to carry it out at the expense of truth.

One cannot question the legitimacy of his effort by claiming that before its dispersion the Jewish people contributed nothing to art, science, and philosophy. Who would dare deny that the Book of Job contains thoughts that are as much in the nature of philosophy as of religion? There is nothing surprising, therefore, that in a tolerant Spain the Jews in the Middle Ages were able, in cooperation with the Arabs, to construct a system of metaphysics that influenced European thought from the Middle Ages to the present.

No doubt, an apology always runs the danger of not being objective, but Mr. Lehrmann is aware of this danger, and he strives to remain faithful to historical and scientific truth. It is possible to disagree with his conclusions without doubting his well-founded convictions.

The spiritual debt that Europe incurred toward the Jews is undeniable, especially if we credit them with the appearance of Christianity. But, even disregarding this point, Mr. Lehrmann is perfectly right in demanding in the name of justice and human brotherhood a more equitable treatment for the Jews than to be forever the victims of massive deportations or bloody persecutions, as has been the case throughout history. More particularly, the treatment that Nazi Germany inflicted on the Jews must never be repeated, for its horror surpasses anything we can imagine.

It is true that the Jews are not the only victims of modern times. The spiritual integrity of many small states has been attacked, and they have been stripped of part or the whole of their territory, crushed by the economic, strategic, or ideologic interests of the Great Powers.

In the future, the organization of the world must be so constituted that it will be impossible for any country to carry out the wholesale expulsion or systematic massacre of its Jewish citizens.

In addition, in order to preserve their spiritual heritage, the Jews ought to be granted everywhere the right to have their institutions to strengthen the solidarity which, in spite of their dispersion through the world, binds them in the same way that ecumenism maintains Catholic unity, and federation that of the Protestants.

If Jewish unity is to be effected simply by a resurrection of the spirit and the language of their ancestors, a solution, it seems, can be found.

But, if the preservation of Jewish unity depends on the possession of a territory that is to be the earthly homeland of the Jewish people, a satisfactory solution is, as we well know, very difficult to envision.

I do not want to discuss this painful problem. On the subject of Zionism, about which Jews themselves disagree, I will only repeat that it has already scored a great success, that of reviving the Hebrew language of the Bible as a living language used in Israel in everyday life: at home, in school, and in the university.

Mr. Lehrmann does not overlook any of the psychological, historical, and political aspects of the questions outlined above. He describes in incisive terms the drama acted out in the soul of the modern Jew; he examines Mendelssohn who, even though he assimilated European culture, remained faithful to the religion of his forefathers; he analyzes the case of Heine, who renounced his Jewish allegiance and suffered because of it; finally, he studies the position of André Spire, for whom the restoration of the Jewish nation required the possession of Palestine.

Through the generous conviction with which he expounds his ideas, the honesty of his research, the broad-mindedness and loftiness of his views, Mr. Lehrmann pleads his cause persuasively and forces the reader to think about it. His publications will no doubt help to show the need to find a just and dignified solution to the spiritual and political problems of Israel.

Arnold Reymond
Member of the Institut de France

La Rouvenaz, Pully-Lausanne

# Preface

A previous work, *The Jewish Element in French Literature,*
contained under that title three themes: the works of Jewish authors;
the influence of the Bible, Jewish themes, and Jewish works on
Christian authors; and the political and religious problems that the
presence of Jews among Christians raised throughout history, and the
attitude of Christian authors in the face of these problems. These
three investigations, conducted simultaneously, allowed me to present
a review of French literature from the Middle Ages to the present
and to examine Jewish works in French from the beginning to the end.

This volume proceeds from the same inspiration, but instead of
dealing with a single nation I have broadened the scope to include
various countries. In a series of portraits and essays, which have already appeared in Swiss, German, and French journals, I have
studied the intellectual situation of the Jews, past and present, in its
relationship to the cultural and social milieux of Europe. It has been
my object to undertake an impartial and not an apologetic study,
just as in my work on French literature, in which Christians and
Jews, the latter not without disappointment, noted the absence of personal bias.

Nothing reassured me more about the objectivity of my method
than this observation from a newspaper, which reflects the prevailing
tone of all the critics: "This book, by a Jewish author, is written
with the greatest intellectual balance, and strives exclusively to estab-

lish objective facts, free from any apologetic tendency. Its pages reflect his quiet conviction that Judaism, after a period of shallowness, will meditate once again upon its values, and will survive the indescribable trials it is enduring. The pure light of this faith, its simplicity, indeed, its humility, have a gripping effect on the reader, who is immersed in a beautiful, clean, intellectual atmosphere." *(Die Weltwoche, Zurich)*

However, the following pages, written during Europe's most tragic hours, did not perhaps maintain the proper balance and scientific detachment. Never was Montaigne's dictum "Knowledge without conscience is nothing but the ruination of the soul" more pertinent than at present, and the author's conscience, revolted, shuddering at the sight of events, may sometimes have cried out in a way that jars the tranquil atmosphere of scholarship.

But as a whole, my works, following hard upon a period of hostile caricatures of Judaism, help to restore objectivity in the assessment of the spiritual role of Israel in Europe, and since this rehabilitation is a moral task as well as a scientific necessity, this study must take its place in the discipline known as moral sciences.

Western civilization is a rich and complex fabric, in which the Semitic thread is as important as the Hellenic thread. "Through Christianity," says the sociologist E. Troeltsch, "the Jewish doctrine became the soul of European life, even where the roots of our civilization remain unsuspected."[1]

It is, of course, less easy to trace the Jewish thread in the vast field of European thought than in the circumscribed field of, say, French literature. While the historian can still treat his subject in the form of a homogeneous synthesis, this approach does not lend itself to the infinitely complex network of European civilization. Consequently, I have presented a series of apparently independent essays, which, however, support and complete each other, in order to compose a broad portrait of the Jewish contribution to the formation of the European genius. That is the *leitmotiv*, the guiding thought, that insures the unity of the following chapters.

1. *Gesammelte Aufsätze zur Geistesgeschichte und Religions-soziologie*, vol. 4 (Tübingen, 1924).

However, the scope of the subject is sure to raise the objections of those who do not like a writer to depart from the beaten paths of scholarship. In our age of specialization it is no doubt preferable to stick to the strictly defined fields of scientific research. Still, the circumstances of these recent times have forced numerous scholars, spiritually or politically alienated, to exercise their talents in the margin of officially approved subjects. Those conditions, transformed into virtues, favor the choice of a theme such as the present one, which, if it is unrewarding for the author by forcing him to work outside the conventional framework without the support of a well-established scientific convention, yet remains worthy of attention. By undertaking a piece of research that is thorny and parsimonious in terms of material reward, I have been led by the hope of helping to cast some light on a series of problems surrounded by prejudice, of adding to our knowledge a few elements of truth humanized by a personal background not irrelevant to the subject under consideration. I have been encouraged by the unfailing understanding and kindness of several Jewish and Christian friends, among whom are the distinguished author of the Foreword, admirable master of a spiritualist philosophy exemplified in his daily life, and, above all, Graziella, my good spirit. May they find some satisfaction, if not in the success of the work, at least in the faith that inspired these pages and directed my efforts.

# Jewish Influences
# on European Thought

# 1

# Introduction

# Jewish Mediation through the Ages

To study the Jewish contribution to European thought means to examine, as Bossuet did for antiquity, the fate of the Jewish people from the vantage point of world history. Indeed, no other individual history has been involved to a greater extent in general history. I mean by this not the visible succession of wars, conquests, and treaties, but the progressive manifestations of civilization. The Jewish people participated in all its decisive phases. It witnessed Sumerian, Egyptian, Babylonian, Persian, Hellenic, Roman, Arabic, and the specific subject of this book—European civilization—in their successive hegemonies. Paradoxically, it is the Wandering Jew who constitutes the element of stability in the flow of human events. He was, through time and space, the link between people to such a degree that his history became itself a universal history. Let me elucidate this point.

It takes an effort to really understand the living conditions of the past. Today the world seems a whole in which all the parts seem inextricably bound. Wars are no longer localized. Social or political crises in one corner of the globe affect the whole fabric of mankind. The stock market in London or New York reacts immediately to disturbances in the public life of the most distant region, just as a seismograph records the slightest earthquake 10,000 miles away. Civilization, with its vices and virtues, has taken on a universal character, and even though allegiance to regional traditions has, luckily, not yet disappeared, the ways of life are alike in every latitude.

Similarly, the exchange of spiritual values takes place in normal times at a speed unknown in the past. The same philosophical problems are discussed in the seminars of the Sorbonne, in Istanbul, or in Philadelphia. Periodicals publish reports on all the special questions in all the sciences. Any new discovery in medicine is immediately known everywhere. The globe is today a universal organization that would be capable, according to Bergson's vision, of becoming "a machine for the creation of gods," evolving, if men were willing, toward its perfection.

Material conditions were not always so favorable to the creation of a civilization. Continents and nations were in the past quite distant and inaccessible. Each people was surrounded with its own Great Wall of China, and the fortunate birth of a culture in one region of the earth had only weak repercussions on the neighboring countries. The usual way of establishing international contacts was war, a fact that has inspired certain theoreticians to advocate war as a creative power and an agent of progress. It is so only indirectly. If the Roman legions did indeed build roads that subsequently connected the Mediterranean peoples, it was a defeated nation like Greece that used these roads: *Graecia capta ferum victorem cepit* (Greece, though conquered, conquered its fierce conqueror).

A more productive link was trade. The ancient traders were the true promoters of the cosmopolitan spirit. Their commercial centers laid the groundwork for spiritual centers. The life of the spirit no doubt follows laws *sui generis*. The fact remains that its development depends to a large extent on economic, political, and geographic conditions. It is not by accident that Athens, Alexandria, Marseilles, Naples, Genoa, and Venice became focal points of culture. Admittedly, the commercial spirit is not by itself creative, and not all commercial centers have assumed a cultural character.

War and trade have occasionally been positive factors in the propagation and exchange of spiritual values. This is not their inherent role. There have been periods of unreserved warfare that did not further civilization. Trade too was often unable to fill the voids that have marked the spiritual history of mankind. Peoples and continents have sometimes existed without mutual comprehension. Vital epochs would have sunk into the abyss of oblivion if another factor, almost fateful, had not intervened to link separate nations. Entire civilizations would have disappeared with the societies that created them if there had not existed then, without the means of modern technology, mediators for the transmission of human thought in space and time.

These were the Jews. They filled the gap left by war and commerce in the contact between nations. The historical and sociological conditions of their role are also a product of war and trade: of war because this stiff-necked people, eternal rebel, jealous of its national liberty, waged war against all the great powers of antiquity, Egypt, Assyria, Babylonia, and Rome; was militarily beaten; and suffered the consequences of physical defeat, deportation, and dispersion. The destruction of the first Temple led to expulsion into the countries of the Near East. The destruction of the second Temple led to exile into the countries of Western Europe. Titus sent hundreds of thousands of Jews to North Africa, to Italy, and to Spain, from where they reached other European countries. The historical and sociological conditions are a product of commerce because the Jews are *the* people credited with a special gift as brokers and traders, that is to say, as intermediaries for the exchange of merchandise and valuables. This the Jews *were,* whatever the reasons that encouraged or even conditioned the development of these activities. Let us note, however, that they were able to transfigure the conditions of their existence. The establishment of spiritual values was not an incidental result of their mercantile activities. They were consciously the brokers of a nobler merchandise, "the traveling salesmen of philosophy," as Renan called them. Several times, at critical junctures in the history of ideas, the Jew has intervened in a decisive manner as intermediary. By the uninterrupted continuity of his three-thousand-year history, this people was predestined to serve as a link between a succession of dissimilar nations.

This was the case during biblical times when Judaism gathered the best elements of ancient civilizations. Judaism is heir to the Semitic world in which it lived. It incorporated its best elements. While rejecting everything that conflicted with its concept of God, it assimilated, from the times of the migration of its patriarchs Abraham, Isaac, and Jacob to the first captivity on the banks of the Euphrates, this Semitic civilization. It then filled it with the thoughts of the prophets to make of it this grandiose system of ideas from which early Christianity launched its extraordinary destiny. The Bible is not only the history of monotheism, but the reflection and the reservoir of the civilization that the tribe of Israel encountered, rejected, or integrated into its monotheistic creed during the 2,000 years of its existence in the Orient. This book is the only monument that the Hebrews bequeathed us in remembrance of 2,000 years of spiritual struggles and victories. But all the treasures stored in it came back to life in every epoch and in every region, so that the West was impregnated by this Oriental book, not only in its religious manifestations, but also in its social structures. It modified, according to Ernest Troeltsch, "the soul of European life, even among those who are unaware of the roots of our civilization. Not that its spiritual activities are based exclusively on Hebrew influences, but they were directed, inspired, nourished, regulated by them." One thinker avers that for anti-Semitism to be consistent its defenders would have to relinquish all their social customs and adopt Chinese traditions.

Judaism, however, did not exhaust its energy by creating the Bible. It did not produce any other book of such magnitude and universal scope, but it continued as a dynamic creative agent. It joined with other movements; it inspired them and was inspired by them, and by virtue of its social situation spread the new seeds through the world. The Jews, present everywhere, are therefore present at the crystallization of new civilizations for which they perform maieutic services. When the splendid city of Alexandria was the center of Hellenic thought, a powerful Jewish colony played an active part in the city and increased its influence. Both Jewish and world history are honored by Philo. The Jews in his days were the undisputed authorities on Plato, but a Platonism enriched for the first time by biblical thought. Furthermore it is in Alexandria that the Bible, transcending its national limits, assumed a universal significance through the famous translation of the Seventy. This Greek translation made by Jewish scholars paved the way to monotheism in a pagan world.

When Palestine was still struggling desperately for its existence as a Jewish independent state, there were already synagogues in all the cities of the Empire. Even imperial Rome had welcomed about one hundred thousand Jews, in great part Roman citizens, who participated in the literary and artistic life of the metropolis. Flavius Josephus, during the Jewish War, went over to the Roman side and became the historiographer of one of the most dramatic episodes of the Empire. According to Juvenal, the aristocracy often met at the synagogues and adopted many Jewish rites such as circumcision. Society, tired of an empty paganism, had become Judaized to such a point that the Apostles found fertile soil for the propagation of the new doctrine. It is only since the Council of Nicaea that Christianity formally separated from its mother religion.

After the fall of the Roman Empire, Greco-Roman thought found a refuge at the court of the Caliphs Al Manseur and Haroun al Rachid. Near Bagdad was located Sura, which, together with Pumpeditha, welcomed the great Jewish academies where the Talmud, cornerstone of Judaism in exile, was composed. The doctors of the Talmud did not collaborate directly in the works of the Arabs, but the works of Jewish theologians, especially those of Saadia Gaon, were to have a great influence on the Jewish thinkers of Spain, and subsequently on Christian scholasticism. A more direct collaboration between Jews and Arabs was reserved to the Western phase of Islam. This era occupies a particularly brilliant place in the history of mankind, if we do not insist on giving precedence to bloody battles and vast territorial conquests.

The Spanish era is considered a golden age in history, the greatest accomplishment of the Jewish genius and the Semitic spirit since biblical times. Its characteristics reappeared: the incorporation of foreign ideas into the Jewish system, the eagerness to transmit its accumulated treasures to a burgeoning culture, performing for it a maieutic role. In Spain, Judaism accomplished the most successful synthesis between its own spirit and the surrounding society, while in France, Germany, and Poland, the equilibrium was broken by an excessive withdrawal, with the resultant ghetto mentality, or by a disproportionate assimilation. Spanish Judaism, while it cultivated the tradition stemming from the Bible, collaborated with the Arabs in all the contemporary fields of knowledge. It is a golden age, not only in Jewish history, second apex after the composition of the Old Testament, but also in the history of civilization, a shining example of what two different peoples can accomplish if they are imbued with a spirit of tolerance and mutual respect.

The role played by the Sephardic Jews transcends in importance all the other phases of postbiblical Judaism and therefore requires a close examination. They functioned in a most critical period of Western history. After the fall of the Roman Empire, Europe had lapsed back into barbarism, and offered a depressing spectacle. Savage hordes wandered over the ruins of the Greco-Roman world. Most of the Hellenic and Roman cities, with their academies, their theaters, their artistic treasures, and the organization of their civic life, had been destroyed. Europe was then prostrated in the long night of its history, a night that lasted over five centuries. Charlemagne's empire was organized only horizontally, not in depth. In the Roman cities of France and Italy that had escaped destruction and that had more or less retained their ancient political organization, the population mingled with the invaders and adopted the crude habits of the victors. Even the Church had to lower itself to the level of the barbarians to have an influence on them. True Christianity was known only to a small elite of the clergy. The masses may have believed in God, but they also feared the devil and demons. Violence and cruelty infiltrated the doctrine of mercy and grace. It is with means borrowed from the barbarians that the Church fought the enemies of her doctrine. It opposed with iron and fire all free expression of thought. As a consequence, all spiritual life was stifled. It is during that time that the Judeo-Arab reign held sway.

The expansion of Arab domination from the Orient to the West, across all of North Africa, displaced the spiritual and political center of gravity from Babylonia to Spain. Córdoba took the place of Bagdad, and gained even greater fame than its spiritual sister. Avenpace and Averroës were the intellectual princes of their time and renewed Aristotelian philosophy. All the sciences and the arts, including the medical arts, were encouraged by the enlightened caliphs, assisted by their Jewish viziers, Chasdai ibn Chaprout in Córdoba, Samuel ibn Nagdela in Granada, philosopher-diplomats carrying out Aristotle's dream. They founded academies of Jewish and profane learning. They utilized their political connections with the Orient to introduce with the diplomatic mail, so to speak, precious manuscripts, immediately translated into Hebrew and soon after into Latin. The Jews distinguished themselves simultaneously in rabbinical studies, philosophy, and logic. They studied mathematics, astronomy, geography, and European languages. Writing in Arabic as well as in modernized Hebrew, and later in Spanish, Ibn Gabirol, Maimonides, Judah Halevy, and Abrabanel, were certainly Masters of the Synagogue. Their prestige has survived to the present, thanks to their recasting of the legislation of the Talmud, their rationalistic and spiritualistic commentaries of the Bible, their liturgical creations, and their Zionides that echo their secret and most profound Jewish nostalgia. However, these same rabbinical authorities were writing philosophical works debated in Arab academies, and a little later, in those of Christendom, at a time when the Arab and Christian worlds were fighting with fanatical rage. Scholasticism reached its apogee about two generations after the great era of Judeo-Arabic thought. Its purpose was to reconcile science and faith. Up until then, the Church had demanded unconditional belief in dogma: *Credo quia absurdum* (I believe because it is absurd). Later the Church stopped requiring blind obedience from ignorant people and addressed itself to their intelligence: *Intellego et credo* (I understand and believe). The ideas of Judeo-Arabic philosophers were to be of great help to Christian philosophy, which was then only laying the foundation of a systematic philosophy.

A mysterious author, much admired and discussed in scholastic circles, was a certain Avencebrol or Avicebron. His *Source of Life,* with its theory of the divine will as the creative force of the universe, was greatly admired and violently attacked in the controversies between Thomists and Scotists. "His name and style are Arabic, but he must have been Christian." Guillaume of Auvergne had the right instinct when he placed him between an Arab and a Christian, but the description also symbolizes the role of intermediary of the Spanish Jew between Islam and Christianity. Modern philology has succeeded in identifying Avicebron with the Jewish poet and philosopher Ibn Gabirol.

Maimonides' fate was happier. His ideas were not only discussed, but largely accepted. The author of *The Guide for the Perplexed* had written this work to give his coreligionists, shaken in their beliefs by the assault of Aristotelian theories, some guidelines. It is obvious that his philosophy was to play a prominent role among Christians plagued by the same doubts. Thomas Aquinas leaned heavily on Maimonides on the questions of the relationship between faith and revelation, the attributes of God, Providence, Creation, and also in biblical exegesis, with the rationalization of the biblical concepts of orginal sin and punishment. Scholasticism, Christianity's new creation, was greatly indebted to Jewish thought and mediation, just as primitive Christianity was created throught the intermediary of Saint Paul, quondam Saul.

This spiritual mediation was supplemented, and perhaps superseded, by a concrete mediation between the Muslim and Christian worlds, which were then fighting fiercely and did not even know each other's language. If Greek was hardly known in Europe, Arabic was almost completely unknown. The Jews are by force of circumstances a polyglot people. Each branch speaks a different language, while all have in common the language of the Bible: Hebrew. This fact was not without importance for literature. When, toward the end of the Golden Age, the fanatical Almohades persecuted learning, burned books, and sometimes authors, the Jews had a simple way of protecting literary works: they copied Arabic writings in Hebrew script, and thus saved precious books right under the nose of the persecutors. Let us note that the Jews knew Arabic while the Arabs did not know Hebrew, and that they knew, as the case may be, Italian,

French, Latin, without reciprocity. The weak thus often have a more powerful weapon than the strong.

In this case, the Jews did not merely transcribe Arabic works into Hebrew letters, they translated them into Hebrew, and then into Latin. The classic land of translation was Provence, where conflicts rarely took a tragic turn. From there, famous translators spread their influence to Sicily and to Naples. Thus, men such as Tibbonides, Jacob Anatoli, and Kalonymus performed great services for European learning at its inception by translating philosophical, astronomical, and medical works. Literature as well benefited from the oriental inspiration transmitted by the Jews. Collections of fables appeared and were greeted with great interest, especially in France, where this genre was developed to the point of becoming, with La Fontaine, the most impeccable expression of the French spirit. The leaders in this medium were Rabbi Berachya, then other Jews, who, following the example of Saint Paul, left the national territory to intervene on the international stage: Jean de Capoue, and the author of the famous *Disciplina Clericalis,* Pierre Alphonse.

If, as a whole, the scope of the Jewish cultural mediation can be recognized only retrospectively, there is a field where the Jews' supremacy was acknowledged by their contemporaries: medicine. From the ninth century on, there existed a school of medicine at Narbonne. A branch of this institution was the medical academy of Montpellier, which became the center of medical science. The teaching was done in Arabic and Hebrew. In the twelfth century these languages were replaced by Latin and Provençal. The Jewish graduates of Montpellier were not only the doctors of popes and kings, but they also attempted to spread and popularize their science. When the Jewish contemporary of Dante, the poet and doctor Immanuel of Rome, wrote a satire of *The Divine Comedy,* he sent to hell not only the charlatans, but also Hippocrates himself, because he had kept his high calling a secret. If the Arabs developed medicine, the Jews applied it and transmitted it to Europe.

In Spain there were no longer Jews or Arabs. Their Most Catholic Majesties, Ferdinand and Isabella, after using the knowledge of the Hispanized Jews, completely restored Christianity to Spain. Torquemada undertook to light up his country's road to the future with living tapers. Some of the persecuted adopted the law and the faith of the stronger enemy and lived as disguised Jews, as *Marranos*. Others scattered to every port where Spanish ships docked. What had been called a "dream of flowers in the history of mankind" really seems to have been only a dream when one considers the material and spiritual poverty that prevails among the Arabs repatriated to North Africa. The stories that circulate among them about the great days in Andalusia are taken for one of the marvelous tales of *A Thousand and One Nights*. The Jews also took along the memories of a bygone era. For them, however, it did not die, but was transformed under their eyes, and with their help, in Italy, France, and Germany, into other forms of spiritual life. The Judeo-Arabic pre-Renaissance prepared the ground for the European Renaissance, a grandiose flowering of civilization whose momentum has been maintained until the present. The Renaissance was made possible by these liaison agents, who, according to Michelet, "were for a long time the only link between the East and the West, thus both frustrating fanaticism, Christian and Muslim, and keeping open permanent channels of commerce and enlightenment."

The decline of Spanish Judaism was a forerunner of the decline of Spain. For the Jews the sunset was immediately followed by a new dawn. The Abrabanels, father and son, symbolize for the time this law of Jewish history. The father, Isaac Abrabanel, talmudic scholar and minister of finance of Ferdinand of Aragon, left Spain with the main body of emigrés. His son, Juda Abrabanel, Italianized as Leone Ebreo, won fame in his new homeland, filled with spiritual excitement, for his *Dialoghi di amore,* which appealed to the idealistic aspirations of the men of the Renaissance, although these Platonic dialogues were visibly inspired by Jewish ideas. Or perhaps because of this, for the Jewish spiritual tradition, especially the Kabbalah, deeply fascinated the contemporary mind. Men hoped to find in it the formula of the mystic harmony between man and the universe. Thus Hebrew teachers were as prized as Greek teachers. Jewish scholars were appointed to honorable positions at the universities, whose curriculum corresponded to Rabelais's program: "I want you to learn languages to perfection, first Greek, then Latin, and finally Hebrew for the Holy Scriptures.''

In Eastern Europe the Jewish masses played the role of intermediary less serenely. They were encouraged by completely agricultural countries to flee the bloody persecutions in Germany during the times of the Crusades, and also the Black Plague, in order to give their feudal lords a merchant class necessary to the operation of the economy. Spiritually, they were completely absorbed by the Talmud and the wondrous world of Hasidism. The spiritual flowering of Hasidism took place in a closed society out of contact with world history. That is why this development cannot be included in a history written from a universal perspective. The mediation of the Jews took place on the economic front, a role that provoked the hatred of the peasants, who were exploited without knowing exactly by whom. It inspired the notorious tzarist system of using the Jews as deflectors of popular anger, a system of safety valves that worked relatively well until 1917.

That was the sad epilogue of a long record of mediation that seems to have been the historic destiny of the Jewish people. For, through the momentum of modern technology, the world has rapidly evolved toward the organization outlined at the beginning of the chapter, which, however removed from a true spiritual organization, does not need the cosmopolitan action of the Jews. One or two of them, unaware of the new situation, still felt the atavistic need to draw nations spiritually together—for instance, Heinrich Heine, who assumed the unsuccessful mission of *agent de liaison* between Germany and France by picturing for the Germans the *Französische Zustände* (the French way of life), and by explaining German philosophy to the French. If nations have a sincere desire for mutual understanding, it is not the means to achieve it that are lacking. The great Jewish philosophers and scholars who, from Spinoza to Bergson, influenced modern thought, the great writers who, from Proust to Zweig, drew portraits of their time, worked as Frenchmen, Germans, and Englishmen, without knowingly using the Jewish tradition, without attempting a mission of *rapprochement*. As for the international projects of a Karl Marx, they are of an entirely different nature from the one I have treated here. From this point of view, the cosmopolitan role of Judaism is ended.

Jewish history was to be tied once more, in a resounding and particularly tragic manner, to universal history during the last World War. The fate of the Jews served as a preview to that of mankind as a whole. The world would not have had to pay such a terrible price for the preservation of its freedom had it recognized immediately the interdependence of the anti-Jewish crusade and the crusade against civilization.

Modern society, growing out of a long evolution, has a tendency to organize itself on the principle of democratic justice. Everything that imperils this principle must inevitably shake the whole community. It was, therefore, mandatory to react resolutely when one member of the human family was attacked in the name of an ideology incompatible with the democratic spirit. Once the first violation of this principle was tolerated, it became necessary, in order to preserve a false peace, to sacrifice one nation after another, without escaping, for all that, the final decisive confrontation between two totally conflicting views of life. Thus the bloodiest chapter of world history was not influenced but symbolized by the corresponding chapter of Jewish history. The Jews participated in the struggle for the defense of Western civilization in a forward position, with the consequent death of six million of their members.

May this catastrophe, which meant the almost total failure of the West, have at least one positive result, that of making the nations of the world understand the indivisible unity of their fate, and realize that they are not merely a flawless technical organization, but a living organism affected throughout by a blow struck at any of its parts. A disaster like the one we have witnessed will not permit any partial solution to our human problems. How are the Jews to be dealt with? Humanity no longer needs Jews as intermediaries. Other countries can absorb only a limited number of them. Well, let them be given the country of their ancestors! Let those who want to go there for spiritual or economic reasons be allowed to build their country freely according to their traditions. Let no one raise obstacles to a people in search of its historic homeland. And if it produces again on its ancestral soil a Maimonides, a Spinoza, a Bergson, an Einstein, they will not express their lofty thoughts in Arabic, Spanish, Latin, German, or French, but in the language of the Bible. If their ideas deserve universal recognition, they will be propagated because there are Jews who remain in their adopted country, but are attached to their spiritual legacy and, like André Spire and Edmond Fleg, want to bring the intellectual activities of Israel to the attention of mankind. The world will then be a better judge of the Jewish contribution radiating from the arid land rejuvenated by the sweat of its legitimate owners.

# 2

## *Judeo-Arabic Thought in the History of Philosophy*

The West is the homeland of science and philosophical speculation. The East is the cradle of religious faith and mysticism. The meeting of the speculative West and the mystical East was decisive for the whole evolution of human thought. Among the oriental people that Alexander had brought into contact with Greek civilization, only the Jews assimilated the positive elements of Greek thought and produced a fruitful synthesis, while the introduction of Greek ideas among other people of the Orient did not produce a Greco-Oriental philosophy. The successive encounters between Hellas and Judea over the last two thousand years are commemorated by names such as Philo, Maimonides, Leone Ebreo, Spinoza, Hermann Cohen.

During antiquity the West and the East faced each other like two seemingly irreconcilable powers, like the two blocs that divide the world today. The orient, with its genius for the transcendental, the infinite, the absolute, but also for authoritarianism in politics, expressed itself in organizations dominated by the will of one person, indifferent to the individual. The West, with its genius for analysis, detailed research, respect for the individual in a democratic state, but also with a tendency to carry to extremes this analytic penchant, evolved toward the disintegration of religious, social, political, moral, and intellectual bonds, toward skepticism, atomization in everything, political and moral anarchy.

One country, located at the nerve center of the Orient, condensed the best qualities of Asia without its negative aspects: Judea, on the borders of Asia and Europe, facing Greece, the forward post of the West. Judea, small and multicolored like Greece, defending herself all through her history against the absolutism of the great powers of the Orient; Judea, freeing herself from the absolutist spirit in human affairs, transfiguring it, and applying it to her relationship with an absolute and monotheistic God. Like the Greek thinkers, thinking of a community of free citizens, the prophets preached in Israel their ideal of rearing a nation of priests.

The meeting of the Greek and Jewish genius produced a mental attitude that up to the present has proved to be a rampart against the destructive intellectualism that Western thought engenders independently, against the tendency toward anarchy, against a passion for analysis, which degenerates into decomposition and suicide. During antiquity and the Middle Ages, this meeting gave birth to a philosophical system that classical philosophy had not suspected, in spite of the great variety of its tendencies. It is religiously inspired philosophy, and it proved to be a barrier against the hybrid nature of the human mind.

The first encounter took place in Alexandria, center of Greek culture and the location of an important Jewish colony. Philo the Jew built a bridge between Moses and Plato (who according to a pious legend was a disciple of Jeremiah), and adapted Western learning to the theological system of his ancestors. He introduced oriental fervor, a mystical accent, into Greek thought, and, for the first time, he applied rationalistic categories and allegorical interpretations to the Holy Scriptures. The new Greco-Jewish cosmology, marked by mysticism with its doctrine of intermediaries between God and the world, spirit and matter, had a decisive influence on Plotinus, the creator of Neoplatonism, and on Christianity. Alexandrian Judaism, through the philosophical works of Philo, as well as the classic translation of the Bible by the Seventy, took its place in universal thought. It left no trace on Jewish history. At that time the Jewish people, its existence threatened by the iron regime of Imperial Rome, was busy defending its individuality and its ideals by the detailed codification of biblical tradition. That was the function of the Talmud. *Primum vivere, deinde philosophari* (First live, then philosophize). The important thing was to remain alive, to consolidate Judaism through time and space. In a period of spiritual upheavals and political turmoil, the moment was not propitious to philosophy.

The second encounter of the genius of East and West took place under more auspicious circumstances. The Arab Empire, forged by the dynamic impulse of a new religion growing out of the Bible, not only annexed a vast territory, but also appropriated the arts and sciences of the preceding centuries. Aristotle, who synthesized the knowledge of ancient Greece, was almost entirely translated into Arabic, and Plato, the other radiant pole of ancient thought, was also partially translated. Under the tolerant reign of enlightened monarchs, the Abassides in the Orient, and the Almoravides and Omeyades in Spain, all could participate in the political and intellectual life of the realm. The children of Israel, the only group that maintained its spiritual unity, enjoyed a spiritual independence that was never surpassed in their postbiblical history, and rivaled the children of Ismael in all the branches of knowledge. Thus was born this marvelous Semitic renaissance, which approaches in its scientific, artistic boldness the Latin Renaissance, which in fact it often inspired. In pure philosophy, the grandiose syntheses of Arab and Jewish thinkers furnished many elements to the Christian philosophers of the thirteenth century, for in both cases the central problem of philosophy, given the dominant position of religion in the Middle Ages, was to define the relationship between reason and faith. Even though the Muslim and Catholic worlds were locked in a far from spiritual struggle, Semitic thought reached Christian scholars mainly through Jewish channels. Arabic philosophy disappeared like a meteor without making any imprint on Islam, and its works were preserved only in Hebrew translations, or transcriptions into Hebrew characters, directed at Jewish readers.

This intermediary position between the Arabic and Christian civilizations is characteristic of the religious philosophy of the Jews in general. Although it is closer to the Arabs' than to the Christians', it has, however, some clearly distinctive traits. Still, Judaism and Islam have a common bond in their greater freedom in religious speculations than Christianity, which, of the three biblical religions, has the most rigid dogmatism, forbidding to reason access to certain regions by a categorical: *Noli me tangere!* (Do not touch me!) Islam and Judaism do not recognize any mystery dealing with divine reality, such as the Trinity. Thus, the Arab philosophers wind up with an extreme rationalism and draw from Aristotle his ultimate conclusions, even though they maintain, like Averroës, that they are only formulating the deepest meanings from the pliable text of the Koran. There was no formal obstacle in the doctrines of Islam to the bold and ingenious theories of the philosophers, but these theories seemed so dangerous to religious practices that they provoked the violent reactions of orthodoxy, expressed in philosophy by absurd theses such as those of the Ascharites, the thunder of an Al Gazzali, who undertook the systematic destruction of all philosophy, and the banishment of the great and solitary Averroës. The sudden disappearance of philosophy from among the Muslims justifies Ernest Renan's assessment: "Philosophy has always been a foreign intruder among the Moslems, without significance for the intellectual education of the people of the Orient."[1]

Neither were the Jewish philosophers writing in Arabic stymied by the formal restrictions brought by religious dogma to the development of metaphysical speculation. The revelation on which the Jewish religion is founded does not dwell on the nature of God. "I am he who is" is the formula by which Moses grasped the divinity, and "I am the Lord thy God" is the first commandment, by which God reveals Himself to His people. The others have a purely moral character. It is true that this absolute biblical morality, postulating free will and implying theodicy, faith in a divine justice, is anchored in a super-rational beyond, interpreted by visionary prophets. But these Jewish philosophers who insisted on a rationalistic interpreta-

---

1.   Ernest Renan, *Discours et Conférences* (Paris, 1887).

tion of the visible universe were entirely free to follow Aristotle's lead, and they dedicated themselves wholeheartedly to the task of relating the Jewish tradition to the scientific concepts of the time. They did not, however, capitulate unconditionally to Aristotle's authority, in spite of his popularity in Israel because of his philosophical monotheism and his ethics, which, according to legend, he had studied in the Temple after the occupation of Jerusalem by Alexander. Maimonides, in contrast with Averroës, disavowed the ancient master whenever the principles of positive religion were endangered. He recognized his pertinence in the "sublunar" world, (we would say with Kant "the world of experience"), but denied it in questions such as the eternity of matter, and defended the creation *ex nihilo*. It is in this limitation of Aristotle's validity, of speculative reason and experimental research, that the originality of the Jewish thinkers of the time resided. Whether their religiosity was mystical or rational, they defended their religious principles, not by a dogmatic veto, but—a new departure in the history of thought—by philosophical arguments. Their reasoning was accepted to a large extent by the Christian doctors of the thirteenth century insofar as it fitted into the religious structure of the Church, and, while Averroës remained suspect, Maimonides was respectfully acknowledged by Albert the Great and Thomas Aquinas.

After this general definition of Judeo-Arabic philosophy, let us trace its three major trends:

1. *Neoplatonism,* with a tendency to reach the absolute by intuitive contemplation, by an illumination of the soul crowning scientific speculation. Its purest representative for the period under consideration was the Jewish poet Salomon ibn Gabirol, known in the history of philosophy as Avicebron.

2. *Aristotelian rationalism,* whose leading exponents were Averroës and Maimonides, looked for earthly perfection, union with God in pure, logical, and abstract thought.

3. *Ethical voluntarism,* emphasizing moral action and immediate religious experience, grants the soul an understanding of the infinite that theoretical knowledge is incapable of reaching. This aspect of

religious philosophy was represented by the Arab Al Gazzali and the Jew Juda Halevi.

These three spiritual attitudes had their Christian counterparts in Augustine, Thomas Aquinas, and Pascal. Let us take a closer look at them and try to assess their significance in the general history of thought.

1. Neoplatonism, which we have encountered in Philo's system, was an Oriental variant of Plato's doctrine, transplanted into Spain by Salomon ibn Gabirol, first Judeo-Arabic philosopher to become widely known in the West. Philo's *logos,* hellenized form of the word of God referred to in the Bible, is found in his work in the form of a universal will, emanating from God and filling the universe with a creative urge. In modern times, the idea of a creative will was developed with a great deal of vigor by Schopenhauer and Bergson. The latter, especially, resembles his Spanish coreligionist by the breath of optimism that enlivens his doctrine. The ultimate consequences of this theory of perpetual creation by successive irradiations are basically in the same spirit as the biblical religions, based on the idea of a personal God, separated from the universe, but acting on it. The Schoolmen appreciated these pantheistic implications, and fought against the doctrines of Ibn Gabirol (whose religion was otherwise unknown during the whole Middle Ages), which proves that this classic poet, this "pious nightingale," as Heine called him, did not worry about the consequences of his Jewish faith. The Synagogue was kinder to him than the Church, either because it did not recognize all the pantheistic implications of his thinking, or it did not insist on forbidding new ideas, even the boldest, as long as they did not conflict directly and unequivocally with tradition and religious practices. That is why the Kabbalah—this other great neoplatonic system, an ingenious attempt to capture the supra-rational by rational formulas, a book consecrated to the mystical contemplation of Maase Bereschit, the work of creation—passionately studied by the men of the Renaissance and that greatly influenced Giordano Bruno and Spinoza, has remained in favor among the Jews, in spite of its pantheistic tendencies, as an esoteric commentary on the Bible. The

Synagogue showed itself intransigent toward Spinoza only because he insisted on categorically emancipating philosophical reflection from all positive religion, and relegating the latter to an inferior position.

2. The most powerful philosophical trend in Semitic Spain, was, however, "peripatetic rationalism": The strength of Aristotle's logic held an irresistible attraction for Arab and Jewish thinkers, whose passion for dialectics had been expressed through the interpretation of the Koran, and especially in the Talmud. In the wake of Aristotle, Averroës summarizes and brings to its culmination the speculations of the philosophers Al Farabi, Avicenna, Avenpace, and Abubekr. Similarly, Maimonides encompasses the theories of Saadia, Abraham ibn Daud, and Bachya ibn Pakuda, and inspires those of Levi ben Gerson (Gersonides) and Chasdai Crescas in their attempts to reconcile certain aspects of Greek doctrine with the Old Testament. Averroës, the great Arab commentator, passionately discussed, even in Christendom, the man "che il gran commento feo" (who made the great commentary), and pushed to its limits the rationalistic interpretation of his ancient master. He reduced immortality of the soul to the union of the human mind with the eternal spirit in the act of knowing, of reasoning reason. Eternal happiness, the reward of the just, lies in the infinite happiness of the knowledge of eternal laws. Predestination, so dear to the Muslims, is equivalent in philosophical terms to the relationship between relatively free will and external causes regulated by unchanging natural laws. Religion in his eyes is not useless as long as it guides men until the moment they become capable of understanding the hidden meaning of the Scriptures. Only those incapable of speculation settle for the images of prophetic revelations. The prophets of all religions possess a parcel of the truth. We must, however, adopt the one most in keeping with reason, which to Averroës was Islam in his time.

It is in this philosophical attitude toward religion that we must seek the origin of the parable of the three rings, the subject of one of Boccaccio's most beautiful tales, also treated by the author of *Nathan the Wise* in a similar spiritual context. There are three similar diamonds, three faiths, each of which claims to be the true one. But, while they cannot all be simultaneously true, can they all be false? Here is the origin of medieval skepticism, which gained strength in spite of the condemnation of Averroism by the Muslims as well as by Christian orthodoxy—skepticism from the orthodox viewpoint, but not absolute skepticism toward religious values. The Averroist apology of reason as a divine force, as a revelation indispensable to man, was enough a little later to fire up the humanistic scholars who, when they unearthed the treasures of pagan antiquity, could not tolerate the idea that this civilization was only "a splendid vice," and would be excluded from salvation because it was not enlightened by historical revelation. Revelation, argued the new generation, occurs in anyone who uses his God-given reason, this *lumen naturale* (natural light), illumination of the soul beyond dogma and cult. This whole orientation of European thought, leading to the *Cogito ergo sum* (I think, therefore I am) and to the *amor dei intellectualis* (intellectual love of God) is found in Averroës' rationalism, not only as a precursor, but also as a concrete influence on Spinoza, who studied Averroës in Maimonides' version.

The latter enjoyed a more favorable fate than his Arab master. It is true that a rabbinical condemnation of his *Guide for the Perplexed* was issued at Montpellier a century after his death, but it was only a minor episode of no consequence for the fame of the "second Moses," whose reputation as a brilliant authority has endured through the centuries, both outside and inside the Synagogue. This philosophical rabbi, in spite of his profound admiration for Aristotle, did not surrender to him indiscriminately. He vigorously defended the basic principles of Judaism, but as a philosopher, not as a theologian, that is to say, with the weapons of logic and reasoning, sharpened not only by the subtleties of the Talmud, but also by pagan knowledge. He smoothened certain difficulties, for instance, the anthropomorphic passages of the Bible, by an allegorical interpretation, for which his supreme mastery of the whole biblical and rabbinical literature was of immmense help. He saw no difficulty in adopting the Aristotelian structure of the universe, in translating "the intelligences that move the spheres" into the angels mentioned in the Bible, and in relating the one God of Abraham, Isaac, and Jacob to the "prime mover" of the philosophers. However, to the idea of a mechanistic universe, governed by inexorable natural laws, existing for all eternity, he opposed the biblical tradition of the creation *ex nihilo,* arguing that the eternal laws of nature that lead to the belief in the eternity of the world only came into being with the creation of that world, that these laws in their totality are subject to a law of spiritual purpose, translated in biblical language by the idea of providence. Similarly, he defended other crucial questions of monotheism. To save the dogma of revelation, he developed ingenious theories on the nature of prophecies and their relation to reason. This is all he needed to gain the acceptance of Christian philosophers, led by Saint Thomas, who leaned on the argumentation of "Rabbi Moyses." His influence in the following centuries is, let it be noted in passing, an indication that Judaism was not, as Bergson misunderstood, a purely national doctrine made for a closed society. This aspect came out only in times of forced isolation. Even after it gave birth to two universal religions, Judaism continued to develop ideas that formed a bridge between the spiritual movements of the time.

Jewish medieval philosophy transcended scholastic philosophy. The last representatives of Jewish peripatetism lived and taught in the luminous Italy of the Renaissance. This is the case of Elias del Medigo, professor at the University of Padua, who translated and annotated for his disciple Pico della Mirandola several works by Averroës, and wrote for him, in Latin and in Hebrew, treatises of religious philosophy, such as *The Examination of Religion (Behinat Hadat).* Even better known was Leone Ebreo, Spanish emigré, author of the famous *Dialoghi d'amore,* in which, it must be said, prevails a Kabbalisitc neoplatonism, but which I mention in my aside on the role of Jewish thought in the movement of ideas at the close of the Middle Ages. This dynamic period, in search of new spiritual horizons, eager for a faith not imposed by ecclesiastic authorities, but having its source in one's personal conscience, and in the development of the forces of the soul and of reason, was bound to welcome, not only the pure peripatetism of Aristotle and Averroës, but also the new version produced by the modifications of Jewish religious speculation. Jewish moderation toward peripatetic philosophy, the adher-

ence to a revealed religion, but amplified by individual revelation
—this combination of traditionalism and liberalism—all were meant
to appeal to the fifteenth and sixteenth centuries, oriented toward a
faith freed from dogma and cult. Jewish rationalism was also moder-
ate in the sense that, in spite of the emphasis put by Maimonides on
knowledge, reason was not considered an end in itself but rather a
means of convincing men to do good. This corresponds to the other
tendency taking shape from the very dawn of modern times, to seek
the quintessence of religious faith in the practice of moral and civic
virtues.

This ethical rationalism, like the pantheistic trend, is also found in
Spinoza. Although for him perfection resided in knowledge, in the
intellectual love of the infinite, he called his major work *Ethics,*
revealing perhaps his debt to his master Maimonides, for whom he
professed so little respect.

3. Neoplatonic mysticism and Aristotelian rationalism, as adapted
to the doctrines of the Koran and the Old Testament, whatever their
importance in Semitic thought and their repercussions on Western
thought, did not exhaust the philosophical content of these religions.
There were thinkers who reflected the feelings of many of the faithful by claiming that neither peaceful contemplation nor intellectual
knowledge expressed the spiritual essence of the revealed religions,
that they are only substitutes for the inexpressible happiness felt by
the true believer. This third trend had its spokesmen—among the
Arabs in Algazel, and among the Jews in Bachya ibn Pakuda,
Chasdai Crescas, and above all, Juda Halevi.

Algazel, himself a thinker of genius, used all subtlety to destroy
the theses of the philosophers. His arguments embarassed Averroës
himself, who answered with a *Destruction of Destruction.* If
Algazel's attitude was suspected of lacking sincerity, this was certainly not the case of the author of the *Kuzari,* whose life was in
perfect harmony with his religious and philosophical convictions.
Juda Halevi, driven by an invincible yearning for the Promised
Land, where the glory of God visited the prophets, relinquished family, friends, and wealth. The pious pilgrimage from which he never

returned is like a concretization of his thinking, of his fervent heart aspiring for union with the creative forces of the universe. Speculation along the lines of Aristotle did not satisfy him, and he renounced it in disappointment, exclaiming: "Don't yield to Greek seduction; it bears only flowers, no fruit." He declared war on metaphysics, for it only traces the shadow of the infinite, which the believer grasps by immediate intuition. To reason, which attempts to define the divine essence, he opposed the answer of God to Moses: "You shall see my back, but my face cannot be seen" (Exod. 33:23). These words, in the eyes of Juda Halevi, are the quintessence of Jewish philosophy. They constituted a veto, not to scientific research, for Juda Halevi could appreciate logic and mathematics, but to all attempts to know God through metaphysical speculation. We know that God is, not what he is. His very dignity demands that he should not be recognized by man. No positive attributes apply to God, and he is knowable only by his reflection in the world. Such a reflection is the principle of justice, even if this justice is manifested only in the third or fourth generation. The Bible is a successive revelation of the principle of justice in the history of nations. Through justice, an essentially unknowable God manifests his will on earth, and the man who contributes to the reign of justice acts according to divine will. The commandments and the interdictions of the Talmud and the Bible help him in this task.

This, however, is still only the rational aspect of religion. It does not deal with its deeper meaning. God is indeed present in every act of justice and charity, and in that sense every man acting virtuously lives according to God; but he does not live in God, he does not know the happiness of the believer to whom God reveals himself. The prophets received this grace, the immediate intuition of the divinity; in revelation they reached the perfect communion with the Supreme Being. However, every sincere believer, and not only the prophets, as Algazel claimed, can feel intensely the presence of God if he observes the sacred ritual that will constantly turn his thoughts toward him, if he obeys the commandments introduced by historical revelations and developed by the doctors. Pious intentions and psychic attention forever directed toward the sublime develop in the believer the prophetic gift, the ability to perceive the divinity. Juda Halevi described with incomparable sensitivity the symbolism of the Jewish ritual, whose purpose is to divinize the profane, to endow daily life with a holy character. Indeed, one does not have to be a Rembrandt to notice the beatitude, the radiance on the face, of a pious Jew about to celebrate Passover or some other rite, or the mother when she blesses the Sabbath light. It is easy to see where Juda Halevi received the inspiration for his religious philosophy. He remained faithful to his time in that he attributed only to his own people the prophetic gift, this gift of superior, uncompromising religiosity. Israel is the heart of mankind, the most sensitive organ, which suffers with any disease affecting any other part of the body, but it is also exclusively capable of the highest spiritual exaltation. Aware of the danger of this particularism, Halevi softened it by interpreting messianism as the journey toward the kingdom of God, common to all people.

By describing the character of Jewish religiosity and showing that the sources of knowledge transcend natural reason, he grasped the nature of religiosity in general, of the sacred, that special field, inaccessible, like pure poetry, to reasoning and analysis. This author, whose piety blossomed under the dual influence of Hasidism and the Kabbalah, probably had no influence on gentile thinkers, for his concern was completely Jewish, that is to say, it concentrated on the definition of the living thought of biblical Judaism. Yet, he was endowed with an inspiration that gave him an insight into the supranatural aspects of religion, which allowed him to formulate the reasons of the heart.

The Judeo-Arabic period, which defined the relationship of philosophy and faith, also discovered the field of the sacred. Modern thought has elucidated this discovery of pure religiosity with Kant, who gives it a negative definition by distinguishing it clearly from metaphysics and morality. If, according to him, religion is inaccessible to reason and scientific knowledge, it nevertheless affirms its reality in the subjective certainty of the religious individual. Subsequently, Schleiermacher defined religion as an irreducible experience of consciousness, as the immediate contact with the absolute. Modern psychology has formulated in this field the notion of "religiöses Erlebnis" (religious experience). We thus understand the opinion of Etienne Gilson on the Middle Ages, who notes that "from it stem directly the scientific doctrines with which critics attempt to undermine it." Let me be permitted therefore to outline rapidly the present-day situation of the problem raised by Judeo-Arabic philosophy.

The nineteenth century had lost interest in the examination of the religious question. Religion had ceased to occupy the central position with which reason and science had to find a *modus vivendi*. For, in the meantime, modern science had been born, ready to assume the functions formerly performed by religion.

> Ein neues Lied, ein besseres Lied,
> Ihr Freunde, will ich euch dichten.
> Wir wollen hier auf Erden schon
> Das Himmelreich errichten!
>
> (Heine, "Deutschland, ein Wintermärchen")

> A new song, a better song,
> Friends, I shall compose for you.
> We shall set up here on earth
> Already the Kingdom of Heaven.

"A new song"—comments such as these have at least created a special atmosphere, which we have been breathing for more than a century, composed of a kind of mystique of science, of an intoxication that it caused, mixed at times with the cult of reason, and the certainty that it would fulfill every one of our desires. Paradise regained, thanks to science, or rather, thanks to the sciences; for the harmonious edifice of the Middle Ages, where all the spiritual disciplines converged toward unity, had yielded to the infinite multiplicity of modern aspirations. Spinoza had postulated the separation of philosophy and religion. The nineteenth century went further, by a radical division of the various scientific branches. Technical progress imbued the new generation with pride and confidence. Philosophy did not find more favor in its eyes than religion. These were merely steps in the evolution of mankind, which had yielded to concrete, irrefutable research, had yielded to the age of positivism. If one religion still counted, it was positivism itself, proclaimed by Auguste Comte. The new scientific era, the modern religion, was to make men happier than the historical religions had made them. This was the hope of the Taines, the Renans, who, nonetheless, realized the limitations of their ideal, for the progress they dreamed of was confined to a limited framework, to a closed circle, governed by the determinism officially formulated by Darwin and Spencer. In the past, all religious or philosophical opinion shared a common belief in a transcendental power, whatever its nature or effect on the world. While the physcal cosmology was geocentric, the spiritual cosmology located the center of gravity beyond mankind. Now man had become the measure of all things, but the hope invested in him by the elite was disappointed. As Arnold Reymond noted with resignation, "mankind left to its own devices was incapable of finding its salvation."[2] As in Goethe's ballad, which foreshadowed the destiny of his people, the magic instrument that man created for himself overwhelmed his creator. The apprentice sorcerer had thrilled at the prospect of imposing his rule over the earth, thanks to the magic wand of his scientific technique. Twice in a generation, the nation that had transformed technique into an idol unleashed the most scientific war imaginable. The technique of destruction took on gigantic proportions, and the organizing genius of that race managed to engineer the disappearance of several million human beings in factories skillfully erected for that purpose, with a swiftness that all the epidemics of primitive times and backward countries never managed to equal. What a tragic lesson for mankind, revealing the ultimate consequence of the hybrid faith in salvation through technology!

However, the reaction against the cult of science, the rehabilitation of a spiritual philosophy and religious thinking was not long in appearing. Infallible science lost its prestige, and not only because of the catastrophes that it occasioned. Scientists themselves stripped sci-

2. A. Reymond, *Philosophie spiritualiste* (Lausanne, 1942).

ence of its prestige. Contemporary physics has abandoned the concept of a mechanical universe and has restricted the validity of the laws of nature. In mathematics, Jules Henri Poincaré has shaken the staunch confidence in the infallibility of scientific laws by stating that scientific formulas are convenient but not true, and Edouard le Roy has emphasized the conventional and symbolic character of the scientific expression of the truth. Concurrently with this review of values, a new philosophy aimed at a spiritual synthesis of scientific efforts, leading to a new formulation of the religious problem. "It cannot be otherwise," exclaimed Karl Joël; "there must be a living, organizing principle as the basis of the world." For me, the symbol of this new scientific orientation is found in a scene in which I saw Albert Einstein, in the winter of 1932-33, explaining some aspects of his theory in a synagogue in Berlin.

In France, Emile Boutroux sapped the deterministic system in which the soul had been confined and cleared a productive path to metaphysical and moral thought. The religious philosophy created by the Jews now belonged to all nations. If philosophers of Jewish origin have abandoned this specialty nowadays, they are still associated with every intellectual activity. Even today, two Jews have sparked the contemporary revival of religious speculation. One, Hermann Cohen, the head of the Neo-Kantian school of Marburg, attempted to interpret the doctrine of Judaism in the light of Kant. His efforts were continued by Martin Buber and, especially, Franz Rosenzweig. The other, Bergson, was less well-versed in the Jewish tradition than in the New Testament, and only on his deathbed did he find the occasion to affirm his solidarity with his persecuted brethren. His philosophical works, however, filled with memories of Ibn Gabirol and kabbalistic elements, revived religious speculation in general, and there is no better way to summarize the meaning of his investigations than by evoking the vision of the present-day position of manking expressed in his last work:

Machines operated by gasoline, coal, and hydraulic energy, transforming into movement the potential energy accumulated over millions of years, have given our organism such a vast existence and such tremendous power, so disproportionate to its dimensions, that surely nothing like it had been expected in the structure of our species. But, in this body so excessively swollen, the soul remains what it had been, too small now to fit into it, too weak to direct it. The magnified body awaits an addition of soul, and the mechanism needs a mystique. It will serve mankind in proportion to its power only if humanity, which it has bent farther toward earth, manages through it to straighten up and look toward heaven.

# 3
# *Medieval Judeo-Romance Literary Relations*

Judeo-Romance literary relations are far more complicated than those of Latin countries with other literatures. France, England, and Germany had cultural centers clearly defined politically and geographically. Jewish centers were harder to circumscribe, but their existence cannot be denied. They varied in origin and importance, their unity lying in their common Hebrew culture. In view of their dispersion throughout the world, Sartre has questioned that unity. He has declared: ''They don't have the same fatherland, they have no history. . . .'' They have only ''an identical situation.'' Nevertheless, the Jewish population, scattered throughout Europe is a homogeneous whole, interacting with its milieu on innumerable occasions, at times deliberately, at others unwillingly. The confrontation often takes place in one and the same person, such as the French descendant of the Marranos, Montaigne, the Italian Manoello Immanuel di Roma, or the Spanish emigrant Abrabanel.

Jewish themes in national literatures sometimes come about simply from the presence of Jewish communities in the host countries. Sometimes the Jewish element exerts an active influence on its surroundings through classical Hebrew, or through the activities of Jewish authors. Hebrew has the same international character as humanistic Latin. It serves as a medium of communication for people of like mind in various parts of the globe.

## FRANCE

French literature exhibits several clearly recognizable phases of foreign influence in its long history. Although it has strongly affected other literatures through its richness and distinctiveness, it must be admitted that this distinctiveness needed the infusion of foreign elements. Its great variety stems directly from continuous contact with extraneous cultures.

This process of interpenetration, welcomed by literary critics like Thibaudet and Brunetière, which they illustrate with examples from modern times but which began in the Middle Ages, was not always a harmonious and peaceful one, and often took place, just as it did in Spain, in a tragic atmosphere.

There were the usual alternations of prosperity and misery, golden ages and persecutions until 1394, when the Jews were expelled from the whole French realm, with the exception of Provence and Avignon.

The first Jewish congregation may have originated in old Massilia (Marseilles), which maintained trade relations with Alexandria. It was followed by others in Avignon, Arles, Bordeaux, and Narbonne. Under the Merovingians there were forced baptisms. But with the growing power of the *maire de palais* (roughly, the prime minister), Jews were not molested, and achieved important economic positions, especially in the port cities. Charlemagne recognized the importance of Jewish trade and granted it a role in his empire. In 787 he summoned the Zakan family from Italy, and in 801 the scholarly rabbi Machir from Baghdad. They and other scholars who immigrated under Charlemagne's immediate successors founded important Talmudic schools in Lorraine and in Southern France.

An intimate relationship was struck with French letters by a characteristic branch of Hebrew literature, the fable. According to talmudic sources, Rabbi Meir, who lived in the second century, knew three hundred fables, many of which were no doubt of Arabic and Indian origin. About 1200, Rabbi Berachya ben Natronay and Isaac de Corbeil published a collection of these fables, including stories by Aesop, some of Indian origin as well as the talmudic fox legends *(Mishle Shualim)* for the instruction and edification of devout Jews. Another collection of this kind had been published by Pierre Alphonse, who had converted to Christianity in 1106. He was originally known as Rabbi Moses, but he renamed himself after the saint of his conversion day, Saint Peter, and his godfather, King Alphonse of Castile. He defended himself against the reproaches of his former coreligionists through fictitious dialogues between his two selves, the Jew Moses and the Christian Peter, dialogues that signal the advent of "religious dialogues."

His main work was the collection *Disciplina Clericalis,* soon after translated into Old French under the title *Discipline de Clergie,* which also appeared in a rhymed version as *Chastiement d'un père à son fils (Admonition of a Father to His Son).* In the style of *Chastiement des dames (Admonition to Ladies)* by Robert de Blois, a sort of Emily Post for society ladies, Pierre Alphonse gives pedagogical instructions through practical examples and Oriental tales. His book is one of the channels through which the wisdom of the Orient entered Europe. In France these fables were the forerunners of the classic works of La Fontaine. While Joseph Bédier questions this, Gaston Paris and especially Montaiglon, who has collected them, are of a different opinion:

> The real intermediary is the cosmopolitan nation *par excellence,* and the only one in the Middle Ages, that is to say the Jews, Oriental themselves in spirit and in tradition, who alone knew Arabic and who alone were able to translate it into Latin. . . .A very curious and very positive clue is the *Disciplina Clericalis* of *Pierre Alphonse.* (A. de Montaiglon, *Recueil des fabliaux,* vol. 1 [Paris, 1872], Avant-propos.)

Jews can be spoken of as mediators in literary matters, as they doubtless have been in international trade, science, medicine, and philosophy, because of their peculiar social position. They always spoke the language of their surroundings, but cultivated Hebrew as a cultural language, so that it served, as did the Latin of the later Humanists, as a medium for overcoming linguistic, political, and religious boundaries.

A phenomenon of a completely different nature also resulted from this bilingual situation—the conservation of the earliest forms of speech by writing them in Hebrew script.

While the process is informative for the other Romance languages, it is especially significant for French linguistic history because of the antiquity of the vocabulary handed down in Hebrew transcriptions, and because the linguistic development in France was subject to far greater changes than the other Romance languages. The gallicisms handed down in Jewish writings are among the oldest documents of Old French, and go back to the eleventh century. A hundred years before Chrétien de Troyes, Rabbi Shlomo Jizhaki (Rashi, 1040-1104) lived in the same city. His commentaries on the Bible and the Talmud have remained the standard work to the present day. In his Hebrew explanations, there are numerous French glosses whose rendering in Hebrew transcription is unusually informative for the vocabulary and pronunciation of Old French. After preliminary research by Eduard Böhmer, this area was opened up for French literature by the works of Arsène Darmsteter and G. Blondheim. Darmsteter's *Gloses et glossaires hébreux-fraņais* is the first Old French dictionary for the eleventh century. He alone collected 3,000 French words in Rashi's commentary to the Bible. Inspired by this example, other publications followed. However, this branch of knowledge is far from having been fully investigated. The University of Basel library owns a manuscript (A III 39) of a Hebrew-French glossary of several texts of the prophets.

Up to this time French words were interspersed in the Hebrew text. Later the procedure was reversed and Hebrew expressions were inserted in a French text, similarly to Franco-Latin texts. Two documents from the thirteenth century are especially informative in this respect. One is from a prayer book for the Jewish holidays, written completely in French, but with Hebrew spelling. The other is the famous *Complainte de Troyes,* the most poignant Franco-Jewish work of the Middle Ages.

By comparing it with a Hebrew elegy of the same period, Darmsteter was able to show that it was written by the same author: Jacob, son of Juda of Lotra (Lorraine). Both elegies describe the fate of thirteen martyrs who were burned alive on Shavuoth 5048 (1288). Behind this *auto-da-fé*, which had been organized by the Inquisition during the Middle Ages' darkest period and which caused a great sensation in France, was the accusation of ritual murder on the part of the Dominicans, the hounds of heaven. The accused refused to save their lives by abjuring their faith. They died by encouraging one another and defying their executioners. Isaac Châtelain, his pregnant wife, his daughter-in-law, "qui tant était belle" (who was so beautiful), Simon the Cantor, "qui si bien savait orer" (who could pray so well), Isaac the Priest, and the others, all perished. The following line, translated from the Hebrew, is about him:

Prechors vinrent R. (Rabbi Ichak Cohen) rekerir
K'i se tornat ver lor creace o il li kevanret périr
Il dit: Ke avès tant? Je vol por Gé morir;
Je suis Cohen, e offrande de mon cors vos ofrir

Preachers came to invite R. Isaac
To adopt their faith or be forced to die.
He said: Why are you so wrought? I want to die for God.
I am a Cohen (priest) and wish to make an offering of my body.

Another scene is filled with touching concern:

Deux frères sont brûlés, un petit et un grand;
Le plus jeune s'effraie du feu qui lors s'éprend:
"Haro! je brûle entier," et l'aîné lui apprend:
"Au paradis tu vas aller; j'en suis garant."

Two brothers are being burned, one little and one big;
The little one is afraid of the fire starting up:
"Horrors! I am burning all over," and the elder tells him:
"You will go to paradise, I can guarantee it."

In contrast to this scene of mortal fear, there is one of great courage, where the group sings together as if marching to a ball:

D'une voix tous ensemble, ils chantaient haut et clair
Comme des gens de fête qui dussent caracoler. . .

With one voice they sang loud and clear
Like at a feast those about to dance.

The song ends with a plea for mercy for the innocent victims.

The theme of conversion played a large role not only in clerically influenced politics, but also in literature. Fictitious religious debates were often devised, ending, of course, with the victory of the Church over the Synagogue, just as in Strasbourg the proud cathedral overshadows the humble synagogue, which, however, has not lost its dignity despite its material setbacks. Nothing was more tempting to a Christian than to triumph over a Jew, the most tenacious of all unbelievers. In *Pèlerinage de Charlemagne (Charlemagne's Pilgrimage),* this is naïvely expressed when a Jerusalem Jew is so dazzled by the sight of Charlemagne that he immediate runs to the patriarch and requests to be baptized:

Un Jueus i entrat, qui bien l'out esguardet;
Com il vi le rei Charle, commença à trembler;
Tant out fier le visage, ne l'osat esguarder;
A poi que il ne chiet, fuiant s'en est tornez;
Et si montet l'eslais toz les marbrins degrez.
Et vint al patriarche, prist a aparler:
Alez, sire, al mostier, por les fonz aprester;
Orendreit me ferai batizier et lever. . . .

A Jew entered, and looked at him carefully;
As he saw King Charles, he began to tremble;
Such a proud face had he, that he dared not gaze at him;
He nearly fell, and ran away.
Running forward, he ascended the marble steps.
And came to the patriarch and began to speak:
Go to the monastery to prepare the baptismal fonts;
I want to be baptized and christened immediately.

In reality the Christian attempts at conversion were anything but successful, since they were undertaken with the weapons of dialectics, in which the Talmud-trained Jews were past masters. Often they were able to disentangle themselves from difficult situations by shrewd argumentation, as the following story illustrates.

Pedro of Aragon (1094-1104), in general well disposed toward the Jews, asked a Jew in his court one day which was the best religion. The latter appeared a few days later somewhat the worse for wear, and complained that two brothers had received a precious stone from their father, and had asked him which stone was worth more. In response to his remark that their father must know that best, they had beaten him. "For this they shall be punished," said the angry king. "May your ears hear what your mouth is saying, O King!" said the Jew. "Jacob and Esau were also brothers who received a precious legacy from their father. Send a messenger to the Father, the Great Jeweler, and ask him to tell you the value of the stones."

Unfortunately, the French were not so well intentioned. They did not readily allow the Jews to defend themselves, and usually circulated only their own tendentious arguments, as the following interpretation of the parable indicates. It is called *Le Dit du vrai aniel (The Story of the True Ring)*. An Egyptian possessed a ring with magic powers. Of his three sons, the oldest was a depraved skeptic, despised by God and man. The second was not much better, but the third had all the desirable virtues. Before he died, the father had two imitations of the ring made, gave each son a ring and informed the youngest of the trick he had played on the older brothers. When the latter saw that they had been deceived, they punished him and damaged the genuine ring. But God sent three princes to save him and returned to the ring its magic powers.

The moral of the story is that the persecuted youngest son is Christianity, driven from its rightful inheritance. The tomb of Jesus is in the hands of infidels through the fault of the Pope and those in power, who are concerned only with their own interests. But three brave princes, the King of France, and the Counts of Artois and Flanders, were chosen by God to free it from persecution. The tale ends with a summons to a crusade, supposedly under Philip the Fair.

A popular genre of the time was the religious debate that reflected the theological tournaments, in popular and sometimes vulgar style, as in the *Disputation de la Synagogue et de la Sainte Eglise* by Clopin, a minstrel of the thirteenth century. Both sects insult each other, the Synagogue being called a "vieille ribaude folle" (old foolish wench), and the Church a "garce et chétive folle" (a slut and wretched madwoman). After further Homeric insults, the Synagogue demands obedience from the Church, since "tu issis de m'escole" (you are the product of my school), but is refused: "Tais-toi, folle vieille froncie" (Be quiet, mad, wrinkled old woman), for after it ceased to be chosen by God, it went on to lead Jews astray and distort the truth: "Querre les moules aux rissoles" (look in the wrong place). The poet, who has heard this conversation in a dream, awakens before its conclusion. Apparently he does not even dare dream of such miracles as the conversion of the Synagogue.

This bigotry resulted, if not in the destruction of the Synagogue, at least in its reduction to impotence. For the attacks continued. In 1242, for instance, the Talmud was burned. This was the death blow to the intellectual life of French Jews.

Ultimately religious accusations were replaced by reproaches of a social nature. The polemics became increasingly bitter, for what was attacked was the position of the Jews in a changing economic system. The bourgeoisie was destroying the feudal structure, trade developed, money gained importance as a means of exchange, and the Jews were forced by all kinds of discriminatory rules into the lending business. Before that, they had been landowners like Rashi, who made a living in Champagne from his vineyards. Religious and economic hostility combined to form an explosive resentment, which vented itself in repeated local expulsions until the final one in 1394.

A graphic illustration of anti-Semitic animosity, nourished by various sources, is shown in the works of Abbé Gautier de Coincy, a moralist of the first half of the thirteenth century. His stories, taken from Latin sources, contain long, banal discourses on abuses in public life, in the Church, and even in the monastery. His indignation is directed especially at the Jews because of his Christian outrage at their unbelief, and their blindness to questions involving the Savior and the miracles he performed.

> Plus bestial que bestes nues
> Sont tuit Juif, ce n'est pas doute,
> Aveugle sunt, ne voient goute,
> Quar miracle, ne prophecie,
> Ne raison nule com leur die. . . .
> Ce méesme qu'a leur yex voient,
> Ce que prophecie avoient,
> Ne voudront croire, quand le virent.

> More like animals than the animals themselves
> Are all Jews, there is no doubt.
> They are blind, they do not want to see anything.
> No miracles, nor any prophecy,
> Nor any reason that one might give them. . . .
> Even what they see with their own eyes
> What the prophecies announce,
> They would not believe them, even if they saw them.

But more than their religious callousness, he is angered by their wealth and possessions, which they have obtained through the complicity of the men in power.

> Certes hauz homs qui les endure,
> Ne doit mie onc durer

> Any prominent man who tolerates this state of things
> Does not deserve to live long.

They have sold Christianity out of greed and handed over Jesus once again, more shamefully than Judas did. If he, Gautier, ruled the land, he would not allow one single Jew to remain.

> Vers eus sui dure si durement
> S'estoie roys pour toute roie
> Un seul durer je n'en lairoie

> I am so bitterly opposed to them
> That if I were king, not in one place
> Would I allow any to remain.

Gautier saw the bad economic conditions without detecting their real cause. The people lived in poverty, the upper classes in magnificent pleasures, and in between were the Jews, who had made a virtue of money lending since they were excluded from trade and from owning property. On the other hand, the Church did not forbid them to charge interest, and thus helped them to a favorable position in a changing society. That they often served as fronts for their powerful employers and as convenient safety valves for diverting dissatisfaction (as in czarist Russia during the twentieth century), Gautier was to perceive only after their expulsion:

> Car Juifs furent deboneres
> Trop plus, en faisant tels afferes
> Que ne sont ore chrestien.

> For the Jews were much more honest
> In handling that type of business
> Than the Christians are now.

In the Old French literature of the twelfth and even the thirteenth centuries, there is still a residue of tolerance, a hope for the salvation of this stubborn people through conversion. In the fourteenth century naked hate takes the ascendency. *Revenge* is the title of a mystery play of the time. It might well be the title of the hate propaganda of the fourteenth and fifteenth centuries in general. It no longer mirrored public opinion. It influenced and directed it, in a typical process described by Joseph Chénier: "At the beginning, the mores of a nation shape the spirit of its poetical works; soon its poetical works shape the spirit of the nation." This particularly applies to dramatic literature, which has a direct contact with the public.

Medieval theater had originated in a kind of pseudo-liturgy, and served as instruction and edification of the people through the portrayal of the life of Jesus, a sort of extended dramatized sermon. On the platform set up in front of the church, where the various episodes of the Passion took place, the actors dressed as Jews had their assigned place, where they accompanied the action with malicious gestures. In scenes familiar to religious tradition, the Pharisees, worried

about their prestige and their revenues, were shown in debate with
brave reformers:

> Pis y a: notre revenu
> En diminue et notre avoir

> And there is worse: our income
> And our wealth diminish.

Mainly because of this material concern, they want to bring Jesus to
trial, and they plot a means to do it:

> Il nous faut songer la manière
> De le charger de quelque crime
> Soit de blasphémie, soit de schisme,
> Ou d'autre grand cas, tel ou tel,
> Qui soit exécrable et mortel.

> We have to think about the manner
> Of accusing him of some crime
> Either of blasphemy, or of schism
> Or of some other great offense
> That is execrable and fatal.

The action was embellished with all sorts of scenes that represent
the Jews as allies of the devil. Betrayal for thirty pieces of silver was
an especially popular *coup de théâtre* and helped create the type of
Jewish usurer who still appeared in Marlowe, Shakespeare, and their
successors. The dramatic climax, however, was the crucifixion, with
the Jews gloating at the savior:

> Le roy des juifz, Dieu te sault!
> Se tu es filz au Dieu d'amont,
> Qui est venu sauver le mond,
> Descend de la croix, par ma loy,
> Et nous croirons trestous en toy.

> King of the Jews, may God save you!
> If you are the Son of God
> Who came to save the world,
> Descend from the cross; by my law,
> We shall all believe in you.

The effect of such scenes on a naïve public can hardly be exaggerated. These performances did not serve any aesthetic end, but were used for edification and religious teaching. The spectators saw in the Jews of their environment the direct persecutors of the Christian deity. The scenes often led to persecution and the Easter season came to mean a time of dread for the Jews of every province. In Toulouse there was a widespread custom of publicly beating a Jew. Once the Vicomte Chappelain d'Aymerie even executed the act with such religious zeal that the Jew collapsed and died. "The people dream up horrible mysteries: Christ is insulted, deicide is repeated, Christians are insulted, their blood is drunk, and the people call vociferously for the death of the Jews. . . .They forget that Christ was born a Jew, the Immaculate Virgin was Jewish, the first apostles were Jewish: they only see in them the persecutors of Christ, and, in turn, they would like to crucify them." (Vaublanc, *La France au temps des Croisades* [*Paris, 1844*], *1:280.)*

In the light of such naïve realism, the state and the church had to intervene and ban the Medieval theater. Five years after the prohibition of 1553, the first Renaissance tragedy in classical style was performed and the spirit of antiquity replaced that of the Middle Ages. But in the process Jewish antiquity was also discovered. Jewish writings were no longer studied simply as justification and prefiguration of the Christian doctrine of salvation, but as an independent source of Western thinking and monotheistic *Weltanschauung*. Calvin wrote his commentaries on the Pentateuch and the prophets without regard to Christian apologetics, "in order not to seem ridiculous in the eyes of the Jews." (A.J. Baumgartner, *Calvin hébraïsant et interprète de l'Ancien Testament,* 1889). The Old Testament inspired the leaders and martyrs of Protestantism, for example, Coligny and Agrippa d'Aubigné, warrior and poet of the Huguenots.

The new access to Hebrew writing also had a direct formal result, namely, the enrichment of the French language, not so much in its vocabulary as in its mode of expression. New figures of speech and images were introduced through imitation of the biblical style. Old French sufficed for the communication of the concrete objects of everyday life, but not for rendering the realm of the abstract, a Jewish skill acquired through the Bible. In Christendom only the clergy possessed, through the medium of Latin, a concept of such nuances in thinking and feeling. Through new translation into the vernacular, the latter was enriched by innumerable new expressions, which rapidly became consecrated through constant use. One thinks of such phrases as "adorer le veau d'or" (worship the golden calf), "être le bouc émissaire" (to be the scapegoat), "ne pas entrer dans la terre promise" (not to enter the promised land), "une brebis égarée" (a lost sheep), "aussi nombreux que les étoiles du ciel" (as numerous as the stars in the sky), "s'appuyer sur un roseau" (to lean on a weak reed), "se prendre à son propre piège" (to be caught in one's own trap), "celui qui sème le vent moissonnera la tempête" (he who sows the wind will reap the whirlwind), "la rosée du ciel" (the dew of heaven), "le soleil de justice" (the sun of justice), "le pain de la misère" (the bread of want), "la voie d'iniquité" (the path of iniquity), "la fontaine de sapience" (the fountain of wisdom), "l'art de la vie" (the art of living).

Such direct borrowings were supplemented by imitation of style, a process that has been continuous and contributed to the formation of a language glittering with a wealth of expressions.

On the other hand, Old French and Provençal expressions were borrowed by the Jewish dialects, for example, *benshen* from *bençun (benedictione), oren* (orare) for "to pray," *shalet* from *cha(u)lt* (the special method of preparing the Sabbath food.)

Modern literature has a patriarch, who, not by his works but by his personality, gives proof of the Franco-Jewish interaction: Michel Eyquem de Montaigne, son of a French nobleman and a Jewish mother, whose family, Lopez de Villanuova, had found refuge in France from the Inquisition. Fortunat Strowski attributes to Montaigne's lineage his suppleness and universality, which he introduced into French literature: "No doubt, Montaigne learned from all these Paçagons, changed into Lopez de Villanuova, to consider himself a citizen of the world and to look beyond the Garonne, or even France." ("La Jeunesse de Montaigne," *Revue des Cours et Conférences* [Paris, 1938].) Be that as it may, it is noteworthy that with him the tendency to constructive criticism, well-meant irony, and perceptive balance enters French literature, known later as "esprit français."

The biological combination of Gallic and Jewish characteristics constituted Montaigne's genius. Just as fruitful was the spiritual synthesis of two traditions, from which the classical tragedy originated. For Aeschylus and Sophocles were not alone in acting as midwife for French drama. Biblical thinking and motifs also had their influence and invested the Hellenistic heritage with new strains. Of one of the first Renaissance tragedies, *Saül furieux,* Jean de la Taille states that it is taken from the Bible, but performed in the style of the ancient tragedians. This formula occurs in French tragedy from its beginnings to its climax in Racine, author of *Phèdre* and *Andromaque,* but also of *Esther* and *Athalie.*

The *leitmotiv* of classical drama is human fate. This precisely is the question on which the Greek and Hebrew world differ. Sophocles and Aeschylus portray and lament man's helplessness vis-à-vis the almighty gods, whose whims play havoc with all human undertakings. The result is resignation, hopelessness, fatalism. This view is challenged by the biblical belief in a providence above all human aspirations, but generating hope and trust in a mankind purified through suffering.

Racine's Orestes sinks into despair:

Grâce aux dieux! Mon malheur passe mon espérance.
Oui, je te loue, ô ciel de ta persévérance.
Appliqué sans relâche au soin de me punir,
Au comble des douleurs tu m'as fait parvenir.
Ta haine a pris plaisir à former ma misère.
J'étais né pour servir d'exemple à ta colère.

The gods be thanked! My misfortune goes beyond my expecta-
    tions.
Yes, I praise you, o Heavens, for your perseverance.
Relentlessly endeavoring to punish me,
You have led me to the ultimate grief.
Your hatred has taken delight in shaping my misery.
I was born to serve as an example for your wrath.

Similar is the rebellion of the ill-fated King Saul:

> Oh! la belle façon d'aller ainsi chercher
> Les hommes, pour après les faire trébucher!
> . . . . . . . . . . . . . . . . . . . . . . . . . . . . . . . . . . . . .
> Mais je vais, puisqu'ainsi en mes maux tu te plais,
> Finir au camp mes jours, mon malheur et ta haine.

> Oh! What a beautiful thing to seek out men,
> Only to trip them afterwards!
> . . . . . . . . . . . . . . . . . . . . . . . . . . . . . . . . . . . . . . .
> But, since you enjoy my tribulations, I am going
> To finish at camp my life, my misfortune, and your hatred.

But here in deepest despair begins Saul's purification, which leads to his submission to God's decrees:

> Oh! Que sa Providence est cachée aux humains.

> Oh! How his Providence is hidden from human beings.

Even clearer is the conversion, out of the darkest despair, of Zedekiah in Robert Garnier's play *Sédécie ou les Juives* when his triumphant enemy Nebuchadnezzar kills his children and blinds him:

> Astres, qui sur nos chefs éternels flamboyez
> Regardez mes tourments, mes angoisses voyez.
> Mes yeux ne verront plus votre lumière belle,
> Et vous verrez un roy privé de liberté,
> De royaume, d'amis, d'enfants et de clarté.
> Qui vit si misérable? Autour de cette masse
> Voyez-vous un malheur qui mon malheur surpasse?

> Heavenly bodies, that burn above our heads,
> Look on my torments, see my anguish.
> Never again will my eyes see your beautiful light,
> And you will see a king deprived of his freedom,
> Of his kingdom, of his friends, children, and light.
> Who lives as wretchedly? Among these masses
> Do you see a misfortune that surpasses my own?

From this anguish, infinitely greater than that of King Oedipus, the

Jewish king struggles to a humble confession. When the Prophet Jeremiah exhorts him: "Il en faut louer Dieu tout ainsi que d'un bien" (You must praise God as if it were a blessing), he draws himself up with a new faith in God born of despair:

> Toujours soit-il bénit, et que par trop d'angoisse
> Jamais désespéré je ne le déconnoisse.
> Je scay bien que l'ai mille fois irrité,
> Que j'ay son ire esmüe, et que par mon seul crime
> J'ai incité au mal toute Jérosolyme.

> May he ever be blessed, and may I never deny him
> Through the despair of exceeding misery.
> I know I have irritated him a thousand times,
> That I have provoked his anger, and that by my crime alone
> I have incited to evil all Jerusalem.

This is no feeble acceptance of brute force, but a confession of guilt and repentance to a biblical God of justice and forgiveness. This Old Testament idea was to attain full significance in the culmination of French Classicism, the plays of Racine. At the same time, this poet wrote an inspiring plea for religious tolerance, which marked the knell of the Middle Ages in literature and was the harbinger of Jewish emancipation, the play *Esther*. It tells of the exile, ostracism, and deliverance of the Jewish people.

# SPAIN

Long before the "Wandering of the Nations" and the occupation of Europe by new inhabitants, there were Jews in the lands that were to make up the Romance cultural realms. It may only be legend that after the destruction of the temple in Jerusalem by Nebuchadnezzar (586 B.C.), a number of refugees had arrived on the Iberian peninsula and settled in Seville and Toledo. But it is thoroughly possible that there were already Jewish settlements under Hadrian in various places in Spain.

At the beginning of the fifth century there were certainly numerous

Jewish communities. Under the rule of the Visigoth their position had not been unfavorable. It became critical only when religious persecutions began shortly after the Visigoth's conversion to Christianity. Although the anti-Jewish measures were at times relaxed, it is understandable that the Arab invasion of 711 was greeted by the oppressed Jews with great expectations.

The expansion of Moorish power led to an explosion of cultural life on the peninsula. It brought the dawn of the "Golden Age" of the Jewish-Arab symbiosis from the ninth to the twelfth century, which had its repercussions on the Christian population of the country.

During the hundreds of years of conflict between the Christian North and the Muhammedan South, alternately military and political, two centers developed, Toledo and Córdoba, both marked by strong Jewish influence. When Alfonso VI of Castile conquered Toledo in 1085, the anti-Jewish animosity born during the Visigoth hegemony was revived. However, gradually Jewish and Arabic intellectuals and specialists were called on. The Cid's heroic deeds were first described to posterity by a Jew, Aben Alfange.

Gradually the Arabic centers of culture, Córdoba and Granada, overtook their northern counterparts and branches of knowledge developed by the Arabs spread through the Christian regions, aided decisively by those Jewish intellectuals proficient in languages. In Toledo, the famous academy expanded, with its great translators' school, where Christians, Moors, and Jews worked together in peace. Later, it was mainly Jews who translated into Hebrew and Latin the culture blossoming in Moorish Spain. At that time the philosophical writings of Salomon ibn Gabirol, known in Christendom as Avencebrol, were translated into Latin under the title *Fons Vitae*. Even more brilliant was Maimonides' *Guide for the Perplexed*. It anticipated Scholasticism, whose main representative Thomas Aquinas discussed and took over the religious-philosophical arguments of "Rabbi Moyses." According to an observation of the historian Michelet, the Jews were in the following historical situation: "the only link between the East and the West that maintained a permanent contact of trade and light between the two worlds, thus frustrating the two fanaticisms, both Christian and Moslem.''

With increasing domination, Christian fanaticism also grew, and led the Jewish population to pay lip service to Christianity in order to retain its role in the life of the nation. The forced converts, *conversos,* remained conscious of their Judaism and practiced it as a family tradition. This situation has persisted to the present day in many Spanish families. Tens of thousands of Spaniards were Christians and Jews at the same time.

But then the Inquisition came upon the scene and subjected Spain to a continuous process of "purification." While some Jews met secretly in cellars to hold Jewish services, others became stooges of the Inquisition as fanatic preachers of their new faith. Rabbi Salomon Halevi became Pablo de Santa María, bishop of Burgos, and induced Benedict XIII to enact anti-Jewish decrees (1412), and to arrange the religious dialogues of Tortosa (1413-14) at which other apostates proselytized vigorously among their fellow Jews. "The Chrisitians have the power," Moses de Toquesillas warned the Jews of Toledo, "and they can silence the truth with one single blow." For this reason the great scholar Nachmanides was "the loser" in the famous Barcelona Debate of 1263 against the apostate Pablo Cristiani, in spite of his intellectual superiority.

Even with Christianity Jewish influence in Spain is reflected in the literature of the time. Over-zealous converts like Pablo de Santa María (whose wife, incidentally, remained Jewish) were able to utilize their Jewish background in a new intellectual sphere. For instance, the Jewish-Christian historian relied on Jewish commentaries of the Bible for *Historia Universal,* a world history from Adam to Juan II in verse. This influence persisted in the awakening Spanish literature until the expulsion in 1492, when the exiles took a piece of their homeland with them into their adopted countries.

Spanish-Jewish history had its golden age under the reign of Don Pedro. At that time a certain rabbi at the royal court was famous as a troubadour. Born at the close of the thirteenth century in Castile, Rabbi Santob, "el Judío de Carrión" (the Jew of Carrion) dedicated his book of instructions to the king: *Proverbios morales,* or *Consejos (advice) y documentos del Rabbi Don Santo.* The rabbinical instructions begin with the verse:

> Señor Rey, noble, alto,
> Oy este sermón
> Que vyene de syr Santob
> Judío de Carríon.

> Lord King, noble, mighty,
> Hear this sermon
> That comes from Sir Santob
> The Jew from Carrion.

Various maxims follow, derived and sometimes literally stemming from the Talmud (Mishlei Shlomo, Midrash, Pirkie Abot):

> Que non ya ome pobre
> Synon el codicioso,
> Nin rrico synon ome
> Con lo que tiene gozoso.

> No man is poor
> Except the greedy,
> No man is rich except
> He who is content with what he has.

Another rabbinical saying from the *Proverbs of the Fathers* is interpreted as follows by Don Santob:

> El mundo, en verdat,
> De tres cosas se mantyen
> De juyzio e de verdat,
> E paz, que dellos vyen.

> In reality, the world
> Rests on three things:
> Wisdom and truth,
> And peace which stems from these.

The practical rabbi ends his collection as he had begun it, with his full name:

> Aquí acaba el Rab Don Santob.
> Dios sea loado.
>
> Here Rabbi Don Santob ends.
> God be praised.

A quick end was put to idyllic relationships such as those between this rabbi and his king by the increase in religious persecutions. Converts known as Marranos increased markedly after every persecution. Conversion made inroads among the upper classes anxious to protect their privileges. Others took on new names during times of terror, but otherwise practiced their Jewish customs much as before.

Their lot was mourned by Antonio de Montoro, the last great troubadour, who lived in Córdoba under Isabella of Castile. He lamented the fate of the recent converts, ridiculed and soon thereafter persecuted, who were insulted as Jews even after their conversion:

> Adorando a Dios y Hombre
> Por muy alto señor mío.
> Por do mi culpa se escombre
> No pude perder el nombre
> De viejo, puto, judío.
>
> Pues Reyna de gran valor
> Que la santa fe acrecienta
> No quiere Nuestro Señor
> Con furor
> La muerte del pecador
> Mas que viva y se arripienta.
>
> Worshipping the God in human form
> As my exalted Lord
> Who redeemed me from my sins
> I was not able to shed the name
> Of old, obscene Jew.
>
> Noble Queen
> Elevated by your holy faith,
> Our Lord does not want
> Furiously
> The death of the sinner
> But that he live and repent.

Antonio also turned angrily on the dramatic poet Rodrigo Cota, one of the authors of *La Celestina,* who ridiculed his former coreligionists.

Jewish literary gifts now turned against themselves. Many converts succeeded in gaining the highest offices in the political and ecclesiastical hierarchy (e.g., the bishop of Burgos), and were also able to gain recognition in literature. They emphasized their Christian loyalty by anti-Jewish polemics to assure themselves the protection of the Church. One of them was Juan Alfonso de Baena (near Córdoba), who under the reign of Juan II of Castile published a collection of the poems of his time, entitled *Cancionero del Judino Juan Alfonso de Baena.* In this collection are found poems of the convert Pero Ferrus, who treated the Jews sarcastically. The rabbis of Alcalá retaliated:

> Los rrabyes nos juntamos
> Don Pero Ferrus a responder,
> E la rrepuesta que damos
> Quered la bien entender,
> E dezimos que es provado
> Que non dura en un estado
> La rriquesa nin menester.
>
> . . . . . . . . . . . . . . . . . . . . . . .
> El pueblo y los hasanes
> Que nos aquí ayuntamos?
> Con todos nostros afanes
> En el Dio siempre esperamos.

> We rabbis are gathered here
> To answer Don Pero Ferrus,
> Please listen carefully
> To the answer we are going to give,
> And we say it has been proven
> That neither wealth nor distress
> Will last for ever.
>
> The people and the cantors
> That are gathered here
> Most fervently
> Will always trust in God.

Meanwhile the fate of the "converts" had deteriorated to a fantastic degree. After the Grand Inquisitor Torquemada, under Ferdinand of Aragon and Isabella of Castile, had carried out the total expulsion of the Jews from Spain (now completely Christianized after the conquest of the last Arab stronghold), his hunt for the new converts took on the character of a furious pogrom. Any denunciation sufficed to deliver suspicious persons over to torture and usually the funeral pyre, *auto-da-fé*s, where mass executions became folk festivals. Therefore great numbers of Marranos soon began individual flights from the clutches of the Inquisition to Holland or Italy, where they returned to their Jewish beliefs, as was the case with Spinoza's family. In France, the camouflage was retained. In the Italy of the Renaissance, the refugees soon found the opportunity to help shape this movement of intellectual renewal, for example, Juda Abrabanel, alias Leone Ebreo, who wrote *Dialoghi d'amore*. Other emigrants retained their Spanish speech for a long time. In Ferrara a literary masterpiece was produced in 1553 in the Bible translation of Absalom Usque, the *Bible of Ferrara,* which Lessing admired so much that he said it would be worth learning Spanish just to be able to read it.

Salomon Usque (Salusque), born in Lisbon and resident in Venice, wrote a play *Esther,* which was translated into Italian. He also translated Petrarch's sonnets into Spanish (1567). He wrote poetry in Italian and in a Spanish permeated with Hebrew words. The emigrants had amplified their mother tongue with numerous Hebrew expressions and created a new idiom known as *Ladino,* spoken to the present day. One of his poems is:

Adonenu Elohenu
Bara es Mosce Rabenu
Para darnos toratenu
Que empieza con Anochi.


Mose ala lasamaim
Sin achila e sin maim
Trujo las luchos snaim
Que empiezan con Anochi.

> Misinai ba a relumbrar
> Con hazozrot y Kol sofar
> A Israel hizo temblar
> Cuando el Dio dijo Anochi.

> Our Lord, our God
> Created Moses, our teacher,
> To give us our Torah,
> Which begins with "Anochi[I]."

> Moses went up into the mountain
> Without food and without drink
> And received the two tablets,
> Which begin with "Anochi."

> Down from Sinai came the lightning
> With trumpets and sounds of the shofar
> And Israel trembled
> When God said: "Anochi."

Another refugee from the Inquisition was David Abenatar Melo, who fled from Madrid, where he had lived outwardly as a Christian, to Amsterdam, where he died in 1646 after returning to Judaism. He was known as "harmonosio traductor del Psalterio misterioso" (the harmonious translator of the mysterious Psalter). His translations are filled with his personal experiences, such as in the 30th psalm:

> Nel infierno metido
> De la Inquisition dura
> Entre fieros leones de albedrio,
> De allí me has redimido,
> Dando a mis males cura,
> Solo porque me viste arrepentido.

> Thrown in the hell
> Of the cruel Inquisition
> In the clutches of ferocious lions,
> From there who have freed me, O Lord,
> You have healed my wounds
> Merely because you saw my repentance.

Other Marranos wrote heroic legends in the style of the time and chose for them Jewish themes, to celebrate their ancestors in the spirit of the *chansons de geste*. Jacob Usiel published a poem in twelve cantos in Venice in 1624, under the influence of Tasso, entitled *David, poema eroico*. Miguel de Silveyra, who had studied in Coimbra and Salamanca, published shortly afterwards the epic *El Macabeo* in Naples. It is filled with longing for the Holy Land.

The most brilliant representative of this Marrano literature was Antonio Enriquez Gómez, called the "Jewish Calderón," exceedingly prolific as epic and lyric poet, and writer of comic and serious plays. Born in Segovia of Marrano parents, he was persecuted by the Inquisition in spite of a promising career in the Spanish army, "accused" of Judaism, and burned in effigy in Seville in 1660. He gives us a gripping picture of the Inquisition.

> Hungrily it plots torment,
> Seeking murder at every step;
> There is no peace in the whole world
> Because of its sharp Argus-stare.
> It spreads disaster everywhere.

> (M. Kayserling, *Sefarad*)

Several of his plays deal with biblical themes: *El Rayo de Palestina, La Prudente Abigail, El Trono de Salomon*. His epic *El Sansón nazareno* is dedicated to the martyr Juda el Creyente, and is about Don Lope de Vera, who had himself circumcised and took the name of Juda. He died in Valladolid in 1644 on the funeral pyre. Gómez glorifies his martyrdom:

> Yo muero por la ley que tu escribiste,

> I am dying for the law that you wrote

Finally, we should mention the name of Daniel Levi de Barrios. He fled Spain and after long wanderings settled in Amsterdam, where Spinoza's family was living at the time. While in Italy he had returned to Judaism. Many members of his family were victims of the Inquisition. His dirges are about them and the play *Contra la verdad no ay fuerça* (Force Will not Prevail against the Truth) is devoted to the martyrs burned alive in Córdoba in 1665 or 1667. His best works are considered to be *Flor de Apolo* and *Coro de las Musas*.

For the record, I shall mention here the claim that the author of the world-famous *Celestina* is also of Jewish descent. Fitzmaurice-Kelly, in his *Spanish Literature* (London, 1925, p. 128) says: "If, as has been claimed, the young Rojas is the author, it would be a brilliant triumph for the Jewish spirit."

A great deal of Jewish blood still flows nowadays in the veins of great Spanish families, but there is no visible Jewish presence in Spain. After all that has happened, and in spite of a great past, the Sephardic emigrants felt no desire to return to a country that had long been their homeland. But its presence remained in their language, which also expressed their Messianic hopes.


# I T A L Y

Of all the Latin countries, Italy presents the picture of the most serene intellectual and social relations between its Jewish and Christian citizens. It never committed the Church-instigated excesses of France and Spain. This may be due to the natural disposition of the Italian people, or the proximity of the Holy See, which relaxed the severity of the application of the canonic laws.

The Jewish community in Italy goes back to the second century before Christ. When the emissaries of the Maccabees sought the protection of Rome against the Syrians, they found a Jewish community there already, rapidly expanding through vigorous missionary activities. In addition to the capital, there were congregations in Naples, Salerno, Ostia, Ferrara, Ravenna, and Milan. The catacombs of Venosa, where there was a talmudic school, and an inscription in Tarento, confirm a highly developed community life.

The Jews owed their position to Caesar, and, generally, they retained their privileges under the Empire. Even after the conquest of Judea, according to Mommsen, Judaism was granted the status of a sanctioned religion. In Rome there were Jewish houses of worship, which, according to Horace and Juvenal, were meeting places for Roman patricians. The spread of Jewish customs and theology provided fertile ground for the activities of the apostles. Besides participating in the arts and sciences, with the historian Josephus as the most prominent example in this field, Jews also actively cultivated religious writings. The "Wise Men of Rome" enjoyed great respect as far as Babylon, the birthplace of the Talmud.

Even after the introduction of ecclesiastic restrictions and the increasing missionary zeal of the Church, Italian Jews were still treated more benevolently than Jews in other lands. While the Middle Ages threatened to go on forever in the rest of Europe, a new age was dawning in Italy. Emperor Frederick II made his Neapolitan court a haven for intellectuals without regard to religious beliefs. He welcomed Spanish and Provençal Jews, whom he commissioned to translate the works of Arabic and Judeo-Arabic philosophy into Latin and Italian. His activities had an exemplary effect on Italian princes, who, with Jewish help, also translated Arabic writings into Latin and Italian. The most famous representatives of the Provençal school were Jacob Anatoli and Kalonymos (Maestro Calo). In this way legends and motifs from the Orient, Talmud, and Midrash found their way into Christian literature, for example, the three rings as a symbol of religious tolerance in the tales of Boccaccio.

When with the "dolce stil nuovo," a new, secularly oriented type of poetry appeared in Italy, it had an influence on the Jewish writers of the time. Immanuel the Roman (Manoello, 1270-1330) introduced new art forms, as well as erotic elements, into the hitherto strictly puritanical Hebrew writings. His collection *Sefer Hamachberot* (collected writings) paves the way for the *Decameron,* but the last canto, *Ha-eden weha-tofet* (Paradise and Hell), is about the poet's visit to hell, and is modeled after Dante's famous work. (Immanuel was the same age as, and supposedly a personal friend of Dante. His guidebook through heaven and hell is called *Daniel* and may be an assonantic reference to his model.)

Immanuel allows people of good will of other faiths into his

Jewish paradise, just as Dante had reserved a welcome place in his for the Jews of the Old Testament. Doctors, however, who kept their art secret, to the detriment of mankind, are banished mercilessly to hell. To this concept, the duty to share medical knowledge, the Jewish doctors of the Middle Ages owed their privileged position with kings and popes.

Immanuel also wrote Italian poetry, and after his death he was eulogized by the poet Cino da Pistoia. In the Synagogue, on the other hand, his works were proscribed because of their frivolous tone, not to mention his fondness for irreverent, although witty, digressions.

After him, other Italian Jews also wrote poems in the vernacular, for example Salomone Ebreo of Ferrara, whose love poems, unfortunately, have been lost. The first translations from the Bible and the prayer book into colloquial Italian, although in Hebrew script, date from the fourteenth century. They were intended for the use of women and those men who could not understand Hebrew. A penitential prayer of that time in Jewish-Italian dialect is very informative for the history of Old Italian. Cassuto quotes a text from Leviticus as an example of this dialect:

> E li figlioli de Israel *giro* a secco infra lo maro e l'acqui a essi muro della ritta loro e della manca loro. E salvao Domeddeth nella di esso Israel da mano de Mizraim, e vidde Israel quelli de Mizraim morte sopre canto dello mare. E vidde Israel la forza granne che fece Domeddeth in quelli de Mizraim. (Cod. Brit. Mus. or 74 f 3 a. Artom, *un' antica poesia italiana*. Riv isr X. Blondheim, *les parlers judeo-romans*. Cassuto, Un *elogio in antico dialetto giudeo-italiano*, in G. J. Ascoli, *Gedenkbuch*.)
> And the children of Israel crossed the sea without getting wet. And the waters formed walls to their right and to their left. And the Lord God saved Israel from the hands of the Egyptians. And Israel saw the Egyptian dead on the shore. And Israel recognized God's might in what he did against the Egyptians

The rabbi-physician Moses di Rieto, personal physician to Pope Pius II, also produced a Hebrew vision of paradise in terza rima, *Mikdash meat* (The Small Holy Place). It contains discussions about

Averroës, Maimonides, and Gersonides, and culminates in a description of the "Kingdom of the Torah." Parts of it were translated into Italian.

With the coming of the Renaissance, Jewish-Italian relations were considerably strengthened. The hunger for new knowledge and the attempt to satisfy it with the treasures of antiquity led to the discovery of a Jewish culture of biblical, talmudic, and kabbalistic origin. When Pope Nicholas V appropriated 5,000 ducats for the search of the Hebrew original of St. Matthew's Passion, he laid the cornerstone for the great collection of Hebrew manuscripts in the Vatican library. Since printing was highly developed in Italy, soon Hebrew presses were founded in every large city. A few years after the first Italian publications, the famous Pentateuch commentary by Rashi was printed in Reggio di Calabria (the first book ever printed in Hebrew). In Rome and Bologna, professorships were created for Hebrew, considered by many humanists to be more important than Greek. Among the Jewish teachers, Elia del Medigo, Pico's teacher, and Jochanan Alemanno achieved distinction.

Through Pico della Mirandola, fascinated by the mysteries of the kabbala, Johannes Reuchlin was inspired to study Hebrew during his Italian journey, and later in his homeland courageously defended the Talmud against the attacks of the Dominicans. The Sforza family's physician, David de Pomis (1525-88), with his *Apologie,* in which he cited the importance of Jewish doctors to the Popes, obtained the suspension of Sixtus V's decrees against Jewish doctors. To the same pope he dedicated his Hebrew-Latin-Italian dictionary *Zemach David,* which was to facilitate the humanists' access to Hebrew studies. Shortly before this, Leon da Modena had written a Hebrew-Latin dictionary.

Intellectual curiosity about Hebrew culture was reciprocated by the Italian Jews with growing interest in their milieu. More than ever before they took part in the intellectual activities of their country. They gave their children instruction in the fine arts in addition to the traditional education in the Bible and Talmud, and they were open to all the currents of the times.

In Mantua, Asaria (Bonaiuto) dei Rossi wrote the historical work

*Meor Enayim* (Enlightenment) in which non-Jewish sources were used for the first time for research in Jewish history. In addition to Jewish authorities, he also drew on Greek and Roman authors, and Church fathers. This departure alarmed congressional leaders, who restricted the work to those over twenty-five years old.

Salomon Usque, already mentioned, contributed to the awakening dramatic literature with *Esther,* performed in Venice. The theatrical center of the sixteenth century was Mantua, where the Gonzaga dynasty adopted a protective attitude toward its Jewish citizens. Jewish troops must have been well received at court, since the performances had to start earlier on Fridays to be ended by dusk, the beginning of the Sabbath. And they began much later on Saturdays, after the end of the Jewish day of rest.

A productive playwright was Leone da Sommî Portaleone, author of comedies in the style of the time, and an epoch-making treatise of the theater, *The Dialogue on Representational Art,* which stamps him as a forerunner of the famous stage directors of the twentieth century.

But the climax of Jewish-Italian relations was another series of dialogues, the *Dialoghi di amore,* written in a Platonic spirit by Juda Abrabanel, who, under the name of Leone Ebreo, shone in the firmament of the Renaissance. (See Chapter 5)

His father, Don Isaac Abrabanel, was the Minister of Finance for King Ferdinand of Aragon, and provided the material prerequisites for the campaign against the Moors. But when the whole peninsula came under Christian domination, and the Jews were expelled at the instigation of the Grand Inquisitor Torquemada, Don Isaac and his son voluntarily exiled themselves, in spite of the king's efforts to retain Juda, his personal physician.

In Naples, both father and son soon recaptured the prominence they had enjoyed in Madrid. Juda, because of his youth, was especially able to assimilate the stimulating atmosphere of humanistic Italy, and he was to achieve an unusual synthesis of Jewish culture with the Renaissance spirit. *Dialoghi di amore* was written in 1502 and published in 1535. To judge from its sensational success, it fulfilled the long-held hopes of generations of humanists, and accurately expressed the spirit of the times, the enthusiastic belief in Greek and Hebrew antiquity as the source of metaphysical knowledge.

In a mood of profoundly Platonic inspiration, two lovers, Philo and Sophie, talk about the nature of love and reflect about the mysterious power that penetrates and stirs all living things. The physical world is not, as medieval philosophy maintained, an ominous, Satanic force. Neither is it held together by inflexible natural laws, at best a perfected but soulless mechanism, but by the creative will of a godhead, at once transcendant and immanent.

Instead of two opposing forces, love and hate, fighting over the world, as Empedocles taught, one elemental power is driving things to an ever higher synthesis. In organic life, as in the cosmos, the spirit of love prevails and summons the world to harmony and perfection.

Man is, according to the injunctions of the Bible, called to perfect creation by carrying out the tasks imposed on him by his milieu and his fate, not by fleeing from reality to avoid unpleasantness. Thus the world is again united with its creator, who longs for his creatures. Such ideas remind one of the teachings of Polish Hasidism.

Leone's originality consists in rejecting a mechanistic explanation of nature such as science was to develop in the following centuries, rather seeing God's intervention in all phenomena, a consciously, creating, striving godhead, the God of the Bible. By showing man his creative place in the world, Leone not only avoided a destructive naturalism, but also overcame the rigid, static, medieval spirit.

While Leone Ebreo introduced Jewish thought into his new homeland, Rabbi Leone da Modena (1571-1648) did the opposite by translating the first canto of Ariosto's *Orlando furioso* into Hebrew. The Roman poetess Deborah Ascarelli translated Jewish medieval religious poetry into Italian, published in 1602 in Venice with her own poems. In the same city, the literary salon of the beautiful Sara Copia Sullam was well known. Ambitious priests attempted to convert this gifted Jewess, then accused her, after their failure, of denying the immortality of the soul. She defended herself in a publication entitled *Manifesto di Sara Copia Sullam* (1621). Venice was becoming increasingly a center of Jewish life, the seat of a community proud of its Hebrew tradition, yet open to contemporary influence. Here, during the Renaissance, Hebrew and Italian culture reached a synthesis not found elsewhere for two centuries.

Judeo-Romance literary relations are an accurate mirror of the political and social reality. They illustrate the history of tolerance, or more accurately intolerance, in the Middle Ages.

Due to their somewhat unusual social and religious aspects, Judeo-Romance relations during the Renaissance show a certain one-sidedness. Jewish thought's contributions to its surroundings by far surpassed its debts. Church and Synagogue had a similar relationship in the Middle Ages. Jewish religious tradition, thanks to its great age, possessed a stability and authority that made the Church feel insecure. Consequently, the Church's frenzied attempts at the conversion of the Jews and ideological disputations culminating in boundless contempt for the Jewish image. But the Church was never able to strip the Synagogue of its nobility.

What the missionary imperialism of the Church did achieve with its soul-saving zeal and effort to annihilate every alien belief was to stiffen the resistance of the Synagogue, to cause it to isolate itself, and to reject vigorously all outside influence.

The situation was radically different during the period of Jewish-Arabic coexistence in Spain, where victorious Islam showed great tolerance, and allowed the Jews to collaborate on an equal footing in every area through poets and thinkers such as Maimonides, Gersonides, Ibn Gabirol, Ibn Ezra, and Judah Halevi. In this Semitic pre-Renaissance, Jewish intellectual life and its milieu influenced each other decisively.

When, however, the Church enclosed the Jews in ghettos, they retaliated by retrenching beyond even higher intellectual walls. Banishment in France and Spain created a sharp, long-lasting hiatus in the history of Romance-Jewish relations. The only continuation was carried on by Sephardic Jews, by Marrano literature in its broadest sense, and by the use of Ladino in the adopted lands. In

France, all contacts had disappeared, and only the subsequent discovery of Hebrew antiquity restored them.

In Italy under the balmy sun of a pioneering humanism, an almost continuous cultural relationship was maintained, which has lasted until the present. This happy collaboration is one of the sources from which modern civilization is fed.

# 4

# *The Golden Age of Jewish Poetry*

There is a tendency to explain historical development according to biological laws: springtime effervescence, flowering, maturity, decadence. According to the theory of Oswald Spengler, Western civilization is approaching its twilight, just as the Oriental, Hellenic, and Roman civilizations have gone from expansion to decadence. This biological process has been applied to historical development, and scholars claim to have found it in the unfolding of Jewish history. The migration in the desert and the conquest of the land of Canaan would be the stormy period of youth during which Mosaic legislation prepared the future fruits. David and Solomon would represent the political flowering of the Kingdom of Israel. The era of the prophets would be that of spiritual maturity, and the following periods, marked by the destruction of the two temples, those of decline and degeneration. That is how Jewish history has been interpreted, especially by Christian thinkers for whom the old trunk had died and brought to life a new offshoot. But, to the surprise of the world, this old uprooted trunk keeps on producing new flowers. The period of what is known as decadence has been going on for two thousand years, much longer than the national existence, and never stops producing spiritual values, and—in accordance with Ezekiel's tragic promise: "You will live in your blood," with which each new member is welcomed to the ancient alliance—our people recovers from each cruel mutilation physically weakened, but spiritually unconquered.

It is true that during the period of the Diaspora, the evolution of Judaism lacked harmony and equilibrium. Different character traits prevailed following the various changes in the political or sociological situation. At times the Jewish people isolated itself completely from the outside world. Its whole effort was directed to the interpretation of the Jewish law. This was the case in Babylonia, where the Talmud was born. It was also the case later in Poland. Sometimes opposite tendencies prevailed, that of assimilating the surrounding civilization and participating in it, as in Alexandria, or in Western Europe in the nineteenth century. In both cases there is a break in the spiritual balance, a one-sided development. Only once during the period of exile were all the spiritual forces of the Jewish people able to develop harmoniously by the study, the meditation, and the renewal of its legacy, accompanied by the active participation in the scholarly and the intellectual currents of the neighboring gentiles. This creative fusion of the Jewish heritage and foreign influence took place in Spain in a three-hundred-year period, from the tenth to the twelfth century, and is considered a golden age not only in Jewish history, but also in Western civilization, as a "dream of flowers," a pre-Renaissance that ushered in the dawn of Western thought. By one of those rare and lucky syntheses that mark the high points of human development, Jews and Arabs met in a common task, without relinquishing their respective traditions, for their mutual enrichment through a totally spiritual rivalry.

A theme that has been repeatedly treated is the incompatibility of Hellenism and Judaism. By Hellenism is understood the whole orientation that has issued from Greek culture. The events that gave rise to the festival of Hanukkah are used by practicing Jews to prove the necessity of fighting against the Greek spirit. They view it as a seductive and dangerous form of the pagan spirit. This antithesis is reduced to the following formula: Judaism is an ethical principle; Hellenism is an esthetic principle. And it is rarely understood that these are two mutually complementary principles.

The awareness of the greatness of biblical humanism must not lead us to adopt a superior attitude toward Greek achievements, which have also been an admirable attempt to lift man above his fate, to give meaning to a life fettered by the misery of the human condition. The struggle of the Maccabees was a fight for national independence against the imperialistic policy of a neighboring country priding itself on its Hellenism, which in its oriental form contained indeed many immoral traits. That, however, does not diminish the significance of a civilization whose road is marked by names such as Homer, Aeschylus, Socrates, Aristotle, and Plotinus, and which played such a prominent role in mankind's intellectual quest. Judaism, basically oriented toward the good, is a necessary complement to Hellenism, just as the latter, in its nobler version, completes Judaism. From the beginning, thinkers have attempted to create a synthesis between these two attempts to control life. In Judeo-Arabic Spain this synthesis was largely successful. The Arabs were then the heirs and the representatives of Hellenism.

While, after the fall of the Roman Empire under the onslaught of the Germanic hordes, Europe lived for centuries in a state of semibarbarism and intellectual lethargy, the remnants of Greco-Roman culture had taken refuge in Asia Minor, where they had been adapted by the Arabs, who carried them as far as Spain during their expansion through North Africa. Under the reigns of enlightened caliphs in Spain, high Jewish officials took pride in encouraging the development of the arts and sciences. It was the age Aristotle had dreamed of, where philosophers would be kings, and kings philosophers.

The Jews learned from the Arabs everything they had to teach them, studied Plato and Aristotle through Avenpace and Averroës, and filled their philosophy with the biblical spirit, creating thus new systems of thought which, in turn, acted on Western consciousness in the process of regeneration. They studied mathematics, astronomy, geography, medicine, and European languages. They were scholars, doctors, translators. Their activities were soon to be felt in other European countries. They applied the scientific method to the study of the immense store of Jewish knowledge, and it is no accident that the first systematic analysis of the Talmud, the theological *summa* of

Judaism, comes from Maimonides, who, at the same time, was the greatest authority of his time in the field of Aristotelian philosophy.

In this fruitful exchange of cultural possessions, each party remained proudly aware of the values of its own legacy while it assimilated foreign values. All the faculties of the mind, which under different latitudes were deteriorating, flowered splendidly in the Spain of that time. Scientific rules and systematic methods were introduced into Jewish disciplines. For the first time they were applied to the instrument of the Jewish spirit, the Hebrew language. It is then that the Hebrew grammar was written, and studies were undertaken on the character of the holy language. Daring philologists such as Ibn G'anach and his school studied the structure of the syntax of Hebrew, thus elucidating through their findings passages that had until then received tortured interpretations. Through its contact with Arabic, its sister language, the Hebrew vocabulary was transformed and enriched. It created a new medium of expression, transcending the judicial terminology of the scholars of the Talmud, adapting itself to all the requirements of the arts and sciences. Thus was formed the instrument of the noblest art, the language of the heart, poetry.

Jewish poetry in Spain stands out in vivid colors from the tradition of postbiblical Judaism. But in spite of its peculiar and very original character, it remains intimately connected with it. If it created new elements, it is only because it drew its inspiration from the historical past of Jewish poetry.

After the dispersion of the Jewish people, the inexhaustible flow of biblical poetry had spread through all the countries of Europe in a thousand rivulets, one of them irrigating the Andalusian land. Here, in a particularly favorable spiritual and sociopolitical climate, it was to nourish the most beautiful poetic efflorescence. Until then, poetic creation had found only once a soil so suitable to its growth. It was the period of the Judges and the splendid reign of the first kings, period of the organic development of all the powers of the people on the national territory. At that time the resources of the people were not yet spent in its daily effort to defend its home and its traditions. It is the classical age of our literature, the period of the Psalms, which belong to world literature. Soon after, at the time of the prophets, the disintegration of the Jewish state cast its shadow on the people and discouraged the lyrical spirit. The inner tension was released through prophetic visions of such tragic grandeur that we cannot apply to them our usual literary terminology of prose, poetry, classicism, or romanticism. The depressing conditions that followed the destruction of the Temple forced the people to concentrate its effort on the Law, as the guarantee of its existence. Poetic inspiration, although alive, had to be repressed in favor of the study and the revision of the Constitution and the morality of Moses. The legends and the fables of the Talmud were, so to speak, secondary products, although they pursued the same goal of moral education by means of the concrete illustration of biblical precepts. As for our liturgical poetry, the "Piutim," it was too obviously moralistic in expression, and rarely reached the heights of spontaneous lyricism.

The spiritual climate of radiant Andalusia recalled the period of the royal bard. Even the landscape, as Marcus Ehrenpreis notes during a trip,[1] resembles in many respects that of Judea, and must have reinforced in the exiled the feeling of being at home. I have just outlined the political conditions that assured the Jews in Spain a position unique in all of postbiblical history. With freedom of trade and peaceful competition in all the spiritual fields, poetry was able to grow to fruition. It possessed an excellent instrument, a delicate and subtle language continuously being refined, on the one hand by the new science of philology, and on the other by writers of genius.

From the Arabs it borrowed and adapted new poetic forms. The Arabs were the masters of Europe in all the arts. The famous poetry of the troubadours, for instance, is of Arabic origin. Jewish poetry, however, did not follow it in that direction. It did not take as a subject a woman of flesh and blood, of transitory beauty, and of questionable virtue. Judeo-Spanish poetry strove toward a much loftier goal.

> Sie war keine Laura, deren
> Augen, sterbliche Gestirne,

1. Marcus Ehrenpreis, *Das Land zwischen Orient und Okzident (The Land between the East and the West)* [Berlin: Heine Bund, 1928].

In dem Dome am Karfreitag
Den berühmten Brand gestiftet—

Sie war keine Chatelaine,
Die im Blütenschmuck der Jugend
Bei Turnieren präsidierte
Und den Lorbeerkranz erteilte—

Jene, die der Rabbi liebte,
War ein traurig armes Liebchen,
Der Zerstörung Jammerbildnis,
Und sie hiess Jerusalem.

(Heine, Hebrew Melodies)

She was not a Laura, whose
Eyes, fading stars
Lit an ardent flame,
In church, on Holy Friday.

Nor a noble lady
Who in the splendor of youth
Presides over a joust and awards
A laurel wreath to the lucky winner.

The woman the rabbi loves
Has a sign of mourning on her face
And despair in her heart.
She is called Jerusalem.

Not that the joys and sorrows of profane love, the yearning for earthly happiness, and the awareness of its limitations, were unknown to the Jewish poets.

On the contrary. This is the period when they rejected asceticism to pursue the enjoyment of life. That is precisely what distinguished this era from the following, and Spanish Judaism from the Judaism of Central Europe. Individual joys and sufferings, and their poetical expression, however, were transfigured by a noble collective idea and converged toward the historical idea of the Jewish people—Zion, city of earthly and heavenly justice.

I have discovered no new stars and I will simply present the classical constellation to illustrate the glorious era of the Hebrew renaissance: Solomon ibn Gabirol, who brilliantly leads the parade, followed by the three stars who light up the firmament of Hebrew literature: Moses ibn Ezra, Abraham ibn Ezra, and Juda Halevi. The epilogue is represented by Al Charisi who, like Heine during the decline of Romanticism, was the last nightingale of a great era.

Little is known about the practical life of Salomon ibn Gabirol. Born in Malaga in 1021, he seems to have lost his parents at an early age and wandered poor and alone through the land. Deprivation and disappointment developed in him a profound *mal du siècle,* which we also encounter in other poets. This in no way contradicts the description of that period as the happiest of the Jewish exile. General happiness does not exclude private misfortune, unfulfilled desires, sadness caused by the physical condition and the metaphysical limitations of mankind. Ibn Gabirol is inclined to melancholy through his nature, and led to sadness by his fate. At sixteen he complains

If I hear laughter my heart cries.

He is not made for ordinary happiness on earth, as he recognizes, not without a note of pride:

My body roams on earth,
But my spirit soars above the clouds.

This spirit was rich and profound, and compensated him for the disappointments of daily life. Maybe, like Torquato Tasso, he was responsible for a great part of his suffering, but he could also claim:

And when other men in their suffering are struck dumb,
A God blessed me with the gift to express my sufferings.

And he transformed into precious pearls the sorrows of his heart. With his great distress he made little songs, molding the Hebrew language to the nuances and subtleties of his emotions. He won the favor of influential people, such as the noble Jekutiel Alhassan in Saragossa, and even Samuel ibn Nagrela, the Jewish minister in Granada. Under their sponsorship his life became easier, and before dying in Granada in 1070, he had achieved some exterior and inner equilibrium.

Ibn Gabirol is a poet and a philosopher. Poetry was his beloved, philosophy his mother:

> How could I forsake wisdom,
> I, who made a pact with her!
> She is my mother, and I her beloved child. . .
> As long as I live, my mind
> Will fly towards heavenly heights;
> I will know no rest until I have discovered its source.

He synthesized the Platonic myths and the kabbalistic ideas that he had inherited with the Jewish conception of God and the creation of the world, and condensed it all into a metaphysical system, a reflection of his nostalgic soul and daring mind. In the Middle Ages *The Source of Life* was known throughout all of Europe.

This work was written in Arabic and translated into Latin. In Hebrew Ibn Gabirol crystallized his thoughts in *The Crown of Royalty,* in which he reveals himself to be a thinker, a poet, and a fervent believer. In this religious philosophy suffused with poetry, which the Synagogue adopted in its Yom Kippur liturgy, Ibn Gabirol developed the following ideas: God is the primary source from which springs the word of God, the creative will that fills the universe. "You, O God, you have caused your will to radiate, the will that rescues being from nothingness, like the rays emanating from a luminous heart." This divine creative force animates the tiniest creature. When it wanders too far from its source, the divine force is transformed into matter. The intermediaries between pure divinity and the world of the senses are three: universal reason, "the tenth sphere, wrought with the silver of truth and the gold of the spirit," the universal soul, and universal nature. Man participates in all three steps. He is free to estrange himself from the divine source by iniquitous acts, or to commune with the divinity by contemplation and virtue, and to participate in eternal beatitude.

Here in a few inadequate words is the main idea of a vision of the world that synthesizes the allegories of the Bible with Platonic concepts. But with Ibn Gabirol—and that is why I have included these philosophical considerations in my presentation of Jewish poetry —these ideas are not abstract and purely rational. Especially in his liturgical poetry, they are expressed by a surge of sympathy for the whole creation and an ardent love for the creator and the created. Heine calls him:

> . . .diesen treuen
> Gottgeweihten Minnesänger,
> Diese fromme Nachtigall,
> Deren Rose Gott gewesen.
>
> Diese Nachtigall, die zärtlich
> Ihre Liebeslieder sang
> In der Dunkelheit der gothisch
> Mittelalterlichen Nacht!
>
> (Heine, Hebrew Melodies)
>
> A pious singer
> A minstrel dedicated to God,
> A nightingale of devotion
> Celebrating the divine rose.
>
> This nightingale that tenderly
> Lifted its song of love
> In the darkness
> Of the deepest Gothic night.

In Ibn Gabirol's time poetry was not yet completely emancipated, and was simply considered an accessory, an ornament, of the mind and of faith. Soon after, it found its justification in itself, and became an independent genre, encompassing every aspect of individual and social life. With the tribulations of the human condition it forged imperishable jewels.

This development reached its culmination in Moses ibn Ezra and Juda Halevi. Of course, they are also religious poets. But, while religion remains the basis of their lives, it does not shackle their minds with dogma. It is more the inner harmony that gives the song its melody. Besides two hundred liturgical works, Moses ibn Ezra wrote 300 poems on secular subjects, which, of course, included love, for a poet without love is, according to Heine, bread without butter. And not only heavenly love according to the rabbinical tradition that transfigured Solomon's *Song of Songs* and gave it a spiritual sense, but earthly love celebrated by the troubadors, purified, however, of its immoral side.

It was probably during his happy years that he wrote his love poetry, charming and superficial, tied in a "chain," one of the Arabic lyrical forms:

> I asked the beautiful maiden this question:
> "Why don't you love the old man's gaze?"
> "And you," she answered, "why don't you have
> A predilection for the widow?"

Love was decisive in the life of Moses ibn Ezra, and the misfortunes of love, as often happens, decided his poetical fate, making him an unhappy man but a true poet. He loved his niece and his love was reciprocated, but because of family politics she married one of Moses' brothers. He could not remain in the country any longer, for it now seemed a prison to him:

> Far from you the world is a prison, without charm.
> Places where I find no sign of you are a desert
> Your words are honey not meant for me,
> Your breath, a sweet odor of which I am deprived.

He wandered from one country to another. The news of the death of his beloved in childbirth is reflected in a moving epilogue:

> Cruelly the new-born child escapes from the bleeding body
> Of his mother, who feels her strength ebbing.
> Death seizes her, and with a haggard smile
> She begs her husband, who gives her caressing looks:
> "Think of the union of our youth
> And transfer to my tomb your affection.
> Take care of the children, and be both father and mother to
>     them,
> Since death is deaf to my tears and prayers.

And write to my uncle who suffered because of me.
Consumed by the flame of his bitter passion
He wanders, a stranger, through the universe
And seeks relief and consolation for his wounds.
His sad fate refuses him surcease of sorrow.

This probably marks the moment of his conversion from a wordly poet to a religious poet singing of repentance and contrition. His *mal du siècle* was transformed into liturgical elegies, even today very popular in Sephardic communities. His verses demonstrate a mastery of the forms of Arabic origin, although the poetic value of his works suffers from these acrobatics as well as the stereotyped character of the usual liturgical prayers of the synagogue. Still, even there, in spite of the conventional forms, Moses ibn Ezra often managed an intimate note arising from his personal tragedy.

Moses ibn Ezra, who in his treatise on literary theory created a Hebrew poetic art, also developed the practical tool of poetic expression. He introduced a new note in Jewish poetry, the subjective, individual emotion inspired by private life. He is proudly aware of the dignity of his vocation.

The poet is the true king, who wears the scepter and the crown.
He bestows honors on those who are worthy of them, but crushes false greatness.
Beware of the poet's pen: it distills both honey and poison.

The poet is an intellectual monarch. The road now opens to pure poetry, and leads to the highest peaks of Hebrew verse. In the works of Juda Halevi are welded nobility of form, ardent subjectivity, lofty national emotions, and the historical yearning for Israel.

Durch Gedanken glänzt Gabirol
Und gefällt zumeist dem Denker.
Ibn Ezra glänzt durch Kunst
Und behagt weit mehr dem Künstler.—
Aber beide Eigenschaften
Hat Jehuda ben Halevy,
Und er ist ein grosser Dichter
Und ein Liebling aller Menschen.
(Heine, *Hebrew Melodies)*

> Gabirol is a brilliant intellect;
> It is to the thinker that he appeals the most.
> Ibn Ezra is a master of his art.
> The artist prefers him.
> These two talents are united
> In Jehuda ben Halevi.
> He is both a great poet
> And dear to the hearts of all men.

Juda, son of Jacob, is the ancestor of the Jewish people, since the ten tribes of Israel only lasted a few hundred years until the deportation of 723 B.C. The tribe of Juda was joined by a part of the tribe of Levi. The Levites were the pious cantors in the Temple of Jerusalem, those who presented the offerings of the Judean people to God. Thus, by his name, Juda Halevi symbolizes the social and spiritual structure of the Jewish people, and his life and his poems have made him deservedly the most popular figure of postbiblical Judaism, among the Ashkenazim as well as the Sephardim. He incarnates the Jewish soul in exile—laughing and crying, dancing and praying—its ideals and its longing for Zion. Within a lifetime of about 50 years, Juda Halevi experienced all the phases of human existence and crystallized them in immortal works: the pure and innocent love of physical beauty, the love of his people, and the love of God. Without knowing his life in detail, we can reconstruct it through his poems and recognize the harmonious evolution of Platonic love, which, like Jacob's ladder, starts on earth and reaches heaven. Juda Halevi knew the desire and the bliss of earthly love, the pain of separation and nostalgia:

> Since you want to say good-by
> Wait a little, let me look at your face. . . .
> Remember our passionate moments
> Just as I will remember our nights of love.
> And if your image enters my dreams
> Let mine also enter yours. . . .
> Remember. Let the day of remembrance
> Bring back to life him who is dying of love.
> And when the bones of the dead rise again
> Return my soul to my body
> So that it will come back to life. For my soul left me
> The day you left me.

He knew the serene happiness of married love and described in charming lines his wedding day, the waiting of the couple. However, another note is already heard, that of love transfigured, the love of his people:

> Soon the waiting will be over and you will be joined.
> Alas! When will the troubles of my people be over?

Here it is, the Jewish soul, the missing stone in the harmony of the finished house. Even personal happiness under the beautiful Andalusian skies does not make him forget his ancestral home, the land of the patriarchs, the place where God visited the prophets. In vain does he seek in religious practices and liturgical poetry the remedy to his nostalgia.

Glorious Zion, "the navel of the world," increasingly occupies his mind, Zion, not as a symbol, not replaced by Córdoba or Toledo, but grieving Zion, waiting sadly for the return of her children.

Where can he borrow wings? He would carry his heart piece by piece. He would kiss every stone of the spot where the Temple used to be—but Zion will not always be so wretched. It will be restored, the glory of God will return to it, and a crown will be bestowed on the people who will redeem it.

> You and I, together, we will be freed.
> Our triumph will be that of your reign. . .
> May your mercy, O Lord, descend on the afflicted,
> Gather the people scattered to the four corners of the earth.
> May their voices sing out,
> May they march freely towards Zion.

Juda Halevi is not an anemic dreamer, content with prophetizing a distant future. He does not settle for anticipating the future. He wants to participate in it concretely, he wants—and that is what ultimately crowns him with a halo in the minds of his people—to carry out his dream. Here too is a refutation of those who explain Zionism through social pressure. Our poet is compelled to abandon the beautiful land of Andalusia, his friends, his family, his comfortable position as a respected doctor, his fame, to undertake the dangerous journey to the Holy Land, dangerous because it is the battlefield of the fanatical Crusaders:

> What matters to me the sun of Spain
> When my soul is consumed with the desire for the ruins of the
>     house of God.

He did, indeed, embrace it, the sacred soil of the Temple. And he died as he accomplished his dream. It might be historically true that he died on the return trip. But legend is truer than history when it maintains that he was killed by an Arab knight as he kissed the holy ground of Zion.

> Ja. das ist das Zionslied
> Des Jehuda ben Halevy
> Sterbend auf den heil'gen Trümmern
> Von Jerusalem gesungen—
>
> Also sass er, und er sang,
> Wie ein Seher aus der Vorzeit
> Anzuschaun—dem Grab entstiegen
> Schien Jeremias, der Alte—
>
> Das Gevögel der Ruinen
> Zähmte schier der wilde Schmerzlaut
> Des Gesanges, und die Geier
> Nahten horchend, fast mitleidig—
>
> Doch ein frecher Sarazene
> Kam desselben Wegs geritten,
> Hoch zu Ross, im Bug sich wiegend
> Und die blanke Lanze schwingend—
>
> In die Brust des armen Sängers
> Stiess er diesen Todesspeer,
> Und er jagte rasch von dannen,
> Wie ein Schattenbild beflügelt.
>
> Ruhig floss das Blut des Rabbi,
> Ruhig seinen Sang zu Ende

Sang er, und sein sterbeletzter
Seufzer war Jerusalem!

(Heine, *Hebrew Melodies)*

Yes, it is the song of Zion
That Yehuda ben Halevi sang
As he came to die on the ruins of Jerusalem.

He stood there and sang
Like a prophet of old.
He looked like Jeremiah returning from the tomb.

His plaintive song captivated
The birds in the wilderness,
And the falcons filled with pity
Came up to listen to him.

But a Saracen knight
Happened to pass that way,
Sitting arrogantly on his tall saddle,
Brandishing his shining spear.

He plunged it into the breast
Of the poor singing old man.
And loosening the reins of his horse,
He disappeared like a phantom.

Blood poured until death came,
Endlessly the song was heard
Until the final moment: "Jerusalem!"
That was his last sigh.

Legend is the symbolic expression of the memory left by a person. "Legends in poetry become the truth of the people," said Victor Hugo. They contain a psychological truth that replaces the details of history. The death of Moses is surrounded with legend; thus he remains the legislator, the father of the Ten Commandments for all mankind. The prophet Jeremiah, eyewitness to the destruction of the Temple, disappears from the scene as soon as his role is ended. He lives as the composer of immortal laments on the ruins of the Temple. Juda Halevi, glorious interpreter of the yearning for Zion, encounters death during his holy pilgrimage. He thus completes his poetic mission and becomes the real Jewish national poet. He is one of those men who incarnate the soul of a people. He formulated for eternity Israel's self-awareness, faithful to its past and its future. He expressed the soul of Israel through his spirit, his poetry, his life, and his death. He is the national poet of the Jews, but, as the incarnation of Israel he belongs to world literature. And he deserves the monument raised to him by another great poet, Heinrich Heine, born of Israel, but who felt, in spite of his success in the world of letters, the ambiguity of his own existence, detached from the trunk of his people.

> Ja, er ward ein grosser Dichter,
> Stern und Fackel seiner Zeit,
> Seines Volkes Licht und Leuchte,
> Eine wunderbare, grosse

> Feuersäule des Gesanges,
> Die der Schmerzenskarawane
> Israels vorangezogen
> In der Wüste des Exils.
>
> (Heine, *Hebrew Melodies*)

> Yes, he was a great poet,
> Star and torch of his time,
> Light and beacon of his people,
> Appointed to serve as guide,

> Like a column of fire
> To the caravan of exile,
> Like a singing flame
> To the suffering of Israel.

The second generation has an unenviable lot. Living in the shadow of their predecessors, they are not appreciated at their true worth. Those whom we consider the second generation of the Judeo-Spanish literature, Abraham ibn Ezra and Juda Al Charisi, are also poets of great talent. Abraham ibn Ezra is known as a spiritual commentator of the Bible with surprisingly advanced ideas. However, what is an advantage for exegesis and guarantees its originality is a disadvantage in poetry. Ezra's poems are too rational, too deficient in spontaneity to be authentic poetry. They are, however, full of charm and wit. This is how Abraham ibn Ezra sees himself:

> I sweat to succeed and succeed in nothing.
> If I go out in the morning to see the king
> I am told he is gone. And if I persist,
> And come back at night, I hear he is in bed.
> Ah, the wheel of fortune turned backwards the day I was born.
> If I were a coffin dealer, nobody would die, mourning would
>     be in mourning;
> And if I sold candles, nobody would ever see the sun go down.

Al Charisi is an interesting figure. Living at the end of the twelfth century, he was *fin de siècle* in the true sense of the word. He refined and carried to its ultimate perfection the poetry of his time. He is reminiscent of Heine, with whom, incidentally, he has a deep spiritual affinity. Both were overshadowed by more powerful personalities, the one by Juda Halevi, the other by Goethe. Yet their merit must be recognized. Al Charisi was painfully aware of the fate of those who, born too late, can only glean in fields already harvested by others.

> Ah! The blessed times of the Gabirols and the Juda Halevis!
> There was then an appreciation of noble poetry.
> But the beautiful muse today has lost its home!

And the poor poet wandered not only through his own country like the troubadours from one court to another, but also over the three continents that were known at the time, just as Moses ibn Ezra had done before him.

This romantic instability was not unrelated to the political events of the times. Various upheavals had taken place, and greater upheavals were in the offing, which were to lead later to the emigration of all the Spanish Jews. Arab domination was waning, and like all forms of decadence, was accompanied by the destruction of freedom of thought and conscience. Christianity was advancing victoriously, and once in power, it had no compunction about the means of consolidating its power. The golden age of Jewish exile was abruptly followed by an age of iron and fire. Torquemada's stakes, living torches, lit up the road of Catholic Spain. In the name of a doctrine that preaches love for our fellow men, the Spanish Jews were subjected to the sword and the flame unless they found salvation in flight or baptism. Among those pseudo-Christians, the Marranos, many made a name for themselves as important Church dignitaries or writers; but, often, the suppressed Judaism was kept alive in the souls of the false converts and expressed itself, sometimes rather strangely.

Among these poets of Jewish origin let me name Miguel de Silveyra, who lived in the sixteenth century and celebrated the Maccabee heroes, defenders of the independence of Judea, in a work of Jewish inspiration, filled with nostalgia for Zion. He was greatly admired by Lope de Vega. So too was Enrique Gómez, one of the most prolific poets of Spanish literature. Suspected by the Inquisition, Gómez escaped to Amsterdam. And for the official *auto-da-fé* the inquisitors had to settle for burning his portrait. Many of his numerous comedies took their names from the Bible: *El rayo de Palestina (The Splendor of Palestine), La prudente Abigail,* a fragment, and *Aman y Mardocheo.* Just as Miguel de Silveyra had countered the *chansons de geste* in honor of Charlemagne with a biblically inspired poem, *the Maccabees,* so Gómez described the heroic life of the Hebrew Samson in the epic *Samson Nazareno.* From a purely aesthetic viewpoint the play leaves much to be desired. Its interest lies in the ardent profession of Jewish faith, expressed indirectly through the mouth of the dying Samson:

> Yo muero por la ley que tú escribiste,
> Por los preceptos santos que mandaste,
> Por el pueblo sagrado que escogiste,
> Y por los mandamientos que ordenaste,
> Yo muero por la patria que me diste,
> Y por la gloria con que el pueblo honraste;
> Muero por Israel, y lo primero
> Por tu inefable nombre verdadero.

> I am dying for the law you wrote,
> For the holy precepts that you ordained,
> For the holy people that you chose,
> For the commandments that you prescribed.

I die for the country that you gave me,
And the glory with which you honored your people,
I die for Israel, but primarily
For your true, ineffable name.

Is this stanza anything but a tribute to the innumerable martyrs sacrificed on the altar of the Inquisition? It is not surprising, therefore, that the "Holy Office" became suspicious of Gómez. His work permits us to note the manifestations of the golden age of Jewish poetry even in the great era of Spanish literature.

The great majority of Jews fled the persecutions by sailing to other shores and settling around the Mediterranean. But the glorious period of Andalusia did not die. It was revived in the exiles' new home. The decadence and the renewal of Spanish Judaism is reflected in the fate of the Abrabanels, father and son. While Isaac Abrabanel withered in exile, his son Juda had a brilliant career in the radiant Italy of the Renaissance. Like Juda Abrabanel, many Jews of Spanish origin took an active part in the cultural activities of their time. But their contributions were based, like Spinoza's, on the universality of the spirit, and Sephardic Judaism did not produce any new spiritual center. The center of gravity shifted definitely to Ashkenazi Judaism. However, while it yielded its spiritual hegemony to another tribe, Sephardic Judaism retained a quickness of mind and a colorful fantasy expressed in numerous popular songs in Ladino, that Spanish dialect sprinkled with Hebrew terms which is the counterpart of Yiddish, the German dialect spoken by Eastern European Jewry. In this language they still sing a song in Constantinople that has a glimmer of the ardent patriotism of Juda Halevi and that ends with these lines:

Oración hagamos: venga el Goel,
Seamos reunidos todo Israel,
Y veamos presto binjan Ariel,
Tornaremos seher por grandi umma
De todos nombrados bene ruchama.

Let us pray: may the Redeemer come,
May all Israel be reunited,
May we soon see the rebuilding of the Temple.
Then shall we again become a great people,
Called children of mercy by all.

This wish for a renaissance of Jewish culture on the national soil is the major tie between Sephardic Judaism and Ashkenazi Judaism, a nostalgia that anticipated its accomplishment. Behind a curtain of blood and tears, we glimpse the dawn of a new creative era. The hope nurtured for 2,000 years, that Juda Halevi expressed and renewed by his lamentations reminiscent of the ancient prophets, and that the suffering of 6 million victims had rekindled in the survivors, is on the road to fulfillment. Yes, our martyred generation, which summarizes 2,000 years of suffering, which has known the horrors of slavery and deportation, the profanation of temples, *the auto-da-fés,* the disguise of Marranos, catacombs, and all the forms of death invented by mankind, has seen the resurrection of Zion, the birth of a country destined to become a spiritual home, more radiant even than the splendid Spanish period.

For even the latter, golden age though it was, felt the weight of golden chains. A contribution to civilization can be made under better auspices than in Spain. The new generation, after its return to Zion, far from withdrawing into an anemic isolation, will remain in contact with the world thanks to the messenger of Jewish thought that the Jews of the Diaspora are destined to become. This thought will be anchored in its historical soil, but enriched by the positive values of other people. Israel will have

> tant appris sur les routes du monde
> Qu'il n'aura plus peur de son vieux péché,
> Et qu'il laissera ses yeux indulgents
> Jouir du mouvement, des lignes, des formes
> Que jadis il nommait une abomination.
>
> (André Spire)

> [Israel will have] learned so much on the roads of the world
> That it will no longer be afraid of its old sin,
> That its tolerant eyes will be allowed
> To enjoy the movement, the lines, the forms
> That in the past it called an abomination.

It is to this ideal of an alliance between Shem and Japheth, between the noblest elements of these two brothers, that Bialik devoted himself. His poetical work breathes the humanity of the prophets. So do the works of Tschernichowski, who translated the great books of world literature into Hebrew. Although these representatives of the Hebrew Renaissance belong to Ashkenazi Judaism, their spirit is identical to that of Spanish Judaism. And in all the pioneers of East and West who irrigate with their sweat the arid soil of Israel lives the spirit of Juda Halevi, who blesses the labor of their hands:

Ufer nur sind wir, und tief in uns rinnt
Blut von Gewesenen, zu Kommenden rollt's,
Blut unsrer Ahnen voll Unruh und Stolz.
In uns sind alle, wer fühlt sich allein?
Du bist ihr Leben, ihr Leben ist dein!

(Richard Beer-Hoffman)

Beneath the surface, deep within us flows
The blood of those who were, towards those who are to come.
The blood of our forefathers, full of unrest and pride,
Fills our being. Can we feel alone?
You are their lives, their lives are yours!

# 5

# *Juda Abrabanel and the Italian Renaissance*

The Jewish contribution to the Italian Renaissance, cradle of modern thought, is epitomized by Juda Abrabanel, called Leone Ebreo. Doctor and philosopher, he lived in Spain, then in Italy, at the end of the fifteenth century and at the beginning of the sixteenth. Separated from us by a period of 500 years, this philosopher nevertheless retains a certain relevance. Juda Abrabanel lived in Spain at the time of the vast persecutions against all those who did not profess the Catholic faith. The government tried to exterminate the Muslims, and it forced the Jews to emigrate en masse to more liberal countries. Juda Abrabanel[1] luckily belonged to that spiritual elite that found in

1. The complete title under which appeared the *Dialoghi di amore* in 1535 is *Dialoghi di amore compositi da Leone Medico di nazione Ebreo e dipoi fatto Cristiano*. On the basis of this title as well as the silence that surrounds Judah Abrabanel's last years, it has been surmised that the author of the *Dialoghi* adopted the Christian faith toward the end of his life. Zimmels proved that Leone Ebreo was still Jewish at the time he wrote the *Dialoghi* (1502-05). That does not exclude the possibility, however, that he converted to Christianity later, around 1520. It is, indeed, strange that the last years of his life are so completely unknown, and that his death was ignored by contemporary Jewish writers. Ludwig Stein also notes that the editor of the *Dialoghi* would not have attempted to add to the title, just a few years after the death of the author, the remark "e dipoi fatto Cristiano" (and then converted to Christianity) if it had not been correct, for it would have provoked the protests of Abrabanel's whole family. However, the fact that Juda Abrabanel is mentioned in the most deferential

its misfortune a source of intellectual enrichment. After being nurtured on the severe Judeo-Spanish tradition, he assimilated the flourishing world of the Italian Renaissance. Whatever he received from his adopted homeland was doubly returned by his writings. His major work, the *Dialoghi di Amore (Dialogues on Love),* written in Italian, gave new luster to the literature and philosophy of Italy.

Even today this work is of strong interest, because it breaks with the traditional philosophy of the Middle Ages and introduces modern philosophy. Juda Abrabanel is one of the first philosophers of the Renaissance, and even among them, he occupies a place apart. Between the pantheistic current of the Renaissance and the religious traditions derived from the Bible, he built a bridge, which, fortified by his genius, provided a solid basis for the subsequent development of philosophic thought.

His life is divided into two great periods, a Spanish period during which he mastered the Judeo-Spanish culture transmitted by his milieu, and an Italian period, during which he had the opportunity to acquire the very different culture of the Renaissance. It is the combination of these two cultures that confers upon Abrabanel's philosophical works their originiality and their importance.[2]

In Spain, Jewish culture had reached a brilliant zenith. During the Arabic domination the Jews enjoyed great freedom. They lived on very good terms with the Muslims and held high positions in the government. There was then a great flowering of Jewish writers and

terms by Rabbi Guedalia Jahia and Rabbi Azaria de Rossi, both from the sixteenth century, and the fact that he was praised by Immanuel Aboab in his *Nomologia* (beginning of the seventeenth century), make us doubt that he changed religion even at the end of his life. Be that as it may, what matters to us is that Juda Abrabanel was Jewish, that he delved into Jewish philosophy, and that he wrote the *Dialoghi* under its strong influence.

2. Juda Abrabanel's authorship of the *Dialoghi di amore* has been questioned. The name Leon was very common among the Jews of the Latin countries, and several philosophers are known who bear the name Leo Hebraeus. B. Zimmels *(Leo Hebraeus, ein jüdischer Philosoph der Renaissance)* distinguishes three: Gersonides (Levi Ben Gerson de Bagnols, who was born in 1288 and died around 1345); R. Jehuda (Leon) of Seville, mathematician and astronomer of the second half of the fifteenth century; and finally our Juda Abrabanel. The first two cannot be considered the authors of the *Dialoghi* since they lived before their composition. Ludwig Stein adds a fourth Leon Ebreo of Mantua, mentioned by Pico della Mirandola the Elder, who authored a work in 1443, thus 60 years before the composition of the *Dialoghi.* All evidence, therefore, leads us to believe that they were indeed written by Juda Abrabanel.

philosophers. When the kings of Castille and Aragon recaptured Spain from the Arabs, they had to maintain a favorable attitude toward the Jews, who were the richest and most educated people in the land.

It is in that environment that Juda grew up, and in which he acquired an intimate knowledge of its brilliant culture. The basis of his education was undoubtedly religion and Jewish philosophy, in particular the philosophy of Maimonides. In addition to this broad background, he also studied medicine, and he became so skillful in this science that several rulers fought for his professional services.

His father, Isaac Abrabanel, was minister of finance of King Ferdinand the Catholic. The king was then waging war against the Moors (1482-92), who still ruled the kingdom of Granada, but his campaign was not going well because the finances of the state were completely disorganized. Isaac Abrabanel succeeded in reorganizing them. Ferdinand, therefore, owed him a great deal of credit for the victory over the Moors, which handed him the whole of Spain.

However, once master of Granada, King Ferdinand, and especially Queen Isabella, who was completely under the influence of the Grand Inquisitor Torquemada, gave free rein to their religious fanaticism. Now that the Muslims had been thrown out of the last corner of Spain, the monarchs wanted a completely Catholic kingdom. They therefore proceeded to the expulsion of the Jews.

The edict of expulsion was signed in 1492. All the Jews were required to leave Spain. Four months later, hundreds of thousands of exiles embarked for other lands. Don Isaac gave up glory and reputation to join the emigrés, and his son followed him a few months later. King Ferdinand, who had impassively allowed the massacre of innumerable innocents, valued his health too much, however, to allow his personal doctor to leave. All the measures he took to retain him prove how much he appreciated him as a doctor. He resorted to every means to prevent his departure, not excluding the most cruel. He tried to kidnap his one-year-old son. Juda learned just in time of the king's scheme and sent his son to Lisbon, at night, "like stolen goods."

From Toledo the Abrabanels went to Naples, where a rich and influential Jewish community had been flourishing for centuries. It welcomed and sheltered the thousands of Spanish wanderers, stripped of their possessions and often starving.

Juda joined the court as a doctor and soon became the king's personal physician, as he had been in Spain. Here begins the second period of his life, where he comes into contact with the culture of the Renaissance, a culture drastically different from the one he had known in Spain. In this Italy of the sixteenth century the Renaissance was in full swing. The austere and gloomy ascetism of the Middle Ages had yielded to a triumphant affirmation of life. The restrictions of the Church against the mind and the body had been rejected, and society was thoroughly and happily committed to life on earth; for people now believed that real life was here, in the tangible present, and not in the distant and uncertain afterlife. Banquets, parties, and external pleasures alternated with the pleasures of the mind. No more was there forbidden knowledge, as in the Middle Ages, when religion had strictly limited the fields of investigation. Scholars had the widest latitude to investigate, study, delve, discover, and there was a widespread dedication to the pursuit of knowledge. Princely courts were the most lively cultural centers, for rulers took pride in attracting the greatest artists, the best scholars, the most educated men, and showered them with favors.

Thus Juda Abrabanel found at the court of Naples a very gay and intellectual milieu. Thanks to his vast culture, he was welcomed in all the circles of poets and learned men, and he enthusiastically joined the general trend. As a doctor he also enjoyed great success. During the Middle Ages medical science had developed more rapidly among the Jews than among the Christians, who were still unaware of the medical writings of ancient Greece. Jewish physicians obtained great renown, also, for the fact that, from the beginning, they had put their art at the disposal of the sick, without distinction of class or religion, showing great tolerance in an era where fanatics preached that it was better to die than to come under the care of a miscreant. Maimonides, who was both a great physician and a great philosopher, prayed God every morning before leaving to examine his patients, to give him bodily and spiritual health "so that I can dedicate myself tirelessly to the service of the rich and the poor, the good men and the sinners, enemies and friends. Grant that I see only man in all suffereing men." Juda Abrabanel succeeded in obtaining almost miraculous cures, among others that of a cardinal whom other doctors had pronounced incurable. He enjoyed, therefore, a considerable influence, and when Naples fell under the domination of a Spanish viceroy who crushed the Jews under a thousand taxes and all kinds of prohibitions, Juda Abrabanel interceded often in their favor. Thus he succeeded in canceling an order of the viceroy making it compulsory for the Jews to wear yellow hats. These are the last reports we have of his life.

Juda Abrabanel belongs to that Jewish elite that, whenever misfortune struck its people, managed to rise above adversity and even took advantage of it. Forced by circumstances to migrate from one country to another, it carried along its wanderings the cultures of the countries it crossed. These Jews thus contributed to the rapprochement of cultures and the progress of civilization. On numerous occasions they had the opportunity (often in spite of themselves, and at the price of personal suffering) to play this role of intermediary. It is one of their most important contributions to civilization.

The thoughts of Abrabanel are concentrated in a book between two- and three-hundred pages long, the *Dialoghi di Amore (Dialogues on Love),* first published in 1535, after the death of the author. The dialogue was a very popular form then for the development of a thesis. One of the interlocutors was the author's spokesman, who presented his ideas and refuted all the opposing arguments advanced by the other interlocutor. It was a rather convenient method of disposing in advance of all criticisms that could be raised against the new theory. This form also gave the exposition greater clarity. Before Leone Ebreo, dialogues were written on theological, didactic subjects, and the like. Leone Ebreo's *Dialoghi* brought back into fashion the subject of *The Banquet*—love—which from then on was discussed by a whole series of writers.[3] The two participants are not two philosophers representing two different schools, Platonic or Aris-

3. H. Pflaum, *Die Idee der Liebe (The Idea of Love) Leone Ebreo* (Tübingen, 1926).

totelian, for instance, but two young men in love. They have theoretical discussions on the love between a man and a woman, and this leads them to speculations on the nature of love, especially the highest form of love, divine love. The work was supposed to be composed of 18 dialogues. Leone Ebreo completed only three; they give us, however, a complete idea of the author's conception of the universe.

This conception is still thoroughly medieval. The earth is at the center of the universe, and the heavens with the sun, the moon, and the planets revolve around it. But, what is absolutely modern in this conception is the spiritualization of the universe by the principles of love, which we might call the life principle.

For Ebreo the universe, as a whole and in its parts, is animated by a current of love. Love gives birth, nurtures, and develops all things in the universe. Love brings them together according to an admirable harmony. Love leads them toward a common goal: their perfection and the perfection of the universe in its total union with God.

It would be erroneous to assume that only animated things are filled with love. Besides the "sentient desire" of the animal, Leone Ebreo distinguishes "the natural desire" characteristic of inanimate things: the law that attracts masses to the earth, that draws iron to the magnet, the river to the sea, are nothing but laws of love, the "natural" love of inanimate things. How are things incapable of feeling and knowing able to love? It is because they are directed by a providential nature that knows everything and directs all sensitive things for their welfare, their preservation, and their fulfillment. "Just as the arrow flies straight to its target, guided not by its intelligence, but by that of the warrior who shot it, by the same token these inferior and apparently inanimate bodies seek their destination and their target not through their own knowledge, but through that of the Supreme Creator, imparted to the soul of the world and the nature of the universe, hence of inferior things. Thus, just as the direction taken by the arrow is derived from an artificial knowledge and desire, the direction taken by inferior bodies is derived from a natural love and knowledge."

Empedocles had already spoken of two opposing powers that alternately joined or separated the various parts of the universe: friendship and hate. But while Empedocles had seen the predominance of the hate principle that separates from each other the elements that should form a whole, Leone Ebreo sees in all things a unifying tendency, and in the entire universe a progression toward ultimate unity.

Here is the poetic language in which Leone Ebreo couched this concept:

> You will see how stones and metals conceived by the earth, when they are removed from the earth, strain to go back to it, and are at peace only after they have found it; thus children look for their mothers and are reassured only near them. And the earth, in turn, produces them, carries them and watches over them lovingly; and plants, grasses and trees have such a great love for the earth, their progenitor, their mother, that they never leave her unless they are forcibly torn away from her. On the contrary, they embrace her tenderly with their arms, with their roots, as children do to their mothers; and the earth not only gives them birth like a loving mother, but also feeds them with her moisture, which she draws from her entrails like a mother who gives her children the milk of her breasts. And when the earth runs out of moisture to feed them, she earnestly asks the sky and the air, with prayers and supplications, and she gets it in exchange for the steam which she releases and which produces rain, the food for plants and animals. What mother would be more tender and fuller of love for her children?

Love also guides the movements of heavenly bodies, so that the whole universe seems to be an immense body, quickened by a kindly intelligence, since it leads everything to its greater perfection.

Thus God in Leone Ebreo's interpretation seems to be the very soul of the universe. This naturalism existed already in the systems of some philosophers of antiquity. Aristotle, even though he distinguished between form and matter, had considered the purpose of the universe immanent in the world. Subsequently, the Middle Ages, with their contempt for earthly life and their adherence to the letter of the Holy Scriptures, had retained from Aristotle's philosophy whatever confirmed their belief in a transcendental God. The Renaissance, on the other hand, adopted the principle, also formulated by

Aristotle, of a final end immanent in nature. All through the Middle Ages, nature was considered a satanic work from which man had to liberate himself by aspiring toward a supra-terrestrial, immaterial world, the only real world. Philosophy did not diverge from the Holy Scriptures, and borrowed from the philosophers of antiquity only the points that could be interpreted in the light of the sacred texts.

As these restrictions weighed heavily on the world of the Middle Ages, a reaction was bound to occur. It occurred with the influx of Greek scholars to the Italian peninsula after the fall of Constantinople. They brought with them an interest in the Greek language, in the authentic texts of the ancient philosophers, rather than the mutilated versions of the Church. These texts finally appeared in their true light and challenged the hitherto uncontested authority of the Church. Meanwhile, the discovery of new lands gave man the feeling of being the master of nature, and not its slave, crushed by a malevolent power. Nature now appeared to be good, beautiful, and useful to man. When man finally succeeded in crossing the Atlantic, held to be, up to that time, a forbidden sea (it was believed that the Hill of Purgatory was on the other side of the Old World), people noticed how false was the image of the world that they had imagined, and confidence in the Church, which supported these images, was shaken even more badly. The critical spirit awakened in man, simultaneously with the confidence in his own power. He believed in himself, in his nature, in nature itself. He dared look at the earth, and he saw that it was beautiful. And he loved it.

This is how philosophy turned once more toward nature and sought in it the explanation of the mystery of life. The new orientation was so radical that it unequivocally abandoned the teachings of religion about a personal and transcendental God who had created the world by a free act at a specific moment. The world was now considered as the overflow of the divinity into time and space. The universe was identified with God, considered only under the aspect of the multiplicity of *sensitive* things.

This return to nature was strengthened by Plato's influence. His work, with which the Middle Ages had been only partially acquainted and which they had used only as an argument in favor of the Christian religion, acquired new importance in the eyes of the humanists. Thanks to the scholars who had come from Constantinople, Plato's philosophy became known in its entirety and in the original text. In Florence, a Platonic academy was founded where humanists gathered to study and discuss the ideas of the master. *The Banquet* was one of the works that gained the greatest favor among the humanists. The fact that Plato starts with corporeal love to reach spiritual love of the beautiful was bound to attract the attention of the humanists, for whom all spiritual speculations had their point of departure on earth.

Plato's influence is an important factor in *Dialogues on Love*. The very idea of seeing love as the directing principle of the unverse can probably be attributed to Plato. Only Leone Ebreo, like many Renaissance philosophers after him, extended this principle, which Plato applied mainly to man, to every element of the universe, conferring on the world an even greater unity than it had in Plato's conception. The universe was thus considered as the explanation of the Divinity in time and space. His conception faced a problem: how to reconcile divine unity with the multiplicity of sensitive things. Several philosophers attempted to resolve it with only partial success. This is Leone's solution.

We have seen him follow the naturalistic current of the Renaissance. This current of love, which in his eyes unifies everything, is ultimately God himself, who is thus inside the universe. However, this philosophy reduces the role of God to that of a natural law, watching, with perfect harmony, over the conservation of the universe, but not for progress; for its existing organization, but not its ultimate perfection. God is the force that makes the plant germinate, the flower blossom and re-create. God drives all living beings to the conservation and the multiplication of their race, but He is not concerned with the goodness or evil of human deeds; the universe only turns on itself, in an eternal closed circle, instead of spiraling upwards toward an ideal goal.

Thus all morality is excluded from this naturalistic system. Leone Ebreo, however, was too conscious of the biblical doctrine to accept this amoral and nonprogressive conception. That is why he added to the idea of an immanent God that of a transcendental God, outside and above the world, and leading it to a certain goal. Leone Ebreo often compares the universe to an individual man. "Man," he says, "is the image of the whole universe." Just as man is subjected to certain natural laws that direct each of his organs, and is endowed with an intelligence that directs the whole, so the world is filled with an inner life that takes care of the conservation and the reproduction of each of its parts, and of a superior spirit that reigns above it and leads it to perfection.

By this extremely original conception, Leone Ebreo ingeniously reconciles the thinking of the Renaissance with the teachings of the Holy Scriptures. At the same time, he removes the difficulty confronting the other philosophers of the Renaissance. God, seen as simultaneously transcendental and immanent, can remain one while he assumes the thousand aspects presented by the universe.

What is the goal toward which the divine spirit guides the universe? According to Leone Ebreo, the purpose of the universe is its ultimate union with the Divinity, an immense, ardent union of love between the creature and the creator. "This ultimate unity is the purpose for which the Supreme Master of the universe and the Almighty God created the world with its orderly variety and unified multiplicity."

Thus, the final union of the world with God is conceived by Leone Ebreo as the reduction of the infinite variety of elements that compose the universe to a divine unity. The universe is only the material reflection of the Divinity. It reflects in its numberless aspects this same divine spirit, but this divine spirit, thus manifested in space under a thousand colors and a thousand forms, is destined to become once more a pure and single spirit, stripped of all material expression: it will become only an immense union of all-encompassing love, supreme synthesis of the stream of love that covers the world in a thousand rivulets, gathered in an immense and powerful sea.

In order to reach this synthesis, the world will have to be divinized, will have to achieve perfection. It was reserved to man to perfect the world, for more than any other creature, he received the capacity for superior love. The human soul, whose essence is spiritual, is coupled with the imperfect body to form the link between the spiritual and physical world and to form one living being.

Our souls are united to our bodies only by our love for the Supreme Creator of the world, and to serve Him, and attract life and intelligible knowledge and the divine light of the superior and eternal world towards this inferior and transitory world, so that the inferior things be not deprived of divine grace and eternal light, and that this immense living being not contain any part that is not alive and spiritualized like the whole. And when our soul accomplishes by this means the union of the whole universe, by obeying divine will, it really possesses divine love; after separating from the body, it achieves ultimate union with the Supreme God. And that is its greatest happiness. But when it fails to understand this function that has been assigned to it, it is deprived of God's love and of union with God, and that is its greatest punishment; for instead of honorably guiding the body and thus ascending to the highest paradise, it remains through its own fault in the lowest hell, eternally separated from God and its own bliss.

Leone Ebreo does not explain his conception of the perfection that the universe must attain to unite with God. It is probably not a perfection to be achieved in nature, since natural laws are already perfect. It seems that this fulfillment pertains mainly to mankind. At any rate, Leone Ebreo assigns a great responsibility to man. The latter is not what the medieval mystics thought: a worthless being, crushed by divine power and dependent on heavenly grace. He, himself, is responsible for his own destiny and for that of all mankind. He must be capable of rising toward perfection and union with God through his own spiritual powers. This conception of man as active, responsible, collaborating with God Himself, was transmitted to Leone by the religion of his ancestors.

How does man reach this superior degree of perfection? It is not by running away from earthly life that he comes closer to God. On the contrary, it is by committing himself to worldly reality that he finds the way to God. Let everyone seek the highest perfection in the situation where life has placed him: he will be performing a divine task. By improving ourselves, we contribute to the perfection of humanity and the divinization of the universe. Leone Ebreo said: "The purpose of each part of the universe is not only the perfection of that one part, but it tends by its own perfection to the perfection of the whole."

But why does God want to unite with the universe? How can God, who is perfect, desire anything? For does desire not imply the lack of something? And if God is perfect, He is therefore lacking in nothing. Once more, Leone Ebreo proves his originality.

Plato, who had inspired all the philosophers of the Renaissance, including Leone Ebreo, had defined love as the desire for a beautiful thing. Since God, being perfect, can desire nothing, He is not capable of love. Here Leone Ebreo diverges from his professed master. The love that God has for the creation is only the wish to increase the perfection and the happiness of His creatures.

> Just as inferior beings love superior beings and want to unite with them for that perfection that they are missing, so do superior beings love inferior ones and want to unite with them so that the latter will be more nearly perfect. This desire does indicate a lack, but not in the superior being who desires, but in the inferior one, and the superior being, through his love, wants to make up the lack of perfection of the inferior being. This is how spiritual spheres love material spheres, to fill their lacunae with their perfection, and to unite them to themselves and make them perfect. . . .Superior beings love inferior ones as a father loves his son; an inferior being loves superior beings the way a son loves his father, and you know how much more nearly perfect is the love of a father than that of a son. Similarly, benefactors have a greater love for those who have received their favors than the latter have for their benefactor, for their love is motivated by material profit, and that of the benefactor by pure moral goodness. Then you know how much more perfect pure love is than utilitarian love. It is, therefore, not without reason that I told you that the love of superior spiritual beings is more perfect than that of inferior material beings. In the universe, the inferior depends on the superior, and the corporeal world depends on the spiritual world, so that the fault of the inferior being causes the fault of the superior being, on whom it is dependent, because the imperfection in the effect proves an imperfection in the cause; hence, since the cause loves its effect, and the superior being loves the inferior, it desires the perfection of the inferior and wishes to unite it to itself in order to free it of its defect, for, by freeing it of that defect, it remedies its own imperfection. Thus, when the inferior being remains separated from the superior, not only is the inferior being unhappy, but so is the superior being himself, just as the father cannot be happy if the son is imperfect. That is why the ancients used to say that the sinner diminishes the Divinity, while the just

man exalts it. It is thus justifiably that not only does the inferior being love the superior, and wishes to unite with it, but that the superior being loves the inferior, and wishes to unite with it, in order that each be without defect, and that the whole universe be united by the links of love, a union that was the fundamental aim of the Creator of the universe in creating the world, with its ordered multiplicity and unified variety.

Thus, not only does the world love God, but God loves the world. Here recurs the idea inspired by the Bible, that not only does man need God, but God needs man: for it is only in a total union of the universe obtained by the self-realization of man that we find the perfection of the whole.

This, in outline, is the philosophy of the *Dialoghi di amore*. It is a felicitous synthesis of Jewish tradition and Renaissance thought. It is the offspring of these two tendencies, so strangely different: fashioned by a mind like Abrabanel's, it did not concern itself with irreconcilable contradictions, but became a luxuriant and flourishing plant that was to nourish future generations with its fruits. And since the task of man is not merely to receive the inheritance of his forefathers, to safeguard it during his lifetime, and to pass it on to his successors, but to make it grow and to embellish it, Leone Ebreo must rank among the great minds who have had a true understanding of their task.

From naturalism he borrowed the idea of a world thoroughly suffused with God, but he transformed this natural God into a moral God, a God of self-realization and progress. By aligning himself with those who had regained their faith in nature, he abandoned the rigid tradition of the Middle Ages; at the same time, he broke the closed and unproductive circle of naturalism by showing man a task, and the universe a goal. He thus laid the foundation of modern philosophy, and his influence produced in Europe such thinkers as Giordano Bruno and Baruch Spinoza.

# 6

# *The Image of the Biblical Jew in Literature*

To understand the extremely diverse versions in which the Jewish subject appears in world literature, we must first of all take into account the decisive break in Jewish history coinciding more or less with the advent of Christianity. Before the Romans' destruction of the Temple of Jerusalem, symbol of the independence of Judea, this history was a national history of a homogeneous state cemented by Moses' theocratic constitution and evolving toward the democratic jurisdiction of the Talmud. After the lethal blows of Titus and Adrian, it became an international history, in which private life was regulated by religious law, social and political life by the laws of the host country. In the national period, Judaism created a universal literature, the literature of the Prophets of Israel, spreading its influence over the whole earth. During the international period of the Diaspora, the Jews produced in substance a national literature—the rabbinical literature; when artificially cut off from the world, they showed the outsider only the hideous aspects of an unbalanced existence, while its true essence remained unknown.

The apparently glaring contradiction between ancient, national Judaism, admired by the world, and postbiblical, international Judaism, misunderstood and slandered, is the source of the widely divergent images that various nations held and reflected in their literature. The biblical Jew appears in an aura of greatness, beauty, and glory (except among a few bibliophobes like Voltaire and his school who, in the passion of their anticlerical campaign, saw in the Bible only a wretched plagiarism of pagan fables). As for postbiblical Judaism, there have been two attitudes toward it. The one that has been overwhelmingly prevalent consists in attributing to the Jews every vice imaginable, and in presenting them as the enemies of mankind. This tendency originated in the Gospels, where the Jews are made responsible for the crucifixion of Jesus. Then there is the type of money-lender, symbolized by Shylock, which survives up to modern literature. The other tendency goes back only to the eighteenth century. It consecrates the effort of that enlightened age to consider the Jew a normal human being, even to discover in him some trace of his former nobility. This attitude finds its apotheosis in the figure of Nathan the Wise, who, unfortunately, inspired literature considerably less than his brother Shylock. There are, in short, with the subdivision I have adopted, three types of Jews in literature (among non-Jewish authors, of course; Jewish authors were eliminated from this particular subject): biblical Jews, the Shylock type, the Nathan type.

If, indeed, the Bible educated the world morally as Hellenism did scientifically, this education (which is still in the making) was achieved not only by the direct means of the religions and doctrines based on the Old Testament, but also by the indirect means of its beauty, an inexhaustible source of literary inspiration. Each generation has attempted to interpret in its own way—in its own image, with its own resources in the arts and letters—the mysterious or picturesque scenes that fill its pages, especially the first book of the Pentateuch. Literary works based on the Bible are, in a way, lay commentaries on this work, whose power is so great that no attack has succeeded in toppling it. The religous and social ideas that constitute its foundation are presented under so many guises —psychological, historical, poetic—that at least one aspect is bound to arouse each reader's interest. The Bible has thus always kept its relevance, and the humanitarian message that is its *raison d'être* has never disappeared from the memory of man: "Ein ewig wirksam Buch" ("An eternally mighty book"). That is how Goethe describes it, and the secret of this eternal youth seems to me admirably illustrated by the naïve commentary of a British minister with whom I was reading the Old Testament. I remember his amused laughter at the unexpected expressions with which each page of this book is so richly filled. "These people are so funny," he told me. "No doubt, the stories of our saints are more moral, but the men and women in those stories are so holy and perfect from birth to death that one becomes discouraged and bored by so much perfection." In the Old Testament, indeed (this is how we could elaborate on the idea of my English minister) there is really no exemplary saint. The most pious make mistakes that are told without mercy, the wisest commit blunders that the chroniclers do not spare them, and the bravest are presented in acts of cowardice that often destroy part of their prestige. Unquestionably Christian saints are paragons of virtue and faith, but the average man feels consoled and encouraged to discover his own weakness among the very men that are distinguished by the loftiest exaltation of the soul.

This is what has insured the Bible's incomparable success in the aesthetic and moral education of the world and its fecundity as a source of other literary works: the touching humanity of its heroes, the great variety of situations, the naïve exposition of psychological conflicts with which each man identifies himself. Yet one can detect the unity of the ideal behind the diversity of the actions taking place. An eternal truth is carried and lived by mortal beings. Sublime ideas are not only proclaimed theoretically, but are implicit in the events described. As in a play by Shakespeare or Goethe, but so much more naïvely, the lesson is not formulated, but must be elicited by the reader. However, an enigma always remains after each interpretation, an enigma that leads him to pursue his investigation ever more deeply and extensively.

The great compatriot of this English minister, Shakespeare, is reputed to be emancipated from the influence of the Bible. This is false, according to a study by Bishop Charles Wordsworth. In his book *On Shakespeare's Knowledge of the Bible* (1864) he proves the influence of the Holy Scriptures on the works of the greatest British poet. We may suppose that Shakespeare not only drew from the English Bible his knowledge of biblical facts and morality, but that he also absorbed the biblical language, that he borrowed numerous expressions, which, thanks to his popularity, entered the vernacular simultaneously with the direct influence of the Bible. However, it is not only the language of the Bible that we encounter in Shakespeare's works, but also its morality. Shakespeare has been wrongly described as amoral. He does not take sides, and the greatness of his art consists in expressing objectively all opinions, but it is apparent that he gives biblical morality a particularly convincing form. He is not only a poet, but he is "certainly one of the greatest moral philosophers that ever lived. . .he drew his philosophy from the highest and purest source of moral truth" (p. 298). The author does not hesitate to say that Shakespeare, without ever having dealt with a biblical subject, is nevertheless more imbued with the Bible than the totality of English lay writers. "Put together our best authors who have written upon subjects not professedly religious, and we shall not find in them all united as much evidence of the Bible having been read and used as we have found in Shakespeare alone" (p. 291).

Bishop Wordsworth notes in this regard that the rationalistic philosophers who fought the Bible relentlessly, Voltaire and David Hume, were also Shakespeare's sworn enemies. Voltaire described him as the "author of monstrous farces that he called tragedies." *Hamlet,* according to Voltaire, was "the work of a drunken wildman." Since then, history has rendered its verdict, granting to Voltaire the title of king of the century, but consecrating Shakespeare as the king of all modern poets.

In the age that followed Shakespeare's, the Bible was the most widely read, most influential book in England. It was the era of Puritanism, whose poet was Milton. His *Paradise Lost* is the imposing monument of a great religious movement that exalted a whole people and marked its whole future. The influence of this literature was such that even religiously emancipated authors expressed their visions and problems in biblical terms. Byron, besides his *Hebrew*

*Melodies,* full of biblical scenes that inspired a wave of imitations on the Continent, wrote a mystery play, *Cain.* The historian Carlyle interpreted the evolution of mankind in the spirit of the Bible, and recognized in the victories and defeats of nations the intervention of Providence. We must also note a literary genre born in England: the religious essay, to which Matthew Arnold, a nonbeliever, gave its most interesting form. In England, theology went beyond the seminary and attracted lay writers.

England did not produce masterpieces of biblical origin that are comparable with Racine's or Dante's. In the aggregate, however, English literature is strongly imbued with the spirit of the Bible. As for her greatest poet, I will return to him through another aspect of my subject.

After Shakespeare's death, the literary hegemony was transferred to France, whose influence spread through all of Europe during the seventeenth centruy. French Classicism is an extraordinary synthesis of the Greek and biblical spirit. It was not Greek fatalism that guided the creation of French tragedy, but the Providence of Judaic writings. The biblical heroes of the precursors of Corneille and Racine, Jean de la Taille and Robert Garnier, after having been conceived "according to the art and the fashion of old tragic authors", undergo a transfiguration that makes them accept their fate humbly and religiously. Yet, there are in these biblical plays scenes strikingly reminiscent of Greek tragedies. When in Garnier's play, for instance, Sédécie, the last king of the Jews, before being blinded, has before his eyes, as a last sight, the massacre of his children, he finds himself in the same situation as King Oedipus in Sophocles' play. But, whereas the hero of the Greek tragedy bitterly accuses the gods and fate of cruelly toying with man, Sédécie, from the depth of his misfortune, rises to a nobility that he did not possess during more fortunate times, and bows to this God who punishes him so severely.

> Je sais bien que je l'ai mille fois irrité,
> Que j'ai son ire ému, que par mon seul crime
> J'ai incité au mal toute Jérosolyme.

I know that I irritated him a thousand times,
That I provoked his ire, and that by my crime alone
I incited to evil all Jerusalem.

How remote is this pious conclusion from the classical model of tragedy.

This evolution is even more forceful in Racine, the glory and apogee of French Classicism. Racine, who had created dramas in the purest Greek tradition, is the playwright who grasped the poetry and the spirit of the Holy Scriptures more deeply than all other classical and romantic writers, French or foreign., The time would come when the biblical inpiration of *Esther* and *Athalie* would be considered their most admirable feature. The rest, the classical form would be relegated to the background. These plays contain the spirit of the religion of Israel and the beauty of Hebrew poetry. They also express with the greatest faithfulness the soul of Judaism in its most characteristic aspects: the active faith that made of Israel the most dynamic religion and nation of the Orient and predestined it to survive in the West: the realistic concept of divine Providence, a positive attitude in the face of events "that refuses to offend God by an excess of trust." This line from the Talmud is to be interpreted as forbidding man to rely on miracles. In Joad and Mordecai are embodied the Jewish belief, both biblical and modern, that we are not to wait for supernatural intervention. The Jews act, and "God does the rest." Racine was thus able to capture the whole substance of the biblical tale he interpreted, presenting Judaism as anchored in the divine, but endowing it with a vitality directed to human activities. There is no separation between the spiritual and the temporal, as Lutheranism especially teaches. In the Jewish religion, as Racine well understood, they are tightly linked, and eternity itself is in the temporal.

In Italy and in Germany classicism does not appear until the eighteenth century, a period unfavorably disposed toward the Bible. And yet Alfieri, the famous author of the tragedy *Saul,* was not able to resist the fascination this figure of the Old Testament held for him, which he defined this way: "No other theme gives a poet greater freedom, a greater outlet for his descriptive, imaginative, or lyrical verve without diminishing the dramatic impact. Expressions that in the mouth of a Greek or Roman would seem exaggerated or strained appear simple and natural in the mouth of a hero of Israel.'' Alfieri, whose poetic style has an almost crude sobriety, rises in his biblical tragedy to a highly picturesque language that reflects its source of inspiration. Another aspect of this inspiration is the way he presents the priest Achimelech. This character is patterned after Joad, and incarnates the dignity and the prophetic courage of the spiritual leaders of Israel. Alfieri, product of the Enlightenment, was not kindly disposed toward the dignitaries of the Church, whom he considered faithful servants of political absolutism. If he nevertheless endowed Achimelech with so much grandeur, he must have been profoundly impressed with the moral radiance of biblical figures.

As for German Classicism, it is Herder who discovered the beauty of Hebraism. For him the Bible is above all poetry, holy and true. In his observations on *The Spirit of Hebrew Poetry* he analyzes passages from the Old Testament from an aesthetic viewpoint. His admiration for Hebrew poetry leads him to deal also with the Hebrew people. He notes that ''its still incomplete journey is the greatest poem of all times, and will probably transcend the last developments in the historical progression of nations.''

Herder was Goethe's master and idol. His influence on the latter was decisive in his orientation toward Hebrew poetry. More than once the favorite child of the gods of Olympus escaped toward the Orient: ''im reinen Osten Patriarchenluft zu kosten'' (''in the pure East, to breathe the air of the Patriarchs''), and Goethe's masterpiece, *Faust,* is the epic struggle between good and evil in the biblical style. He not only adopted its spirit, but according to K. Burdach,[1] conceived the figure of Faust entirely in the image of the author of the Pentateuch, Moses. Let us recall the solemn ''Prologue in Heaven'' that opens the work; the pact of God with the Devil in imitation of the book of Job, which rabbinical tradition attributes to Moses; the apparition of the spirit of the earth surrounded by flames,

1. ''Faust und Moses,'' *Jahrbuch der Preussischen Akademie der Wissenschaften* (1912).

that recalls the burning bush; Doctor Faust's magic, suggesting
Moses' magic; finally, after many a parallel, the blessed death of
Faust, with the distant vision of a hard-working and happy people,
like the death of the lawgiver on Mount Nebo, his eyes gazing at the
Promised Land, a blessing on his lips:

> Im Vorgefühl von solchem hohen Glück
> Geniess ich jetzt den höchsten Augenblick.
>
> Forsensing all the rapture of that dream
> This present moment gives me joy supreme.

The preparation of his tomb by the spirits and the struggle for his
soul between Mephistopheles and the angels recall the rabbinical
legend in which Mephisto is called Samaël. Only a poetic giant like
Goethe could have dared borrow for his greatest work the traits of
humanity's incomparable lawgiver.

The German writers who followed Goethe, Hebbel and Otto
Ludwig, settled for less-demanding biblical subjects. In contemporary
literature, Thomas Mann is the author who has captured with most
remarkable acuteness the psychology of a few figures of the Old Testament in *Joseph and his Brothers*. This tetralogy is based on an
abundant documentation on the mores and the places where Rachel's
dazzling son passed. In addition to the Bible, Thomas Mann, like
Goethe, studied the rabbinical legends and commentaries, as well as
the scientific investigations on the subject. These various sources
were condensed into a work of exceptional homogeneity. While the
author has for the religious ideal of his heroes no more than understanding mitigated by a skeptical smile, he does, on the other hand,
analyze with great insight and love the psychic motives of their
spiritual unrest, especially their religious experience. This is particularly evident in the first volume, *The Stories of Jacob,* which contains a number of episodes and speeches that cannot be found in the
Bible. Yet they do not seem to be inconsistent with the original
story. All of Thomas Mann's elaborations could be integrated without in the least distorting the original characters. The author managed
to explain this atmosphere so foreign to the modern mentality without

destroying its unique charm. How alive are the coarse sons of Leah, as virtuous as she is homely, and the supple and charming offspring of the beautiful Rachel, all gathered around the patriarch, a timid man, almost a cowardly man, always anxiously in search of justice, truth, and God's will, whose moral greatness and strength grew only under the blows of fate.

The story of Rachel's death alone is a masterpiece inspired by the tragic nobility, the moving sobriety of the text, free of modern sentimentality and therefore that much more gripping. This novel by Mann contains the most beautiful German prose since Goethe and renders brilliant homage to the Bible. Through specific episodes, Thomas Mann attempts to explain the Hebrew character in general as it has manifested itself through the ages.

# 7

# The Image of the Postbiblical Jew in Literature

After an extremely brief sketch of the Jews during the adolescence of their history, we sadly tackle the other aspect of this question, that is, the form in which the postbiblical Jew appears in literature. The transition could not be more abrupt or more cruel. As a matter of fact, there is no transition, but a complete break, often in the same author, who, like Victor Hugo for instance, presents both sides in his work. He who had stated "As far as I am concerned, of all the books that are read, only two deserve to be studied, Homer and the Bible" created, on the other hand, Shylock types without any psychological restraint. The break was as complete and the change of scenery as brutal as the disintegration of a proud and free nation into a stateless mass, dependent on the dubious hospitality of other nations because, conscious of the possession of a living truth, it refused to abdicate before the law of pagan or Christian Rome. The defeated Synagogue, supplanted by the triumphant Church yet refusing to recognize what seemed an unquestionable reality, was in itself enough to exasperate its victors, who were unable—even with the methods of the Inquisition, the medieval Gestapo—to force it to

125

abandon its ancient law. This religious grievance was accompanied, then replaced by the anger of seeing these pariahs reach economic prominence that gave them an edge over their masters (an irony of history that transformed moneylending, to which the Jew was condemned as almost his sole means of support, into the seed of a new power, capitalism). Soon religious zeal was reduced to a simple screen that badly disguised the animosity of Christian competitors. Religious and economic grievances blended so that the Jews were accused of all the ugly traits that contempt and jealousy can dream up, especially if these feelings are accompanied by a carefully fostered ignorance. The theater in particular, always looking for a villain to achieve its cheap effects on naïve souls, perfected and consecrated the legend of the grasping, mean, unbelieving, and vindictive Jew. The international terminology of the passion plays, the religious theater of the Middle Ages, faithful mirror of the life and outlook of that period, constantly harps on the treachery, the evil, the duplicity, and the incredulity of the Jews. The medieval theater disappeared without leaving any traces since the Renaissance, except for the hideous figure of the Jewish usurer. The transition between the medieval theater and the modern theater was *The Merchant of Venice*.

In Shakespeare's masterful hands the Jew Shylock (see chapter 8) became completely different from what the author had intended. He had planned the use of a cliché only to develop the plot of the comedy. Shakespeare had selected the figure of the Jewish usurer that went back to the Middle Ages and that was very familiar to the public of the sixteenth century, just as he legitimately used other popular subjects. But his creative genius transformed everything he touched. Through his insight, he gave life to subjects that before him had been only stereotypes. He did it unwittingly, for his genius was more clairvoyant than his interest as a playwright looking for facile effects on the stage. When he chose the subject of the Merchant of Venice, he had no other intention than to use a theatrical scarecrow to spread terror and heighten, by contrast, the charm of the comedy. Along the way, Shakespeare discovered by close examination the whole tragedy of Shylock's fate. Instead of an unnatural monster he discovered an ordinary man, composed of virtues and faults.

Inspiration dictates to the poet more things than—and often different from—he had intended to say. He lives with his characters. He does not manipulate them like puppets. He seeks only to understand their joys and their pains and he can only humbly note what they have to say. So he hears what his conscience tells him: "Of course, the Jew is bad, but if we examine the situation carefully, we discover that it is our behavior toward him that is responsible for his meanness, a behavior that is not much more Christian than his."

Nevertheless, the figure of the Jewish usurer remained a favorite cliché of the theater, a shrill cliché. For Victor Hugo he became a super-Shylock, a freak in the tradition of Quasimodo; a wheeler-dealer for Balzac, Alphonse Daudet, and Paul Bourget. In various guises he has persisted to the present day. It was a very convenient cliché, as was explained by Adolphe d'Ennery, a half-Jewish popular writer at the end of the nineteenth century. When he was asked if his plays contained a Jewish character, he explained: "No, never. And the reason is very simple. The first duty of an author is to please the public, that is to say, to respect his likes and his habits. If I had portrayed a Jew, I would have been compelled to make a usurer of him, a crook, a traitor, in other words, a villain."

This revealing admission applies to all authors whose concern is the public's favor. They are great popular successes, but do not convey a great message. There are several ways of devoting oneself to literature. One is characterized by the expression, "art for art's sake." It is the art of the aesthetes, entranced by formal beauty, that they elevate into a cult. Then there is the category of those writers who write according to the principle of "art for the artists." These are the skillful *litterateurs,* endowed with an unerring flair for success, who know how to exploit the preferences of the general public by posing as champions of its favorite ideas. Finally, there are writers inspired by a lofty humanitarian ideal, which they carry out through the instrument of their art. They do not sacrifice beauty, they do not neglect the public's favor for the sake of their cause, but their maxim remains first of all: "Art for the sake of progress." They want to carry out their ideal, and are not afraid, if necessary, to disturb entrenched opinions, and to face the disapproval of the masses.

It is within this frame of mind that great literature is born, creative literature that destroys ready-made concepts and habits, and that leads humanity to new horizons.

To this category belong the authors who dare present the contemporary Jew in a favorite light, to rehabilitate him. What Shakespeare had glimpsed in passing, what Pascal, ardent and sincere Christian, had noted in his aphorisms almost stealthily, a few eighteenth-century writers attempted frankly and deliberately. Thus Montesquieu maintains in his *Persian Letters* that the Jewish religion was not in the least invalidated by the arrival of Christianity. "It is a mother who gave birth to two daughters who inflicted on her a thousand wounds: for, in the matter of religion the greatest enemies are the most closely related. But however badly she has been treated, she nevertheless takes pride in having given them birth. She uses one to encompass the world, while the other through its venerable age embraces all periods." Montesquieu accentuates this idea, adding his respect for the practitioners of the Jewish religion in his *Very Humble Remonstrations to the Inquisitors of Spain and Portugal,* in which he attributes to Portuguese Jews the following reasoning: "We believe in a religion that, as you yourselves know, was once held dear by God. We think that God still loves it, and you think that he doesn't love it anymore. Because of this opinion you subject to fire those who commit the very pardonable error of believing that God still loves what he used to love. . . ."

It is in the same spirit that Lessing and Joseph Chénier (brother of the unfortunate poet André) wrote their dramas *Nathan the Wise.* A Jew as the center of the action was nothing new. But a Jew not only humanized but idealized, bearer of the loftiest teachings of ecumenical and international love, that was a revolution, although a revolution from above, of limited scope, by an elite that half opened the door to a golden age for which the common people were not yet ready.

The noble ideas of the eighteenth century enjoyed only a brief honeymoon during the fever of the Great Revolution. They were only too quickly falsified and misdirected. Nevertheless, they were revived here and there under other forms. The idea of tolerance, of interconfessional understanding found new defenders. In the nineteenth century, philo-Semitic literature was powerfully reinvigorated by Lord Byron, who expressed in gripping tones the tragic destiny of the Wandering Jew. His *Hebrew Melodies* launched a wave of sentimental pro-Judaism even in Germany, where it received the name of *Judenschmerz,* with Gutzkow and Lenau as its most eminent representatives. In Russia, Lermontov inherited from Byron not only his romantic temperament, but also his fondness for the Jews. A similar influence came from Walter Scott, who in *Ivanhoe* lent Isaac of York and his daughter touching traits. This current was extended by Wordsworth, and culminated in the novel *Daniel Deronda* by George Eliot.

In France Dumas the Younger, Maupassant, Anatole France, and Zola opposed sympathetic Jewish types to Balzac, Daudet, and Bourget. They were succeeded in the twentieth century by Lacretelle with his novel *Silbermann,* and the Tharaud brothers, who, under the influence of the noble and powerful ideas of Charles Péguy, went in their youth in search of the picturesque and spiritualized life of Eastern Jewry. Unfortunately, from 1933 on, they managed to adapt themselves to a new circumstance. The same applies to the author of the ballads *Judah*—Baron von Münchhausen. Let me also mention the German R. Dehmel who, in his superb poem *A Monument to Heine,* denounced the inane lack of understanding of his people of the noble aspirations of the author of *Lorelei.* Maxim Gorki is among the most famous names of the last generation, who dedicated their talents to the emancipation of the Jews. His heart overflowing with love, he described the misery of the Jews under the tzarist regime in various scenes, pogroms among them. He considered the Jews a precious gift to the Russian community.

Have I not forgotten a famous writer whose name is identified with all the important ideas of the nineteenth century? No, I have not forgotten him: By mentioning him last I emphasize that his ideas are still influencing the present and will influence the future. The man who could give all problems, including the Jewish problem, a new and productive insight was Jean-Jacques Rousseau, the lonely dreamer whose dreams inspired the actions of the subsequent generations. Although he was the immediate inspiration of the French Revolution that consecrated the emancipation of the Jews, he did not settle for the form which the National Assembly felt to be the definitive version. However noble and great this individual emancipation, to which the Jews have responded with unswerving loyalty, it is not the last word in the rehabilitation of Israel. This is what Rousseau recognized. He not only foresaw with an intuitive genius that bordered on divination the granting of citizenship to the children of Israel living among other nations, he also postulated the restoration of the Jewish state. For he felt that Judaism still carried an important message that could not be formulated because of abnormal circumstances, and that only a homogeneous community, rooted in the physical and spiritual soil of its ancestors, could fully express.

This is how the observation in the fourth book of *Emile* must be understood: "If someone among us dared publish a book openly favoring Judaism, we would punish the author, the editor, and the bookseller. This policy is convenient and guaranteed to be always right. It is a pleasure to refute people who do not dare speak up. I do not think I will have fully heard the reasons of the Jews until they have a free state, schools, universities where they can safely speak and discuss. Only then will we know what they have to say." This idea was more or less elaborated by his disciple Lamartine, who went to refresh his poetic soul through contact with the Holy Land, and soars to a prophetic vision of the land and its people: "Such a country, repopulated by a new and Jewish nation, cultivated and irrigated by intelligent hands, made fruitful by a tropical sun, producing all the plants necessary or pleasing to man, from the sugar cane and the banana, to the vine and wheat of the temperate zone, to the cedar and the pine of the Alps, such a country, I say, would still be the Promised Land if Providence gave it back a people and a policy of serenity and freedom."[1]

Freedom! That is what grows the most opulent fruit, that produces

1. *Voyage en Orient, Oeuvres complètes* (Paris, 1861).

the milk and honey of the mind and heart. The great Geneva thinker knew it when he demanded for Israel spiritual and political freedom. The return to nature that he preached means also the restoration of freedom, which is the natural state of individuals and nations.

Rousseau foresaw that in a climate of freedom, through the emancipation of the Jews, not only as individuals, but as a people, a new type of Jew would develop, radically different from the one present in Western literature, even at its most favorable. It is the type of the *halutz* who in one generation transformed marshy lands, neglected for fifty generations, into a luxuriant garden. This miracle was possible only for those who knew that they were the legitimate heirs of the soil of their ancestors. The atmosphere of the land of Israel will extend the miracle to its spiritual renaissance. Awira Eretz Israel mahkim. The breath of the land of the prophets quickens the soul. We are witnessing the rebirth of the Jew, a painful rebirth, accompanied by bloodshed and cries of anguish. He will remember the ignominy and the injustice that he suffered in the houses of slavery, prophets, a message of war against infamy, hypocrisy, spurious greatness, arrogance; a message of peace to the humble, to those who did not shed blood and did not bear false witness; a message of of hope to the downtrodden, to those who stumble in the darkness, hope and promise of a kingdom of justice that must be founded on this earth.

This message will radiate to the Jews scattered throughout the world and fill them with the courage to act according to this ideal born in Zion, and once again at home there. Then the world will know what we have to say. Then a new national existence will create once more a universal literature as in the times of the judges and the prophets, whose legitimate heirs we are, in spite of the vicissitudes of our external fate. This way, when the gentile writers want to choose a Jewish subject, they will not establish an artificial distinction between the Jews of old and the contemporary Jews, but will recognize the natural filiation between ancient and modern Zion, will recognize that the land where the cry for justice and peace first rang out is still the Promised Land. "And the nations will recognize that I, the Everlasting, sanctify Israel, since my sanctuary will be in their midst, now and forever" (Ezekiel 37:14).

# 8

# *Pioneers of the Idea of Tolerance: Shakespeare, Racine, Lessing*

I am going to analyze three crucial steps leading to the birth of the idea of tolerance by listening to the plea of three great defenders of the human mind: Shakespeare, Racine, and Lessing. In three masterpieces of English, French, and German literature respectively, each centered around a Jewish character, they took a stand in the eternal trial of the Jews, a trial whose incidents are a barometer of the cultural climate of its time. Shylock, Esther, and Nathan are protagonists in dramas that bear the imprint not only of their author's genius, but also that of their period. They appeared at the end of the sixteenth, seventeenth, and eighteenth century, three centuries that mark the evolution of the idea of tolerance up to its victory in the Declaration of the Rights of Man—ephemeral victory, for there is no final conquest of the human mind, constantly threatened by the revenge of the repressed animal.

*The Merchant of Venice*

*The Merchant of Venice* is the play that presents the greatest diffi-

132

culty for those who, like us, are looking for an understanding attitude about the issue under study. Shylock, the pivotal character, is a Jew afflicted with all the conventional vices imputed to his coreligionists: he is a filthy usurer, without other ideal than money; a bloodthirsty cur, dying to tear out a piece of flesh from the breast of the royal merchant Antonio; a monster hated by his own daughter, Jessica; a scarecrow, whose function it is to enhance by contrast the gaiety and charm of the poetic action.

From a distance, Shylock corresponds precisely to the traditional figure of the Jew on the medieval stage. The Jewish usurer had been portrayed in innumerable plays. It is enough to recall the terrifying mystery plays of the thirteenth, fourteenth, and fifteenth centuries, in which Judas Iscariot, Caiaphas, and Annas were the prototypes of all the variants of the greedy and vindictive Jew. Even in Shakespeare's time, in the Elizabethan theater, which marks, after all, a considerable progress over the mystery plays, there were no fewer than 17 plays portraying this cliché of the Jew.[1] Marlowe's *The Jew of Malta,* written in 1591, is the best known of these dramas that Shakespeare partially utilized for his *Merchant of Venice.* It contains Barabbas, real devil in human shape, who commits crime after crime, treachery after treachery, that he expiates with his daughter by a frightening death meant to soothe the indignant conscience of the spectators. From that play Shakespeare borrowed a few scenes as well as the conventional type of the Jewish usurer.

Another play, published in 1579 and now lost, gave him the plot of his comedy. That play contains, among others, the famous episode of the contract for the excision of a pound of flesh, by which the figure of the Jewish usurer is given monstrous proportions.[2]

1. J. L. Cardozo, *The Contemporary Jew in the Elizabethan Drama* (dissertation, University of Amsterdam, 1925).
2. Let us note in passing that during antiquity this contract was more in accordance with the mores of numerous European tribes and goes back to the earliest Roman legislation concerned with the defense of the creditors' rights, while the Mosaic code prefers to take the side of the debtor. According to Jacob Grimm's *Deutsche Rechts-Altertümer,* an old Norwegian law gave the creditor the right to cut off one of the debtor's limbs, corresponding to the value of the debt, for the various parts of the human body were taxed (which lends credibility to the talmudic interpretation according to which the dictum: "An eye for eye" means the obligation to replace in cash the value of the damaged limb.) This rigorous interpretation of the creditor's rights remained in force until the end of the Middle Ages. Cf. also this significant passage

There is no reason to believe that Shakespeare intended to express a personal dislike of the Jews, that he meant to create a play with anti-Semitic overtones. By choosing the figure of the Jewish usurer, he borrowed without any ulterior motive a literary subject from the Middle Ages, like so many authors after him—Victor Hugo, for instance.[3]

In presenting the Jew as a usurer thirsting for Christian blood, Shakespeare did not invent anything. He was even less interested in initiating a new trend; he simply "copied." For Shakespeare was a plagiarist. He utilized not only old chronicles, but also existing plays. His personal contribution was his genius, a gift for psychological insight, thanks to which insignificant plays became in his hands immortal masterpieces.

Thus, what distinguishes the figure of Shylock from all previous figures of Jewish usurers is precisely the author's psychological insight. It made of Shylock a drastically different character from what he must have been at the beginning. Shylock was supposed to be the scarecrow spreading terror and enhancing by contrast the game played in the crystalline Venetian atmosphere. Like Faust, who made a pact with Mephistopheles while planning to outwit him at the end, Antonio signed a contract with Shylock, the devil in human form, whose disappointment was supposed to amuse the public and insure a happy ending. For the spectator was bound to be happy if the Jew, smeared with all the conventional vices of Israel, received at the end

from the short story by Cervantes, *Rinconete y Cortadillo,* a mirror of Spanish life in the sixteenth century. It refers to a certain Maniferro who bears this name "because he had an iron hand instead of the other that had been cut off by the law." His hand had been cut off because he had stolen a sum of money and was unable to reimburse it. This frequent custom of cutting off a limb of a lawbreaker stems from the same judicial tradition as the practice of the pound of flesh, reflected in various literary versions, among others the *Gesta Romanorum,* in which the pitiless creditor was not a Jew at all. This role, as well as that of the eternal wanderer Ashaver, was assigned rather late to a son of Israel, when, toward the end of the Middle Ages, the Jews inaugurated with the Italians the banking system of money-lending.

3. Victor Hugo, *Torquemada.* Besides, Shakespeare could not harbor anti-Jewish feelings for the simple reason that during the time of Elizabeth and the first Stuarts there were no Jews in England, except a few Marranos fleeing the Spanish Inquisition, who were only too eager to remain unnoticed. English merchants might have met them in the Mediterranean area, but for the majority of Englishmen, the Jew was an abstraction, an exotic being, known exclusively through literature.

a just punishment. However, Shakespeare did not achieve this happy ending because, in spite of himself, he explored the character of the monster and discovered in him a living person, composed of qualities and vices. For the first time, someone examined the other side of the Jewish problem, which up to then had been treated too unilaterally. Genuine poetic works have the virtue of condensing and crystallizing the facts of existence. Shakespeare, in his comedy, conceived the Jewish phenomenon as a problem. The word "problem" implies that two or more aspects of reality are singled out and contrasted, unlike a dogmatic attitude that condemns or absolves in advance.[4]

Shakespeare was thus the first writer to formulate the problem presented by the presence of the Jews in the Christian world. He conducted a modern trial in which the accused, although severely condemned, benefits from extenuating circumstances. Since his time, the problem that he formulated has raised endless discussions, judicial, political, and human. Eminent scholars such as Jhering, Kohler, and Niemayer wrote legal studies on Portia's verdict. For Shylock acted according to property rights then in force, and according to the creditor's recognized sanctions. His procedure is not in the least extraordinary, and anyway is authorized not by Mosaic law, but by the law of the country in which he lived. Portia's verdict and her legal arguments are devious shenanigans[5] unworthy of a judge in charge of enforcing the law.

During his stay in England, Heinrich Heine attended a performance of *The Merchant of Venice* at the Drury-Lane. He noted that he would never forget the pale and beautiful Englishwoman who was crying during the fourth act, and sobbed: "The poor man was wronged." The cry of this Englishwoman is typical of the reaction of the man in the street, who, indifferent to legal discussions over the deal of the pound of flesh, feels that the solution of the drama that

4. These two contrasting attitudes can be reduced to the dichotomy, Middle Ages versus the modern era, or, in political terms, dictatorship versus democracy, and in that sense Shakespeare is modern, much more so than so many twentieth-century men whose dogmatic and fanatical minds reduced infinitely complicated and subtle problems of humanity to sweeping and oversimplified judgments.

5. "Ein jämmerlicher Winkelzug" (a deplorable subterfuge), says Jhering. Cf. *Kampf ums Recht* (Fight for Justice) (Göttingen, 1872). pp. 58-60.

settles everything at the expense of the Jew is not satisfactory. He feels that the Jew is not the monster who deserves to play the role of scapegoat for the sake of the comedy, and that the royal merchant Antonio is not so royal as he ought to be. Shakespeare retouched the black and white contrast that he inherited from the tradition of the theater. The poet discovered both in the hero and the villain motives that made the hero less virtuous and the villain less heinous. Thus, since Kean and Irving, the role of Shylock has been interpreted not as a comic but as a tragic figure, in spite of the contrary opinion of the German Anglicist Brandl and the actor Werner Kraus. A detailed analysis will indicate the grounds for the English interpretation.

From the very first scene Shylock is characterized by two traits that a hardy tradition attributes to the Jews: usury and hatred of Christianity. But right then, Shakespeare is careful to explain the character he creates. The feelings of hatred on the part of the Jew are only a reaction to similar emotions on the part of his partner Antonio. Shylock and Antonio are two merchants, two competitors, whose rivalry arises from an antagonism of principles. The Church forbids the Christian to lend money at interest. Money is a liquid asset. It is a sin to make it grow by itself. The Jewish merchant has a different concept of money, just as it proved to be, subsequently, in Christian society too.[6] "And thrift is blessing, if men steal it not," says Shylock, invoking the name of the patriarch Jacob, who also made a profit on the capital of his father-in-law, the ewes and the lambs, to whose striped and spotted young he was entitled.

We are dealing, basically, with two forms of emerging capitalism—the two enemy brothers, landed capitalism and commercial capitalism. This antagonism was sharpened between Antonio and Shylock by the personal animosity of competing merchants, expressed with varying degrees of virulence according to the period.

Antonio had every opportunity to express his hostility. Shylock was obliged to repress his. And now the proud Antonio needed the services of the very man he had so often slighted. The latter, without

6. Let us recall that as early as the fourteenth century, there existed in Italy the system of *mons*, an incorporated organization that granted interest-bearing loans, since the prohibition of the Church applied only to individuals.

refusing, was delighted to be able for once to reproach his opponent for his haughty and offensive attitude.

> Signior Antonio, many a time and oft
> In the Rialto you have rated me
> About my moneys and my usances.
> Still have I borne it with a patient shrug,
> For suff'rance is the badge of our tribe.
> You call me misbeliever, cut-throat dog,
> And you spet upon my Jewish gaberdine,
> And all for use of that which is my own.
> Well then, it now appears you need my help.
> Go to then! You come to me, and you say,
> "Shylock, we would have moneys"; you say so—
> You, that did void your rheum upon my beard
> And foot me as you spurn a stranger cur
> Upon your threshold; money is your suit.
> What should I say to you? Should I not say,
> "Hath a dog money? Is it possible
> A cur can lend three thousand ducats?" Or
> Shall I bend low in a bondsman key,
> With bated breath and whispering humbleness,
> Say this:
> "Fair sir, you spet on me on Wednesday last;
> You spurned me such a day; another time
> You called me dog; and for these courtesies
> I'll lend you thus much moneys?

Does Antonio modestly acknowledge how lacking in Christianity and nobility his attitude is? Not in the least. Far from adopting an accommodating attitude, he brazenly displays his arrogance:

> I am as like to call thee so again,
> To spet on thee again, to spurn thee too.
> If thou wilt lend this money, lend it not
> As to thy friends; for when did friendship take
> A breed for barren metal of his friend?
> But lend it rather to thine enemy,
> Who, if he break, thou mayst with better face
> Exact the penalty.

He demands that the Jew treat him as an enemy. Confident of his immense fortune, he refuses in advance all consideration in the case of insolvency. That is how he signs the famous deal, vestige of the cruel legislation of antiquity.

It is still only a collateral in Shylock's hands. Nothing indicates that he intends to use it literally. This is where the psychology of the poet intervenes to explain the intransigence of the Jew. Suddenly he is struck by a series of blows, all originating from Antonio's circle. His only daughter is carried off by her lover, a Christian whom love has not blinded to the Jew's ducats. Shylock grieves over the loss of his money that his daughter, much too generous, squanders gaily with her new friends; above all, he grieves over the betrayal of his child, the lack of respect for the family ties, so sacred to the Jews, a lack of respect expressed in the casual way she hands out family momentoes. Shylock is told that Jessica has exchanged a ring for a monkey.

It was my turquoise; I had it of Leah when I was a bachelor: I would not have given it for a wilderness of monkeys.

In a flash Shylock's family feeling appears, as strong as his love of money.

When they meet him in this state of shock, Antonio's friends find nothing better to do than to rail at his misfortune. The Jew, distraught and humiliated, keeps quiet, but when a little later they inquire about the pact that is about to expire, all his controlled anger, his offended dignity, his insulted paternal love, all explode in an unquenchable thirst for revenge. They ask him what good Antonio's flesh would do him. He answers:

To bait fish withal: if it will feed nothing else, it will feed my revenge. He hath disgraced me, and hindered me half a million; laughed at my losses, mocked at my gains, scorned my nation, thwarted my bargains, cooled my friends, heated mine enemies; and what's his reason? I am a Jew. Hath not a Jew eyes? hath not a Jew hands, organs, dimensions, senses, affections, passions, fed with the same food, hurt with the same weapons, subject to the same diseases, healed by the same means, warmed and cooled by the same winter and summer, as a Christian is? If you prick us, do we not bleed? if you tickle us, do we not laugh? if you poison us, do we not die? and if you wrong us, shall we not revenge? If we are like you in the rest, we will resemble you in that. If a Jew wrong a Christian, what is his humility? Revenge. If a Christian wrong a Jew, what should his sufferance be by Christian example? Why, revenge. The villainy you teach me, I will execute, and it shall go hard but I will better the instruction.

The denouement of the play is well known. The Jew will have neither his revenge nor the money he loaned. One half of his fortune is confiscated, and he is forced to be baptized. His enemies disgrace him, rob him, and finally ridicule him, and with all this, feel the satisfaction of having saved a soul. The critic A. Kerr wrote after a performance in Berlin:

> He looked like an animal maddened by cruel treatment. Yet they delighted in beating him, although he was already half-dead. They breathed with relief, and the self-righteous exclaimed: "Ah! the brute! How vulgar thus to force our conscience. This animal is very mean. When attacked, it defends itself." All these people saved from embarrassment by the ingenuity of a woman feel a happiness full of piety when they listen to the sermons on "mercy," this "mercy" that nobody practices, but that everyone feels duty-bound to praise in lofty terms. *(Die Welt im Drama,* 3:300)

Heine, bad Jew as well as bad Christian, but incorruptible critic in matters of taste, noted: "If the only form of Christianity were that taught by an Antonio, Bassanio and Lorenzo, Shakespeare would have written a satire of that religion. Who is that Bassanio? A fortune-hunter, as an English critic said, who outfitted himself magnificently with borrowed money to find a wealthy wife. And Antonio? He appeals to the Jew in the name of Christian charity, but when it is his turn to practice it, he does not even think of restoring the thousands of ducats he borrowed. And his friends? They deplore Antonio's misfortune, console him with a glib line, but one wonders why they made no collective effort to lend him the money he needed. Their love of money is at least as great as Shylock's, who can throw it away, disdain it, to get revenge for the slights he suffered." *(Shakespeare's Mädchen und Frauen.* "Jessica.")

Thus, instead of a happy ending like all the others of Shakespeare's charming comedies, the denouement of this play produces in the ordinary spectator an uneasy feeling. For in this case, Shakespeare did not succeed in restoring order, in distributing rewards and penalties equitably to satisfy the demands of justice. In the brilliant figures of the play there are too many shadows, and in the dark figure of the Jew there are too many human and touching traits. This is not in accordance with the original intent of the poet. He, no doubt, wished to portray an evil villain of the theater, the bloodthirsty monster who suffers a well-deserved punishment by losing his money and his daughter. Such a monster would have justified the denouement. But the genius of the poet, the divine spirit that moved him, was stronger than the skillful dramatist who knew the resources of the theater.

Like Balaam, who in spite of a vile and mean nature, rose to the most exalted prophecies whenever the divine spirit moved him; like Voltaire, whose character was nothing but resentment and pettiness, incapable of loving his fellow men, but whose genius led him to champion a high humanitarian ideal, each man of genius is the spokesman, the instrument of the spirit that inhabits him and sees farther than he. The poet is inspired in spite of himself. Shakespeare had no apologetic intentions. Like Goethe, he was a naïve poet, and a bit of a court poet. Social questions did not interest him, except as psychological phenomena. He sought neither to accuse nor to defend. He only wanted to represent human passions, the conflict that they cause, and the tragic or comic actions that they motivate. He never appointed himself the interpreter of any particular point of view. It is only incidental to his psychological studies, on which his plays are based. But that is why he is so effective. He does not use eloquence to obtain the quick but passing triumph of a thesis. He does not awaken transitory emotions. He appeals to intelligence. His eloquence is the objective analysis of cause and effect in a particular tragic situation. His psychology is incorruptible and leads him to assess the pros and cons to discover extenuating circumstances in criminal actions, to point out sordid motives in apparently virtuous actions. He makes accessible positions around which dogmatism had erected unbreachable walls; he humanizes irreconcible ideologies. He opens new perspectives that awaken indulgence, understanding that leads to tolerance.

In the case of the usurer Shylock, the poet's genius gathered more extenuating circumstances than the unity of the play can tolerate. They can be summarized in the following observation: Of course, the Jew is bad, but upon close examination you will discover that it is your behavior that developed his wickedness. Your behavior, my Christian gentlemen, is not much more Christian than his. This conclusion, while not explicitly stated, is clearly implied in the play and is self-evident to the spectator. It foreshadowed the rallying cry of those who, two hundred years later, intervened in favor of the Jews in the French National Assembly. Robespierre was to exclaim: "The vices of the Jews are due to the degradation into which you have plunged them." Did not Shylock say almost literally "I practice the evil you have taught me"?

The problem has been formulated. If the denouement at the expense of the Jew, who must submit to baptism in order to save his life, does not satisfy our sense of justice, still, for Shakespeare's time, it is a merciful solution. Shakespeare's contemporary, Marlowe, had proposed a harsher penalty, the total ruination of Shylock. Shakespeare borrowed everything from Marlowe's play except the psychology. Psychology thus led Shakespeare to the understanding of the social situation of the Jews in general. Soon after, Cromwell opened the doors to the tribe whose descendents were to produce the architect of the British Empire, Disraeli.

*Esther*

One hundred years after the *Merchant of Venice,* where medieval traditions encountered and clashed with liberal ideas announcing a new era, the poet Racine, at the end of the seventeenth century, created his biblical dramas *Esther* and *Athalie,* the culmination of the art of the greatest French poet, who crystallized the whole passion and religious poetry of Israel in immortal French verse.

*Athalie* was described by Voltaire as "the masterpiece of the human spirit,'' an immensely kind assessment on the part of a philosopher who had an aversion to anything related to the Bible. The other play, *Esther,* was considered a disguised portrayal of Louis XIV's court. It has been claimed that Esther represented Mme de Maintenon; the young Israelites raised in a corner of Ahasuerus's court, among whom Esther forgets her exalted position, represented the young girls of Saint-Cyr; Ahasuerus was Louis XIV; the haughty Vashti, Mme de Montespan. In Haman some saw Louvois, who was falling out of favor. The edict proscribing the Jews supposedly represented the revocation of the Edict of Nantes.

Racine's commentators accepted all the conceivable interpretations of *Esther* except the simplest: the possibility that the poet was actually thinking of the people in question when he dramatized a chapter of Jewish history.

The reason may be found in the fact that during Racine's time the Jewish problem had no relevance in France. A few Jews existed, but there was no organized Jewish life. A few hundred years earlier there had flourished a long-established center of Judaism. Talmud scholarship had produced its greatest masters with Rashi, born in Troyes, and with the Tossafist school. In the South, at the crossroads of civilizations, the Jews, thanks to their business and intellectual contacts, played an important role as intermediaries between the Judeo-Arabic civilization of Spain and medieval Europe.

However, beginning with the fourteenth century, during the decline of the Middle Ages, Europe sank into barbarism, intolerance, and started the persecution of all those who threatened the established order, disguised as religious dogma. France, too, succumbed to this state of mind that led to the expulsion of the Jews, stripped of their possessions.

This is the basis of the belief that Racine, when he wrote his biblical plays, did not think at all about contemporary Judaism, just as no relation is seen between the Greece of today and that of Pericles' time. However, when one reads *Esther* carefully and examines the thesis developed in it, it is hard to imagine that all the events refer only to biblical Judaism or to the court of Louis XIV, rather than to the Jews of the seventeenth century, whose history and European situation resembled so strikingly that drawn by the poet. The lamentations of the chorus on the decadence of the people of Israel do not strictly refer to the Babylonian exile.

> Déplorable Sion, qu'as-tu fait de ta gloire?
> Tout l'univers admirait ta splendeur.
> Tu n'es plus que poussière, et de cette grandeur
> Il ne nous reste plus que la triste mémoire.
> Sion, jusques au ciel élevée autrefois,
> Jusques aux enfers maintenant abaissée,
> Puisse-je demeurer sans voix,
> Si dans mes chants ta douleur retracée,
> Jusqu'au dernier soupir n'occupe ma pensée.

> Pitiful Zion, what did you do with your glory?
> The whole universe admired your splendor.
> Now you are nothing but dust, and from this grandeur
> There remain only sad memories.
> Zion, formerly exalted to the heavens,
> Now cast down into hell,
> May I remain without voice
> If your grief, expressed in my songs,
> Does not occupy my thoughts to my last sigh.

The nostalgia for Zion and the attachment to Jerusalem expressed in this scene are characteristics not reserved to the Jews of biblical times. It is above all the plot, the anti-Jewish persecution ordered by Haman, and Esther's intervention with the King, that give the poet the chance to enter the arena of the Jewish question from the contemporary as well as the historical viewpoint.

Racine shows the full horror with which the word *Jew* filled those who knew this term only through a screen of legends. The horror was more characteristic of Racine's contemporaries than Esther's.

> Vous la fille d'un juif? Hé quoi, tout ce que j'aime,
> Cette Esther, l'innocence et la sagesse même,
> Que je croyais du ciel les plus chères amours,
> Dans cette source impure aurait puisé ses jours?

> You the daughter of a Jew? What, everything I love,
> This Esther, innocence and virtue itself,
> That I considered the dearest love of heaven,
> Drew her life from this impure source?

But Esther emphasizes the noble origin of her race. Her speech is the prototype of a formal refutation.

> Et que reproche aux juifs sa haine envenimée?
> Quelle guerre intestine avons-nous allumée?
> Les a-t-on vus marcher parmi vos ennemis?
> Fût-il jamais au joug esclaves plus soumis?
> Adorant dans leurs fers le Dieu qui les châtie,
> Pendant que votre main sur eux appesantie,
> A leurs persécuteurs les livrait sans recours,
> Ils conjuraient ce Dieu de veiller sur vos jours,
> De rompre des méchants les trames criminelles,
> De mettre votre trône à l'ombre de ses ailes.
> N'en doutez point, Seigneur, il fut votre soutien,
> Lui seul mit à vos pieds le Parthe et l'Indien,
> Dissipa devant vous les innombrables Scythes,
> Et renferma les mers dans vos vastes limites.
> Lui seul aux yeux d'un juif découvrit le dessein
> De deux traîtres tout près à vous percer le sein.

> What does his venomous hatred reproach the Jews?
> What domestic wars have we provoked?
> Were they ever seen marching among your enemies?
> Were there ever slaves more docile to the yoke?
> Worshipping in their chains the God that punishes them,
> While your hand oppressed them,
> And turned them over to their enemies without recourse,
> They implored this God to watch over your life,
> To undo the villains' criminals plots,
> To put your throne in the shadow of his wings.
> Don't ever doubt it, O Lord, he was your support,
> He alone delivered into your hands the Parthian and the Indian
> Scattered before you the innumerable Scythians,
> And enclosed the sea within your vast frontiers.
> He alone delivered into your hands the Parthian and the Indian,
> Of two traitors about to stab you in the chest.

The object of the plea was not only Esther's Jewish contemporaries, but also Racine's, and those of every period, in every land.

The Jewish question has always remained the same in substance. If we change a few details in the speech of Haman, the persecutor of the Jews, we notice identical circumstances in those distant events and the general situation of the Jews, regardless of time or place. Furthermore, poets and philosophers, even if they examine only the most general problems, see them from a certain angle, in the mirror of their own time. Every man, even the most independent mind, is always under the influence of his era and milieu. Racine could understand the situation of the Jews in Persia only if he understood their situation in Europe. Consequently, the dialogue between Ahasuerus and Esther reflects the very special atmosphere surrounding the Jews in Racine's time. Esther's speech shows rather clearly the playwright's position one hundred years before the Jews' emancipation. It is undoubtedly not without a personal bias that this Christian poet dramatized the defeat of anti-Semitism, the triumph of Mordecai's loyalty, the perfidy of Haman, the victory of Esther's virtue over the daughters of Persia.

Of course, as a faithful believer, Racine was obliged to acknowledge the dogma of the downfall of the Jews because of their unfaithfulness to Jesus. But, otherwise, like Pascal and Bossuet, he saw in them the descendents of those who formulated the doctrine on which Christianity was based. Out of his respect for this lofty origin, he pleaded for mercy for Israel. Not a return to its former glory, but a tolerable life for the "witnesses of Christianity," in the name of their greatness of yesteryear, from which they have retained certain virtues. It is a revolutionary thesis for the seventeenth century when we consider that even Voltaire conceded only that "he did not want the Jews to be burned."

Maybe Racine had no conscious intention of pleading the cause of the Jews. He chose the subject because of the appeal of the plot, to please Mme de Maintenon, who had requested a play for her girls' school. As a real poet he found in the subject more than he had bargained for. He found the truth under the convention, and the real poet, like the prophet, can express only the truth. Even if it was by accident— Mme de Maintenon's request—that Racine was led to select the subject of his play, he went beyond the needs of the young ladies of Saint-Cyr. He found himself in the presence of the Jewish question and, like Shakespeare, he divined its tragic depth. For what is great, said Jules Romains, is that we do not know what we are going to think, nor when we are going to think it. A genius knows it even less than other mortals, and most discoveries of genius are fortuitous.

Racine examined the problem as a Christian believer, but taking literally the doctrine of charity on which Christianity prided itself (in whose name it is also true that Torquemada conducted his persecutions), he pleaded for indulgence for the Jews without demanding that they forsake their faith. It is not tolerance according to our interpretation, but it is already a step beyond Shakespeare. The concept of emancipation had made progress, and thanks to Racine it made further progress. The Jew gradually lost the hideous appearance with which the Middle Ages had saddled him. Here and there, he was seen in a softer light, a ray of the century known as the Enlightenment.

## Nathan the Wise

While Shakespeare and Racine discovered the Jewish problem only in passing, Lessing chose it deliberately as the theme of his play *Nathan the Wise,* one of the greatest works of world literature. It is a thesis play, a polemical play written to defend a social and political idea, and yet a pure work of art that inaugurated the great period of German classicism. What makes a work a classic is the felicitous marriage of form and content, the lofty viewpoint from which the subject is treated, the transposition of a particular thesis to a higher level to become a noble humanitarian ideal. That is the purpose and the *raison d'être* of genuine literature. Goethe, Schiller, and all German playwrights, came under the influence of Lessing's masterpiece, just as several generations of writers of comedy were inspired by his other play, *Minna von Barnhelm.*

In *Nathan* we are privy to the noblest, most unequivocal proclamation of the idea of tolerance. Shakespeare was the first to declare that the Jews, in spite of the vices that a stubborn tradition imputed to them, are nevertheless human beings ruled by the same feelings as other men, and must at least be given the chance to repent by forsaking their tribe and accepting the official religion of the state.

Racine, as a biblical poet, considered the postbiblical Jew fallen from his former greatness, but in the name of this past grandeur he pleaded, if not for tolerance, at least for indulgence born of Christian charity.

With Lessing it is not a question of individual forgiveness, nor of collective indulgence, but of acceptance of a religious group whose moral level seems to him equal to that of others. Lessing had the opportunity to know Jews intimately, to judge them individually and collectively. He noticed that their humble social positions as *protegés* did not correspond to their moral culture. He saw in his friend Moses Mendelssohn the incarnation of an ideal to which Diderot and Voltaire dedicated their pens much more than their lives.

A religion that produces a Mendelssohn, he concluded, still has a contribution to make, regardless of the predominent religions and new philosophical doctrines, for neither express anything that it has not already articulated. His Jewish friend, born in the ghetto, observing the law of Moses, yet participating brilliantly in modern thought, was in his eyes a synthesis of the oldest monotheistic religion and eighteenth-century thought. He was the eternal Jew, in whom the social and humanitarian ideals of the prophets of Israel, and those of the wordly prophets, find their natural descendent. There is no need to proceed to a detailed analysis of *Nathan the Wise,* The idea of the play is crystallized in the parable of the three rings, which, since its appearance in the European literature of the thirteenth century, has been given various meanings, and for which Lessing finds the noblest interpretation:

> Each of you received a ring from his father. Let him firmly believe that his ring is genuine. He unquestionably loved all three of you equally. He would not have wanted to mistreat two of you in favor of the third. Well, let each of you, with a love incorruptible and free of prejudice, attempt to show to the world the virtue of his ring's stone by his gentleness, his tolerance, and his sincere devotion to God. And if the virtue of this stone appears in the children of the children of your children, I'll summon them again before this court thousands of years from now. Someone wiser than I will preside and speak for me.

Lessing's play contributed not only to the fostering of an atmosphere of tolerance whose results were only to be felt in the long run; it produced an almost immediate political and social effect. Under Lessing's influence Dohm wrote his essay *On the Civic Improvement of the Jews,* a work that served as a basis for the essay by Abbé Grégoire, awarded first prize by the Royal Society of Sciences and Arts of Metz: *On the Physical, Moral, and Political Regeneration of the Jews.* This study was the prelude to the emancipation of the Jews proclaimed by the National Assembly.

Why did not the subsequent development of emancipation take the direction indicated by *Nathan the Wise?* Why did the children of Mendelssohn, the prototype of Nathan, desert the Jewish camp, and how do we explain the disintegration of Judaism in the nineteenth century, the pseudo-assimilation that produced the reaction of which we were the helpless witness?

It came from the fact that other tendencies, different from those formulated in *Nathan,* prevailed. The idea of tolerance can be based on two different concepts. Voltaire and Lessing, for instance, even though they both promoted tolerance of all religious confessions, started out from two radically different premises. The tolerance of the eighteenth-century French philosophers was, in a way, a result of their general skepticism. They demanded tolerance for all religions because they considered all sects various forms of a fundamental error. Those who lack an absolute conviction are kind to the conviction of others. The eighteenth century, out of indifference to religion itself, fought for acceptance of all particular confessions, whatever their names. This form of tolerance does not stem from a positive appreciation of the religious values we are asked to respect, but from a contemptuous attitude toward religion in general.

In contradistinction, there exists a positive kind of tolerance, originating in a profound respect for the particular form in which the search for truth, absolute and unique, crystallized. In this respect, minds truly positive and free of prejudice, such as Montesquieu in France and Lessing in Germany, respected the beautiful, the good, and the true in all its forms. Montesquieu expressed it thus: "Zeal for the progress of religion is different from the attachment that we owe it. To love and practice it, it is not necessary to persecute and hate those who don't.'' And Lessing formulated the same idea in a famous passage: ''If the creator of the world held in his right hand absolute truth, in the other hunger for truth, and told me: 'choose,' I would humbly pray: 'Lord, give me what you have in your left hand, for pure truth is for you alone.' ''

This declaration is the equivalent of a profession of faith and a refutation of the claims that the parable of the three rings is a demonstration of skepticism: the three rings are false, hence the three rings are deceiving. The skeptical thrust of Nathan's tale refers only to fanatical clericalism that considers itself the repository of absolute truth. He teaches the spiritualization, the humanization of all sincere faith. His conclusions do not lead to an easy reconciliation of denominations, to their fusion in a kind of humanitarian religion *à la* Saint-Simon. According to Nathan, religions and philosophies must converge toward one supreme goal: the education of humanity; but each must proceed with the means consonant with its history and the temperament of its followers.

This injunction was not respected by the succeeding generations. Before the National Assembly Clermont-Tonnerre declared: ''To the Jews as individuals, everything; to the Jews as a nation, nothing.'' This became the guideline of the process of emancipation in France, Germany, and wherever Napoleon brought the spirit of the Revolution.

Filled with the outlook of the Age of Reason, the French Revolution wanted to reorganize society by erasing all distinctions, and just as there were in 1933 groups of Jews seeking a *rapprochement* with National Socialism, there were, during the period inaugurated by the Revolution, Jews who were ready to pay any price to forestall the least doubt about their patriotism. There developed then a frenzied race in a direction that was to lead sooner or later to the baptismal fonts.

Paris, Berlin, and Vienna, became the new Jerusalem. No Frenchman was so Gallic, no German so Teutonic, no Hungarian so Magyar, as the Jewish citizens in these respective states. Ultimately, this false assimilation proved illusory in the light of new theories originating from other criteria than religion.

The Dreyfus crisis that followed had a happy conclusion, which would have been even more fruitful if its lesson had been better understood. The more clear-sighted minds (which are a minority among Jews, as elsewhere) recognized the false direction that the idea of tolerance had taken. They understood (and the existence of Switzerland is living proof of the truth of that concept) that diversity of origins and traditions is more of an asset than a hindrance to a nation. "Note," says even Maurice Barrès, nationalist leader of French youth, "you were made to feel as Lorrainers, Alsatians, Bretons, Belgians, Jews." That is to say, each citizen must draw his spiritual forces from his origins and his traditions. Romanic Switzerland can turn toward the cradle of French civilization without danger to the solidarity of the confederacy, each Catholic can look toward Rome, and each Jew toward Jerusalem.

As the wise Nathan said:

> Es eifre jeder seiner unbestoch'nen
> von Vorurteilen freien Liebe nach.
>
> Everyone should emulate his uncorrupted
> Unbiased love.

This conception, stemming from the revolution that the Dreyfus Case turned out to be, is still valid nowadays. Collective values can be created only if each man retains his individuality, without being forced to disguise it. It is the only true tolerance, the *raison d'être* of each democracy. The Jews must have the courage to identify themselves proudly with Judaism, to free themselves of the ridiculous complex that was their nightmare for 150 years, whether to be Jewish first, and French, German, or Swiss afterwards, or vice-versa. There is no before or after in the biological make up of the individual: everything coexists in the human soul.

No solution *à la* Shylock, consisting in the dissolution of the human family consecrated by 3,000 years of common history. Judaism cannot be forsaken without penalty, even as the prophet Jonas could not forsake his prophetic vocation. And the world will not accept Jews in disguise. Its finer elements respect only those who acknowledge their origin and distinctiveness sincerely and modestly.

Equally unacceptable is the indulgence advocated by Racine in the name of the glorious biblical past, without a positive role for the future. We need, rather, the tolerance preached by Nathan, relating everyone to his spiritual heritage for the collective construction of the future, with the free contribution of Jewish thought to a new civilization. Judaism in the Europe to come must be considered and must consider itself a spiritual minority, contributing its own values to the common treasure of Western civilization.

I have attempted in another work, *The Jewish Element in French Literature,* to define the character of Jewish thought as it manifests itself in the West, to discover what Jewish scholars and writers of various countries and various areas of interest have in common. I noted the prevalence of a dynamic spirit, inherited from prophetism, that has acted as a ferment in the spiritual existence of mankind. This attribute, existing for generations and adapted to literary, philosophical, or artistic fields, is the source of a substantial number of new ideas and useful discoveries by Jews of various nationalities.

Besides this atavistic, unconscious disposition, the Jew possesses a living, conscious heritage that is now undergoing a renaissance in Israel. The existence of a spiritual center in Israel, new crystallization of biblical culture, will give the Jews scattered through the world the assurance and dignity necessary to add their voices to the concert of nations. The Occident needs their collaboration to erect a new civilization whose law will not be condescending indulgence toward one's fellow men, nor even kindly tolerance, but justice for all; a civilization that will no longer attempt to buy peace by sacrificing a minority, but that will have learned, from the merciless penalties that successive concessions have made increasingly universal, that it is one and indivisible.

This literary analysis has given a sweeping view of a long-lasting ideological struggle. The three steps that I have singled out reflect rather faithfully the political and spiritual evolution of modern

Europe. A great poet is first of all a witness to his time before acting on it. He synthesizes the multifarious spiritual, political, and social currents that converge within him, and then gives them a new impetus. Dante is the incarnation of the Middle Ages, as well as a powerful protagonist of modern times. Similarly, with Shakespeare, Racine, and Lessing, we see the confrontation of all the positive and negative influences of the past, present, and future, symbolized by dramatic figures. They fought prejudice with the power of the word that the creator gave to mankind to perfect or destroy the world.

# 9
## *Jews in Literature and Jewish Literature*
### (A Pathway to a Definition)

In this chapter I propose to explore not only a literary topic, but also the general problem of Judaism in the Diaspora in the following ways: by portraying the sphere of influence of Jewish authors or Jewish subject matter in world literature; by defining that which should either be considered a Jewish contribution to Western life in the sense of a widespread influence or only an incidental private phenomenon; by defining the criteria for an actual autonomous Jewish literature; and by clarifying the ambiguity of individual and ethnic traits in the works of Jewish authors.

The answer to questions such as that of Jewish authors and Jewish literature is undoubtedly among the most difficult tasks of the literary historian. Similar difficulties of even greater complexity exist in another field of the arts, music history. What part does the Jewish origin of a Mendelssohn, a Meyerbeer, an Ernest Bloch, a Gustav Mahler, a Jasha Heifetz, a Jehudi Menuhin, and many Soviet Jewish artists play in their musical productions? What is the common denominator for artists of such different times and places? Are they not the product of their milieu, their century, their personality, rather than of their distant Jewish origin? And if such a common element exists for all Jewish musicians, what are their distinctive features? The same question arises in all areas of art and science.

I will, however, limit myself to literature because of the magnitude of the problem. To facilitate the search for a common denominator, I shall try to arrange the extremely contradictory material by dividing it into three different categories. First, we will observe the role of Jewish authors in world literature, then Jewish themes and Jewish figures, and finally, the possibilities and prerequisites of a genuine Jewish literature in the languages of the Diaspora.

What are we to make of the incontestable fact of the exceedingly great number of Jewish authors in the literature of the various nations? In most cases they are nominal Jews or even just of Jewish origin. Creatively, they belong to the milieu in which they lived and for which they wrote. In what way does an Henri Bernstein or a Tristan Bernard, an Arthur Miller, a Stefan Zweig, an Arthur Schnitzler differ from his gentile colleagues? They write for the same public, treat the same material, the same problems, the same conflicts. They are Jews, but they consciously withhold any Jewish note from their works.

Many of them even feel handicapped by their origin and attempt to forget it. One speaks, for example, of camouflage in famous writers such as Montaigne and Marcel Proust. To be sure, both are Jewish only on their maternal side. But the mother, although her name is not inherited, is usually more decisive than the father in the development of the child. Yet in Montaigne's works his mother is not even mentioned. It is as if she did not influence his outlook. This silence suggests the idea of camouflage, especially when one realizes that Montaigne's work is not impersonal. He does not write adventure novels in the style of his time; he is not an abstract psychologist, nor a theoretician of contemporary ethics. He is rather a pioneer, in whom all modern French introspective literature had its beginnings, just as French philosophy starts with Descartes. Montaigne is a pioneer in virtue of his method of ruthless self-examination. He derives his attitudes from the elements of his very own experience, with the people of his immediate environment. Only his mother is shut out of this world, as if she were insignificant, the mother so crucial in a child's life, the mother whom Goethe, not exactly an affectionate son, celebrates in these terms:

> Vom Vater hab ich die Statur,
> Des Lebens ernstes Führen;
> Vom Mütterchen die Frohnatur,
> Die Lust zu fabulieren.

> From Father I have my stature,
> The ability to meet life head on,
> From Mother my serenity,
> The desire to create and tell stories.

Does Montaigne exclude her from his work because she did not know Greek and Latin, and would not cut a good figure in the illustrious circles of his "guild of humanists"? Was she really so insignificant in his intellectual growth that she deserves complete oblivion? Or is the reason perhaps the fact that she, the Jewess López, emigrated with her family from Spain to Bordeaux as a Marrano, like so many other forced converts, and endangered her famous son in that society of violent religious strife? One should not forget that in his century the Jews had long ago been driven out of France and were confined to certain districts in Alsace and Provence. By intentionally neglecting to mention his Jewish mother, Montaigne hoped, no doubt, to allay any suspicion of unorthodoxy.

There is in modern French literature a strange counterpart to this typical case of camouflage in the figure of the novelist Marcel Proust, who likewise stands on the threshold of a new, psychoanalytically oriented literary genre. As the son of a Catholic father from the upper middle class, but also of a Jewish mother from Alsace, he was exposed to social stigma. For in modern times, after the political emancipation of the Jews, an invisible caste system, social banishment, has taken the place of the visible medieval ghetto walls. Proust showed great tenderness toward his mother, whith whom he felt a biological unity. His method of self-analysis, related to Montaigne's but psychologically rather than philosophically oriented, gives him much less opportunity than his forerunner to pass over in silence the figure most dear to him, even if she stood in the way of his social ambitions. In order to solve the conflict between his childlike attachment and his social ambitions, he found the ingenious solution of expressing himself in his novelistic self-confession through two different characters, mainly through the narrator Marcel, who comes from an old settled Catholic family, and to a lesser extent through the figure of Swann, half Jew like Proust and possessing many of the author's traits. Together, Swann and Marcel give a true picture of Proust's soul, or rather of his two souls.

This deception, in accordance with all the rules of the art of war prevalent in the *salons,* was abandoned, however, when the Third Republic and the whole order of French society was shaken by the effects of the Dreyfus Case, where the confession of the accused was used as a pretext to send him to the desolation of Devil's Island, as a scapegoat for the sins of a clique of officers. The split in French society engendered by this affair is reflected faithfully in Proust's novels, in which this period is described. The author had to and wanted to take a stand, like every other contemporary. Therefore the balance between Swann and Marcel so painstakingly struck was destroyed. For at that critical juncture, Proust did not hesitate to take, unequivocally, the side of the Dreyfus supporters, and to acknowledge his maternal side, "this strong Jewish race." His confession of Judaism did not, to be sure, go beyond the Dreyfus episode and he did not draw the same consequences as those who later were to lead in the formation of a self-aware Jewish literature in France.

With Montaigne as well as with Proust, this camouflage is understandable to a degree, inasmuch as they both belonged wholly to the French cultural realm, without any intellectual influence from Judaism. Their Jewish roots were rather a psychological factor—a component of their personality, their temperament, and not of their world of ideas. But this alienation was true even for many authors for whom Judaism was an inchoate influence, where it should have been a living reality. As an example, let us take one of the most successful writers of our century, Stefan Zweig. Although a compatriot and contemporary of Theodor Herzl and coming from the same milieu, he removed himself quickly from the influence of the great Zionist and endeavored only to continue the tradition of Austrian literature without deviation. In this he succeeded for several decades. Only in casting a backward glance on his life, at the "world of yesterday" did he realize his own tragic error and that of his generation. He discovered to his surprise that the Austrian tradition, the brilliant Viennese center of all intellectual fields of the twentieth century was made up almost exclusively of Jews: Freud, Adler, Gustav Mahler, Goldmarck, Oskar Strauss, Emanuel Kalman, Sonnental, Max Reinhardt, Hugo von Hofmannsthal, Arthur Schnitzler, and Stefan Zweig. All these names, however, were famous as Austrians, not as Jews. Stefan Zweig himself was proud to be a bearer of the Viennese spirit. Judaism was only a vague memory for him, at most an anonymous impulse to help construct the intellectual values of the Western world. "Forgotten people, undying spirit," that is how he defined the fate of the Jews, while Vienna seemed to him the capital of Europe, his fatherland. "Oh, Europe, our sacred homeland, cradle and Parthenon of our civilization!"

Nevertheless, once in his life this repressed Jewish consciousness reached a breakthrough, a volcanic eruption. It was during the First World War, when the boot of Wilhelminian militarism threatened to crush his European ideal. Then the cosmopolitan poet revolted, and resisted the chauvinistic mass psychosis in Vienna and Berlin. With what weapons did he revolt? With the words of the Bible, through the figure of the Prophet Jeremiah, with whom he suddenly identified and in whose heroic defeatism he recognized his own position: to stand alone against the mass insanity so painstakingly cultivated by military censorship and war propaganda. In the face of the people, drunk with premature announcements of victory, he hurled the admonition of the godly pacifist Jeremiah: "No war is sacred, no death is sacred. Only life is sacred. . . .Do you not think that peace is an accomplishment, the greatest of accomplishments? Day by day you must tear it from the mouth of liars. . . ." The poet did not misjudge the danger and the hopelessness of his enterprise: "Who is more foolish than he who proclaims wisdom in the midst of drunkards, he who speaks of peace when war is raging?" But he could not remain silent, he who otherwise avoided difficulties like his model, Erasmus. A holy fire had inflamed him. The poet became a prophet and proclaimed his humanitarian ideal through the mouth of a biblical witness to the truth.

It is not accident, not even a literary device on Zweig's part to select the old prophet as a spokesman for his pacifist views. "In choosing a biblical theme, I had unconsciously hit upon something which until then had lain dormant in me: it was the echo of my Judaism, anchored in my blood and tradition. Was it not my people that had been conquered repeatedly by all people, and yet outlasted them because of some mysterious power, the power fo transform defeat into victory through the determination to overcome it again and again. . . .I felt this while working on this drama."

We did not need this confession to see that this cultured man of letters, this proud Viennese, was more personal in this work than in any other book. Here he descends into the maternal regions, into the primary sources of his soul, and thus is formed a work both of Jewish and world literature.

The play *Jeremiah* remains, however, the only document of his rediscovery of Judaism. A tragic situation had laid bare the depths of his being, as the lower layers forced their way up in an earthquake. Similar things had happened to Proust during the convulsions of the Dreyfus Affair. The most famous example of such a conversion is offered by Heinrich Heine, who, after renouncing Judaism, sang *Hebrew Melodies* on his deathbed, the *Matratzengruft* (mattress tomb), and boasted of belonging to the oldest aristocracy of mankind, the people of the Bible. With Stefan Zweig this conversion was of no longer duration than with Proust, for in the years between the two world wars he turned again completely to aesthetic and psychological literature, like André Maurois far removed from present-day problems. The latter is an example of the "unauthentic" Jew who ignores his origins, typical of a whole line of modern writers of Jewish origin who, however, do not belong to Jewish literature.

Perhaps the most fitting summary of the first part of this examination is an expression used by Sartre about the "unauthentic" Jew:

name authors, even internationally known, of Jewish origin but not of Jewish consciousness. These Jews in world literature produced no Jewish literature and only allowed their Jewish contributions to appear unwittingly. I will touch on the question of the extent to which there can be an unconscious Jewish contribution to world culture, and will refer to phenomena such as Montaigne, Spinoza, and Bergson. The latter is an example of an absolutely ''unconscious'' Jew, or rather, of a philosopher who is unconscious of his Judaism, who has absolutely no knowledge of the Chassidic movement that his forefathers belonged to in Warsaw, but whose work is nevertheless characterized by Chassidic *élan vital*. Spinoza seems to represent a thinker who stands in violent opposition to his religious community, but he has, almost unknowingly, introduced into his system thoughts derived from his teacher Maimonides. But I do not want to linger over the question of unidentified Jewish contributions, for my main interest centers on the question of an authentic Jewish literature in the midst of the Western world.

How are we to regard those works that have as their subject Jewish figures or problems, themes from the Old Testament or modern times? Does not the theme ''Jews in literature'' also include Jewish figures such as Shylock or Nathan the Wise, or the biblical plays of Racine, or the novel cycle *Joseph and His Brothers* by Thomas Mann, and the innumerable plays with figures based on Shylock? Here again I can only touch upon a subject that deserves its own examination and that I discuss in more detail in another context. Let us settle for the following statement: Jewish themes in world literature are from my standpoint much more meaningful than authors of Jewish origin but without Jewish identification. These Jewish works by Christian authors are, to be sure, not part of Jewish literature, but a step in that direction.

They enable us to see with increasing clarity what must be the conditions of an authentic Jewish literature in the light of differences of language, nationalities, and characteristics of the Jews in the Diaspora. Which language has priority among the seventy spoken by the Jews? Is it rabbinical Hebrew, by means of which intellectuals have been communicating for two thousand years, like the humanists in Latin? Herder, who collected *The Voices of the Peoples in Song,* reserved a place of honor for the biblical language and its literature, but had little sympathy for the international Hebrew of the intellectuals. He thought it a conglomeration of borrowings from all the tongues with which the Jews had come in contact. Does this process of depersonalization that Herder detected in intellectual Hebrew make it impossible to create Jewish literature in the Diaspora? For without a suitable instrument, without an adequate medium of expression, the soul cannot express itself, cannot create living works.

These theoretical considerations remind us of the Eleatic philosophers, who were struck with the mathematically irrefutable fact that the quick Achilles could never overtake the slow tortoise, even though in practice he would outdistance it with a single step. I also want to take this step by simply casting a glance at the language and literature of Eastern Jewry. Before the Second World War eleven million people spoke Yiddish, a South German dialect originating in the fifteenth and sixteenth centuries. The emigrants took it into their new Slavic homelands and kept it to prevent assimilation, built it up and enriched it until it became an unusually expressive instrument. Such was its hegemony that millions of Russian, Polish, and later, American Jews simply could not imagine that sometime in the future a different language, even modern Hebrew, could become the national language of Israel.

Authors such as Mendele, Peretz, and Sholem Aleichem could express all the yearnings and reactions of the sensitive Eastern Jewish soul. Sholem Asch in America wrote his novels in Yiddish and they were translated into many foreign languages. German-Jewish writings and other innumerable works in Yiddish make up a rich literary production. Even today, in spite of Hebrew's preeminence, the Yiddishists have not given up hope of a renaissance of this folk language many hundreds of years old. But the wheels of history cannot be turned back. With the tragic disappearance of Eastern European Judaism, its language and literature are condemned to extinction, even though it produced a golden age that rivaled the Babylonian and Spanish eras.

If Yiddish literature was a true mirror of the Jewish soul in the Diaspora, it was not the only one. For wherever a Jewish community produces writers and poets who listen to the heartbeat of their contemporaries, who feel their problems, joys, and fears, and give them form in their mother tongue, we see an instance of a genuine Jewish literature. The phrase with which the first man greeted the being created from his rib: "Bone of my bone, flesh of my flesh!" could also be applied to Yiddish, German-Jewish, French-Jewish, English-Jewish, and Italian-Jewish letters. Jewish literature in all languages is of the same flesh and the same essence. I accept without reservation the definition of the great historian of Jewish liturgy, Ismar Elbogen: "All Jewish writings from the oldest times to the present are an organic whole, and the history of Jewish literature includes all the intellectual documents of Judaism, no matter in what language they are recorded." To be sure, it appears in different forms that reflect the degree of emancipation and assimilation of the Jews in the host nations.

After Yiddish, German Jewish literature has the longest tradition. It also belongs to the past, yet it will always occupy a place of honor in the Jewish intellectual history of modern times, independently of the present science of Judaism, which had its birthplace in Germany. German Jewish literature began with Heinrich Heine, or to be more precise, with his *Hebrew Melodies*. (See chapter 10.) Throughout his whole life Heine had denied his Judaism, suppressed it, and tried to shake it off like some crushing burden. He boasted of being a life-loving Hellenist. He did not even consider Judaism a religion, but rather "a stroke of bad luck," until the day he collapsed in the Louvre with the illness that was to hold him in its clutches for seven long years and "suck the marrow from his bones." He lay there helpless, in that high-vaulted hall of the Louvre, in front of the armless Venus de Milo. He suddenly recognized in that statue the symbol of the heathen world-view, a powerless aestheticism, offering no vital help to mankind. There, in his hour of need, he turned again to the God of Israel, the God not of revenge but of justice, whose severity does not exclude forgiveness and salvation. Reaching into the depths of his soul, remembering the first experiences of his youth, the poet experienced again the warmth of the Jewish atmosphere, the enthusiasm of the circle surrounding Leopold Zuntz. Far from the will-o'-the wisps of Parisian life, he perceived anew the rhythm of his blood, the melodies of his heart, expressed in the now famous *Hebrew Melodies,* in which he paid tribute to Princess Sabbath and the religious *Minnesaenger* Juda Halevi, whose holy vow became Heine's own confession:

> Es welke meine rechte Hand,
> Vergess ich jemals dein, Jerusalem!
>
> May my right hand wither
> If I ever forget thee, Jerusalem!

The French see in Heine the wittiest, most French, so to speak, of all German poets, a cross between Voltaire and Alfred de Musset, a mixture of cleverness and deep feeling; if he has made of the German language an instrument of incomparable clarity and sensitivity, all these qualities come to a full flowering in the lyrics of his last years. They express a unique groping for the God of his fathers. In the *Hebrew Melodies* in particular, Heine accomplishes the most intimate synthesis of the Jewish world of the imagination with the German language.

A second peak emerged with Else Lasker-Schüler, Richard Beer-Hoffman, and Nelly Sachs. The visionary Lasker-Schüler had traits of the biblical prophets. She proclaimed very early the end of an era, not only for her coreligionists, but also for her German homeland. She discerned the decadent character of the prewar epoch more clearly than any Christian poet. But she especially felt the tragedy descending on her people, and bewailed it in these somber lines:

> Mein Volk wird morsch
> Dem ich entspringe
> Und meine Gotteslieder singe.
>
> My people is decaying,
> Those who have borne me,
> To whom I sing my songs of God.

She has a vision of the whole horror of the Jewish tragedy. On the other hand, she also expresses her belief in the vitality of this people:

Mein Volk,
blüh ewig, Volk.

Strom, ausgespannt von Mitternacht zu Mitternacht,
Strom, gross und tief von Meer zu Meer,
aus deiner Tiefe stürzen Quellen,
urewig speisend dich,
mein Volk.

Mein Volk, blüh, ewig, Volk.
Du träumst dir Zukunft an die Brust.
Einst wird kein Tag mehr deinen Traum zerschlagen,
die Berge deiner Seele werden in den Himmel ragen
und uns erheben,
uns,
das Volk.
Ich bin ein Baum im Walde Volk.
Und meine Blätter speist die Sonne.
Doch meine Wurzeln schlafen ihren Schlaf der Kraft
in dir,
mein Volk.


Mein Volk,
einst werden alle Dinge knien
vor dir.
Denn deine Seele wird entfliegen
hoch über Schlote, Städte in dein eignes Herz.
Und du wirst blühn,
mein Volk.

My people,
Blossom eternally, o people.
Stream, stretching out from midnight to midnight,
Stream, great and deep from sea to sea,
Out of thy depths spring sources,
Eternally nourishing thee,
O my people.

My people, blossom eternally, o people.
You dream your future in your breast.
One day your dreams will no longer be crushed,
The mountains of your soul will reach to heaven
And lift us up,
Us,

The people.
I am a tree in the forest of the people.
My leaves are nourished by the sun.
Yet my roots sleep their sleep of strength
In thee,
My people.

My people,
One day all things will kneel
Before thee.
For thy soul will fly away,
High over dwellings and cities into thine own heart.
And thou shalt blossom,
My people.

Another poet, Karl Wolfskehl, a member of Stefan George's circle, settled his bitter accounts with the host country to which he had at one time felt so completely bound: He saw no future in a German-Jewish synthesis and warned against looking back like Lot's wife:

Schaut nicht zurück!
Jung lechzt das Land.
Was war, ist Tand,
Ist tot. Ihr seid
Im Wanderkleid.
Fortgehn ist Leid,
Fortgehn ist Glück.
Schaut nicht zurück.

Don't look back!
What was is dead, is paltry.
You are dressed for wandering.
To go forth is to suffer,
To go forth is happiness.
Don't look back.

Many other writers of his background, nurtured by their Jewish legacy as well as their own country felt the same way. A short poem by Richard Beer-Hoffman reflects the essence of German-Jewish literature. The *Lullaby for Miriam* contains no mention at all of

Judaism. It is, aesthetically, the purest type of contemplative poetry, where the rational elements are not simply cast into verse but dissolve in ethereal and tender lyrics. The substance, however, is distinctly Jewish. When I pronounced this poem Jewish, I was asked once if the name *Miriam* justified this point of view. I explained that it could have been Jacqueline or Madeleine without changing its Jewish content in the least. Thus Kafka, totally Jewish in his *weltanschauung,* never treats a Jewish theme directly. Even when, in his sublimating and allegorical way, he describes the essence and unique position of the prayer leader in the synagogue, he calls his tale *Josephine and the Mouse-Folk.* The Jewish soul hovers over his work just as it does over the pictures of Chagall. This is also the case with the *Lullaby for Miriam.* It expresses with enchanting suggestiveness the Jewish conception of the unity of generations in spite of time and space:

> Ufer nur sind wir, und tief in uns rinnt
> Blut von Gewesenen, zu Kommenden rollts;
> Blut unserer Väter, voll Unruh und Stolz.
> In uns sind alle; wer fühlt sich allein?
> Du bist ihr Leben, ihr Leben ist dein!

Shores only are we, and deep within us runs
The blood of the dead, flowing toward the unborn.
Blood of our fathers, full of restlessness and pride.
In us are all men; who can feel alone?
You are their life, theirs is yours.

After the thousand-year nightmare, this poem seems filled with new, deeper meaning. It seems to be a eulogy of the great century of German-Jewish symbiosis, as significant as the Spanish phase of Jewish history. The great episode of German-Jewish literature has come to an end. Nevertheless its *élan vital* flows on to other shores.

French-Jewish literature is inspired by views and feelings that grew out of the Dreyfus Affair and its patriarchs are André Spire and Edmond Fleg. (It has since become a significant branch of French literature, and has received several Goncourt Prizes, the highest recognition in France.) Originally completely bound to the literature of their nation, in which they played an honorable part, they gradually came to discover their Judaism, and interpreted it as a revolt against the empty aestheticism and carefree behavior of their generation, which had led André Maurois and Stefan Zweig astray. Spire, for instance, who had long "looked after the swine with the Hegelians," and subscribed to a powerless and decadent cult of beauty, came under the influence of the English writer Israel Zangwill, and attempted to rouse his fellow Jews and warn them against the temptations of a facile integration. He described his transformation from a "carefree child of France" into a Jew aware of his heritage. (See chapter 15.)

> O pays adorable,
> Toi qui absorbas tant de races,
> Veux-tu m'absorber à mon tour?
> Ta langue modèle mon âme.
> Tu m'oblige aux pensées claires.
> Tu forces ma bouche à sourire.
> Et tes grandes plaines si soignées,
> Et tes forêts aménagées,
> Tes forêts où l'on n'a plus peur,
> Et la mollesse de tes lignes,
> Tes fleuves lents, tes villes, tes vignes.
> Me voila plus qu'a moitié pris.
> . . . . . . . . . . . . . . . . . . . . . . . . . . . . . . . . . . . . . .
> O chaleur, ô tristesse, ô violence, ô folie,
> Invincibles génies à qui je suis voué,
> Que serais-je sans vous? Venez donc me défendre
> Contre la raison sèche de cette terre heureuse.

> O lovely country,
> You who absorbed so many races,
> Do you want to absorb me too?
> Your language shapes my soul.
> You compel me to think clearly.
> You force my mouth to smile.
> And your great plains, so carefully tended
> And your civilized forests,
> Forests no longer frightening,
> And the softness of your lines,
> Your slow rivers, your cities, your vineyards.
> I am more than half caught.

O warmth, o sadness, o violence, o madness,
Invincible genie to whom I am pledged,
What would I be without you? Come and defend me
Against the sterile reason of this happy land.

In another place he takes issue with the uncommitted ideal of *l'art pour l'art*. He also rejects the lure of *joie de vivre*. What the poet sees as the most precious legacy of his Judaism is the socio-ethical responsibility first for his Jewish brethren and then for all outcasts. With him, unlike Beer-Hoffman, it is rather a social than a mystical solidarity. Spire's is not a contemplative nature, but dynamically intent upon the pursuit of the "eternal Tomorrow" to which Edmond Fleg gives practically Messianic emphasis at the end of his play about Solomon Molcho, *The Pope's Jew,* with these lines:

Il faut aller pourtant, fût-ce en la solitude,
Et quand on est tombé, se remettre debout.
Il faut ne se lasser d'aucune lassitude.
Quel que soit le chemin, la lumière est au bout.

But we must go on, nonetheless, even alone,
And if we have fallen, get up again.
We must not get weary of any weariness.
Whatever the road, the light is at the end.

These lines are substantially similar to the ending of the play *Jeremiah,* in which Stefan Zweig interprets the mysterious fate of Israel in these words:

Wir aber schreiten und schreiten und schreiten
Tiefer hinein in die eigene Kraft,
Die sich aus Erden die Ewigkeiten,
Und aus ihren Leiden den Gott erschafft.

But we march and march and march
Ever deeper into our own strength
Which creates for itself eternities out of earth
And God out of its sufferings.

While in Zweig's interpretation this eternal train of wanderers vanishes in mystical distances, dissolves gradually among the nations of the world ("Lost people, undying spirit"), Spire sees new horizons, concrete goals for the Jews, who have been scattered abroad in the Diaspora but not destroyed, who from their contact with other people emerge enriched to build a more beautiful Israel:

L'océan se fendra de nouveau devant toi.
Les chefs de tes tribus ont parcouru le monde,
Ont reconnu pour toi de nouveaux Canaans.
Prends ta hache, Israël; abats ces vieux arbres;
Prends ton pic, prends ta bêche, défonce ces sols vièrges;
Elève des abris, des fermes, des hameaux;
Fais paître tes troupeaux, plante, greffe, ensemence
Et moissonne.
Et parmi le miel de tes abeilles,
Le lait de tes brebis, le raisin de tes vignes,
Tu verras se dresser, convalescente et jeune,
Ta fierté, Israël.

The ocean will open up in front of you once again.
The heads of your tribes have travelled the whole world,
Have explored for you new Canaans.
Take your axe, Israel, cut down these old trees;
Take your pickaxe, take your shovel, tear up these virgin lands;
Erect shelters, farms, villages;
Take your flocks to pasture, plant, graft, sow,
And harvest.
And in the midst of the honey of your bees,
The milk of your ewes, the grapes of your vineyards,
You will see standing convalescent and young,
Your pride, Israel.

Without relinquishing the hope of an "eternal Tomorrow" in the distant future, he shows his people an immediate goal in the poem *Israel*.

Political events now ushered in a new phase of Jewish literature, which developed in many of the lands of the Diaspora. All these branches belong to the same trunk, as I mentioned in connection with Elbogen. According to a rabbinical legend, God created Adam from the dust of the whole earth, but his head from the earth of the Holy Land. Although all Jewish literature expresses some aspect of Jewish history, the most authentic incarnation of Judaism is reserved for re-surrected Israel.

Does that mean a return to a narrowly theological, exegetical, liturgical literature? No, there is no reason to fear the shrinking of the Jewish horizon when we see a new Hebrew literature arising that reflects all the facets of a strong, pulsating life. To stand in im-mediate contact with the problems of existence, to distill the poetic essence from the daily routine, to describe the growth, the progress, the setbacks of a people—that is a worthy continuation of biblical literature. To go beyond one's problems, to lose oneself in a higher, supra-national goal shall lead Jewish literature to new heights.

What Herder said, then, about the poetry of the ancient Hebrews shall also apply to the Hebrew renaissance: "The poetry of the He-brews belongs under the open sky and, where possible, before the eyes of dawn, because it has been the dawn of the enlightenment of mankind." Mankind eternally needs the enlightenment of revelation. May a new source of human compassion spring up in Israel and pour its vivifying waters through the channels of the Diaspora unto the peoples of the earth.

# 10

# Heinrich Heine: A German, French, or Jewish Writer?

Germany's greatest poet, Goethe, spoke of the two souls that lived in his breast. Even he felt threatened by the misfortune that he describes to a friend of his youth: "He could not control himself, and thus his life disintegrated, as well as his writing." But Goethe did know how to control the two steeds pulling the chariot of his fate and how to capitalize on the tension of opposite poles. He, the darling of destiny, was indeed helped by all of life's circumstances to harmonize his existence and his work. Enthroned on Olympus, transcending all the political and social problems accumulating menacingly in his homeland, exempt from all financial worry, he presented a picture of heavenly harmony and bliss.

Not so the other great lyric poet of the German language, in whose youth the clouds burst amid thunder and lightning, and in whose breast, as he lamented, was reflected the strife of the whole world. Heinrich Heine was the last great bard of German Romanticism, its heir and panegyrist, but at the same time the pioneer of a new, militant poetry. In his time, the explosive thoughts of the French *philosophers* reached across the Rhine, and the sociopolitical upheavals of France fascinated him. Meanwhile, the national consciousness of the German lands was beginning to take political shape so that he, the child of the Rhine, the borderland, was caught in a whirlpool of currents and cross-currents. Moreover, he was also a Jew, newly escaped from the age-old ghetto. Even though he behaved like a German and was seduced by the world of fairy tales and sagas, invisible barriers separated him from his homeland. These triple roots did not strengthen his spiritual existence. The circumstances of Heine's life, three irreconcilable elements—Germany, France, Judaism—posed a problem that was nearly as insoluble as the squaring of the circle. This apt comparison may serve to explain the difficulties of an accurate portrayal and evaluation of the poet. His conflicts wrecked his life, but opened up rich sources of inspiration, so that he became a guide for spanning chasms, for reconciling antitheses. Even today his exhortations are of vital significance.

It would transcend the scope of this study to try to follow and document three essential characteristics of Heine and his works in detail. My task is facilitated by the existence of three poems of precocious mastery written by the young Heine. They are the poems *The Two Grenadiers, The Ballad of Belshazzar,* and *The Lorelei,* expressions of the three main themes of life. By a rare stroke of luck, Heine's first verses are like a chiseled prologue to his life's work. He returned consciously to these his most popular, most spontaneous sources for the representation of his being.

Another precocious poet, Schiller, had as a nineteen-year-old, expressed in a raucous cry the craving for freedom of his generation under the weight of Württemberg despotism, and then dedicated his whole life to giving form to this clear impulse. Heine's life was not governed by a single impulse. His inner division makes him a reflection of his generation and its problems, which have grown continually up to our day, so that we, instructed by this mirror, can perceive the historical basis of our own situation.

I

After the repercussions of the French Revolution, the Napoleonic Empire, and the Wars of Liberation, the old order no longer appeared creditable, and the hurried restoration of dynastic power could not recapture its prestige. Too many storms had passed over the same generation, too many emotions had stirred men's souls and left their mark. Only outwardly were the waves calmed by the oil of Metternichian diplomacy. The yearnings awakened in the human breast demanded satisfaction. At times they expressed themselves through Catholic mysticism in romantic longings to escape from the world, at others in sociopolitical ferments and humanistic beliefs in the future.

In Jewish circles these tendencies were combined with attempts at social or religious emancipation. Young Heine, entirely an echo of his times, absorbed all these currents into his soul and condensed them in his poems.

In the poem of the two grenadiers, the Napoleonic experience found its first literary expression, unsurpassed in literature. It is a sort of Nibelungen saga of modern times, an epic of heroism and downfall, a myth of the tragic fate of bravery and beauty, of "noble misfortune," where all greatness is destroyed, but also transfigured.

Napoleon appeared to Europe as a worldly savior, come to redeem mankind from the Middle Ages. In his childhood, Heine had seen Napoleon in all his glory. What Goethe grasped at Valmy as a "world-shaking event" was experienced at that time by a nine-year-old boy in the court gardens in Düsseldorf when the Emperor made his entry. A few days before, when the Prince Elector was there to announce his abdication, young Heine had come home sobbing bitterly, and no argument could console him. He knew what he knew, and the sad fact that the Prince Elector abdicated was not to be glossed over.

The next day, however, a new sun arose. To resounding trumpet blasts French hussars and dragoons in fiery red and sky-blue jackets rode into the city. And right through the middle of the avenue, which it was forbidden to obstruct under the penalty of five Rhenish gulden, he came!—the Emperor, greeted by the populace with fearful respect. The officers were as glorious to look at as archangels; the world seemed freshly painted; every day there was music on the castle square, and little Harry stood behind the drum major, whose drum rolls pierced bone and marrow. Or he marched behind the band, matching their every step. The Jews too cheered the Emperor-

Messiah bringing them their civil rights, and the right to serve in the imperial army. After all, everybody had a marshall's baton in his knapsack, or at least a knapsack. Even Heine's father, a peace-loving, anything but martial citizen, as an officer of the Citizens' Guard wore a fancy uniform with epaulettes and a plume on his three-cornered hat. On the day that father Heine was in charge of the city's security, much Rüdesheimer flowed and many a battery of wine bottles, whose mouths were of the largest caliber, were taken by storm.

What followed was not all wine and roses, and finally the magnificent grenadiers marched off across the Rhine with tattered uniforms and hollow cheeks. But much worse was the return of the lords of the Restoration who had learned nothing and forgotten nothing, and that of three dozen miniature despots whose music-making followed the baton of the "Prince of Midnight" (Metternich). The little words "liberté, égalite, fraternité" were not forgotten, however, and the memory of Napoleon blended with that of the proclamation of human rights, as the herald of which he had conquered the world. That is how his image appeared to the two ragged figures returning from Russian captivity and receiving the sad news of the destruction of the Empire. The song had ended and the dreams and hopes of the little man were gone. France was lost. The arrogant leaders of the Ancient Regime could now again do as they pleased. The inconceivable had happened. They had imprisoned the eagle in a cage, the eagle who had carried the hope of the people heavenward! ". . .the Emperor, the Emperor, he's been captured!" The two grenadiers symbolize two attitudes toward misfortune and servitude. One admits defeat; he renounces all further hope and joins the great throng of the disappointed. The other, however, cannot survive without his ideal. And although he will not see the new era himself, he knows, nevertheless, that it is coming. One day the Emperor will ride again at the head of the people's army over the graves of the fallen, and at the sound of the victory fanfares his faithful will be resurrected and gather around the banner of human rights.

Thus, in a few seemingly artless verses, a newly awakened, secularized messianic faith was given gripping expression.

"Secularized messianic faith" is indeed the proper designation for

Heine's sociopolitical ideal, which is at the same time an expression of his anti-religious revolt, his rebellion against the Judeo-Christian belief in the hereafter. Without considering that the prophetic Messiah idea is not inimical to the world, but includes a heavenly kingdom on earth, Heine attributed to biblical religions the dogmas of earthly renunciation opposed to progress ("Nazarenertum" he called them), on which he declared war.

> Ein neues Lied, ein besseres Lied,
> O Freunde, will ich euch dichten!
> Wir wollen hier auf Erden schon
> Das Himmelreich errichten.
>
> Es wächst hienieden Brot genug
> Für alle Menschenkinder,
> Auch Rosen und Myrten, Schönheit und Lust,
> Und Zuckererbsen nicht minder.
>
> A new song, a better song.
> O friends, I will create for you
> We want to set up here on earth
> A heavenly kingdom.
>
> There is bread enough down here
> For all the children of men,
> And roses and myrtle, and beauty and desire
> And sweet peas as well.

Beyond the glorification of Napoleon as an earthly Messiah, the poem also contains the whole spectrum of emotions that was to be the basis of Heine's lifelong relationship to France, his second fatherland.

For a few years after the composition of *The Two Grenadiers,* France became the land of refuge for him, who, in spite of his fame, had searched in vain for a bourgeois existence in Germany. Like a lark he had soared into the air in his *Book of Songs,* had fluttered about anxiously, and had looked around longingly for a small piece of land where he could settle, for one can sing in the air, but one must live on earth.

But wherever he looked he could find no secure future. The later motif of his homelessness was already beginning to sound. Where would the tired wanderer one day find his last resting place? "If only I knew," he wrote in his diary in 1830, "where I now can lay down my head! In Germany it is impossible. At any moment a policeman would come in and shake me to see if I was really asleep."

Yet, in the same year in which he wrote these gloomy observations, the trumpets were sounding in Paris: "Aux armes, citoyens!"

The July Revolution broke out and France was again in turmoil. The Emperor rode again over the graves, under the fluttering flag with the sacred three colors. The religion of freedom and equality seemed resurrected, and the French were its chosen people. For, in Heine's enthusiastic words, "in their language the first gospels and dogmas are recorded. Paris is the new Jerusalem, and the Rhine is the Jordan which separates the holy land of freedom from the land of the Philistines."

Heine, the emigrant, was acknowledged immediately as an intellectual power, accepted by the *cénacle* of French Romanticism as one of their own, and he received for life, so to speak, an orchestra seat in the great Parisian World Theater.

For the whole world was streaming to Paris, to this "Pantheon of the living," in this beautiful cradle of new social, political, and aesthetic ideas. Here he was no longer outlawed, discredited in newspaper articles, attacked as a trespasser in the sacred groves of national literature. Fashionable periodicals competed for his contributions. One of them published his study of the German Romantic School. He became the single mediator between France and Germany by explaining each people to the other, although his immediate success was more of an intellectual than a political nature.

Through him the French learned that lyricism consists not only of strikingly colorful language, but also of mysticism; that love is not celebrated only in hymns, but should speak, as among the common people, in simple tones directly to the heart. On the other hand, the poet who was seeking to overcome romantic *ennui,* found in Paris and in French High Romanticism the sociopolitical climate that allowed him to proclaim a new secular religion without incurring the danger of arrest by the secret police. In this atmosphere he seemed to recover from the grief he had suffered and the sound of the French language intoxicated him constantly. In Germany the French language had seemed only an attribute of high society, but now, O wonder of wonders, every cab driver spoke more elegant French than any German countess. Oh, what a lovely spell to be under!

## II

Nevertheless, Heine remained a stranger, for "he who would understand a poet must visit the poet's land." He remained rootless, and his spiritual exile was defined a hundred years later by Stefan Zweig's confession: "Twenty borrowed languages do not replace one's own tongue." This was especially true of Heine, whose mother tongue had developed into such a wonderful instrument for the expression of feelings that derived from the traditions of his homeland in contrast to the sophisticated thought drawn from French sources. Therefore he felt that he was, in spite of his intimate connection with France, a German poet from whom, with increasing frequency, sighs of nostalgia were to be heard, such as the following:

> O Deutschland, meine ferne Liebe
> Gedenk' ich deiner, wein' ich fast!
> Das muntre Frankreich scheint mir trübe,
> Das leichte Volk wird mir zur Last.

> O Germany, my distant love,
> When I think of thee, I almost weep!
> Light-hearted France seems gloomy to me,
> This gay people is now a burden.

In these lines lies the whole tragedy of the emigrant, the tragedy of the poet deprived of his legacy. Nevertheless, the German Romantic School found in Heine its consummation and its succession. He sang "the last free wood-song of Romanticism." The irony in his loftiest moods that so upset his critics is nothing more than romantic irony carried to its extremes. It does not deny and ridicule a mystical outlook, but simply expresses a new attitude toward life and society demanded by changing conditions, and announces the end of an era. Heine felt personally involved in public affairs, and developed into a modern writer, *engagé* and progressive. In secret, however, he remained a child of the "moonlit enchanted night which holds all senses captive" (Tieck). His soul had succumbed to his Rhineland home, its mountains and valleys, which he populated with figures and shapes. Out of this intimacy with his native soil he created *The Book of Songs,* which won hearts everywhere, and the saga of *The Lorelei,* which was not to be eliminated from German folk literature by any Imperial Department of Culture or literary criticism.

*The Lorelei* is not simply the high point in the cycle of tales about Father Rhine, not simply the consummation of a tradition, but rather a new poetic field, an original approach to legends. Not that Heine invented the material. A few years before, two other romanticists had celebrated the Lorelei rock for the first time. But they lacked the inspiration. Only Heine's magic wand could free the spirits locked in the rock and awaken them to a magical life of their own.

Perhaps in no other work of world literature is the mystery of creation so visible as in this song, where the poet with a few strokes, as in an etching by Picasso, brings forth an irresistibly evocative picture. With a few monochrome touches, Heine produced a wealth of shades that bury themselves deeply within the soul. With the merest gesture he transports us into a dreamlike landscape filled with fairy-tale figures. The tale is not a new treatment of an old theme. But nature is ancient, as is the Rhenish homeland of the poet. The dreams and yearnings of mankind are immemorial. At times primal human experiences intrude into our consciousness as mythological figures or in fairy-tale form. Such an archetypal experience, also found in *The Odyssey,* is the erotic longing of man for exalted womanhood, until his ship of life is dashed to pieces by the alluring siren song. Thus in the evening sun appears an ethereal figure on a shimmering mountaintop and lures the love-sick sailor away from the security of the shore until his woeful cries are stilled by the impassive waves that lap the destructive rock.

From this evanescent picture Heine created that wonderful, power-

ful melody that has enchanted millions and immensely increased the
fame of the Rhine:

### Loreley

Ich weiss nicht, was soll es bedeuten,
Dass ich so traurig bin;
Ein Märchen aus alten Zeiten,
Das kommt mir nicht aus dem Sinn.

Die Luft ist kühl, und es dunkelt,
Und ruhig fliesst der Rhein;
Der Gipfel des Berges funkelt
Im Abendsonnenschein.

Die schönste Jungfrau sitzet
Dort oben wunderbar;
Ihr goldnes Geschmeide blitzet,
Sie kämmt es mit goldenem Kamme

Sie kämmt es mit goldenem Kamme
Und singt ein Lied dabei;
Das hat eine wundersame,
Gewaltige Melodei.

Den Schiffer in seinem Schiffe
Ergreift es mit wildem Weh;
Er schaut nicht die Felsenriffe,
Er schaut nur hinauf in die Höh,

Ich glaube, die Wellen verschlingen
Am Ende Schiffer und Kahn;
Und das hat mit ihrem Singen
Die Loreley getan.

### The Lorelei

I do not know the reason
Why I am so sad;
A tale of ancient times,
Will not leave my mind.

The air is cool and it is getting dark,
And quietly flows the Rhine;

The hilltop sparkles
In the evening sun.

The most beautiful maiden
Sits wondrously up there;
Her golden adornment glistens,
She combs her golden hair.

She combs it with a golden comb
While singing a song;
It has a wondrous,
Mighty melody.

The boatman in his boat
Is seized with a wild ache;
He does not look upon the rocky reef,
He only looks up high.

I think that in the end the waves
Swallow boatman and boat;
And that was done
By the song of the Lorelei.

Even the literary dictators in the period of Nazi barbarism were not able to banish this song from popular memory and had to settle for the wretched solution of ascribing it to an "unknown author." But the silencing of the Jewish author is the greatest tribute that can be paid a poet: his creation had become, like the oldest tradition, an anonymous component of folklore, and as such, the property of the people.

But it was precisely that achievement that was held against him during his lifetime in the circles of the so-called *Altdeutschtum*—that Teutonism which became tragically important under National Socialism. A citizen of alien blood, recently escaped from the ghetto, could not and should not have been allowed to become a German poet. From the beginning this presumptuousness was to earn the defiant writer the enmity of certain academic and social circles, who wanted to see in his works only a pose, a clever imitation, and passed on this judgment to posterity. It is painful to watch Adolf Bartels furiously attempt to rob Heine of his laurels, or Wilhem Scherer denigrate the popularity of *The Lorelei* by his invidious comparison with previous treatments of the theme. "Heine," he said, "reaped by a skillful pastiche what Brentano had sown."

However, the simple people for whom Heine thought and wrote, and other readers unimpressed by the academic wisdom of orthodox Germanistics, have given us a different judgment. Nietzsche called Heine the first German of European stature since Goethe because in his *Book of Songs* he raised a German literary genre, the *lied,* to European importance. Surprisingly, even Bismarck supported with remarkable willingness the unsuccessful attempt of Empress Elizabeth to construct a Heine memorial in his home town of Düsseldorf. He subscribed to the arguments that Heine's songs had enriched German literature.

Heine's doomed struggle for German acceptance is anticipated symbolically in the changing history of this song. Powerfully and plaintively, the German melody sounds through his whole life, even in glittering Paris. But his anger at the official hostility he incurred in spite of his popularity, or because of it; his violent denunciations of social and political abuses; his accusations against the leaders of the absolutist régime made him extremely unpopular with Metternichian censorship, which declared him Public Enemy Number One. Yet there grew in him through the years an insurmountable nostalgia for the land where he once "cried the bitterest tears," and his songs of homesickness are like stifled sighs:

> Und als ich an die Grenze kam,
> Da fühlt' ich ein stärkeres Klopfen
> In meiner Brust, ich glaube sogar
> Die Augen begannen zu tropfen.

> Und als ich die deutsche Sprache vernahm,
> Da ward mir seltsam zu Mute;
> Ich meinte nicht anders, als ob das Herz
> Recht angenehm verblute.

> And when I came to the border,
> I felt a stronger beating
> In my breast; I think even
> My eyes began to tear.

And when I heard German spoken
A strange feeling came over me;
It seemed as if my heart
Would bleed with sheer delight.

Then he seemed to receive new breath.

Seit ich auf deutsche Erde trat,
Durchströmen mich Zaubersäfte—
Der Riese hat wieder die Mutter berührt,
Und es wuchsen ihm neu die Kräfte.

Since I came to German lands,
Magic fluids stream through me,
The giant has again touched the mother
And regained his power.

Nevertheless, he continues to brandish the cutting sword of his scorn over the national situation, which has not essentially changed since his emigration.

Noch immer das hölzern pedantische Volk,
Noch immer ein rechter Winkel
In jeder Bewegung, und im Gesicht
Der eingefrorene Dünkel.

And still the wooden pedantic race,
And still a right angle
In every movement, and in the face
The same frozen arrogance.

But in spite of his grief over the persistence of the eternal Yesterday, the love of his homeland breaks through repeatedly, as in those lines which are an almost embarrassed prayer:

Der Himmel erhalte dich, wackres Volk,
Er segne deine Saaten,
Bewahre dich vor Krieg und Ruhm,
Vor Helden und Heldentaten.

> May Heaven keep thee, brave people,
> And bless thy seed,
> Protect thee from war and fame,
> From heroes and heroics.

Once again all the bitterness and all the devotion that he feels toward Germany are clashing within him. He sees the disaster brewing, which earlier had led him to give warnings such as the following: "A play will be staged in Germany in comparison with which the French Revolution will seem a harmless idyll."

However, besides these shrill Cassandra calls, besides the justified premonitions of looming catastrophes, there stands his unshaken hope for the future, his appeal to a later generation, which forms the gripping ending of his book on Germany.

> Das alte Geschlecht der Heuchelei
> Verschwindet, Gott sei Dank, heut',
> Es sinkt allmählich ins Grab, es stirbt
> An seiner Lügenkrankheit.

> Es wächst heran ein neues Geschlecht,
> Ganz ohne Schminke und Sünden,
> Mit freien Gedanken, mit freier Lust—
> Dem werde ich alles verkünden.

> The old generation of hypocrisy
> Disappears, thank God, today.
> It sinks slowly into the grave,
> It dies of its pathological deceit.

> There will spring up a new generation,
> Completely without pretense and sins,
> With free thoughts, free desires—
> To it will I proclaim my allegiance.

He was the sharpest critic of German conditions but, precisely because of that, a better friend of this land than the extremists, who repeatedly drove it to ruin through arrogant glorification and incitement against their neighboring country, which had become a second home to Heine and to many emigrants.

But how did the poet solve the problem of being a citizen of two countries, which at that time and for another hundred years remained arch-enemies, in a way that transcended his personal fate? By recognizing the future synthesis of the seemingly irreconcilable antitheses and setting himself in the service of its realization through his untiring efforts to explain each people to the other. "The Holy Alliance of Nations will come about. We will no longer need to feed standing armies of many hundreds of thousands of murderers created by mutual distrust. We shall use their swords and horses to plow, and we shall achieve peace, prosperity, and freedom. To this goal my life is dedicated. It is my mission," he asserted. And he predicted the day when both lands would, like Homeric heroes, exchange weapons and armor as signs of friendship. This exchange of weapons was unfortunately not to occur in such a friendly manner. Now, however, after the reign of folly, the time for reasonable dialogue has apparently come, and Heine's pleas and promises are reaching the stage of realization. The Rhine, instead of being a border and bone of contention, is becoming a link between people. A European family of nations is growing, in which political and economic problems are solved in ways other than by suicidal violence.

### III

Thus Heine solved his personal problem of dual citizenship by attempting a European solution. He had gotten into the impasse of divided allegiance through his Judaism, however—that third component of his identity that made his life "an equation to the third power." It was because of his Jewish origin that all doors in Germany were closed to him, and that he had to go in search of a new homeland. His Judaism was not, as with so many others, just an external characteristic, but rather a powerful ferment of his intellectual personality.

Again it is a youthful poem that symbolically points to his position on the Bible and Judaism, *The Ballad of Belshazzar*. It was written at approximately the same age as *The Lorelei* and *The Two Grenadiers*. But what a difference in tone and style! While the rhythm, for example, in the grenadiers' song is graceful and quick, and one seems to hear *The Marseillaise* and the neighing and hoofbeats of the horses, here we encounter an ascetic, sober tone, a biblical tone.

In a few lines the situation and the atmosphere are almost magically conjured up:

>Die Mitternacht zog näher schon;
>In stiller Ruh lag Babylon
>
>Nur oben, in des Königs Schloss,
>Da flackert's, da lärmt des Königs Tross.
>. . . . . . . . . . . . . . . . . . . . . . . . . . . . . . . . . . . . . . .
>Die Knechte sassen in schimmernden Reihn,
>Und leerten die Becher mit funkelndem Wein . . . .

>The deep of night is coming on;
>In still repose lies Babylon.
>
>But high in the castle of the King
>The royal train is revelling.
>. . . . . . . . . . . . . . . . . . . . . . . . . . . . . . . . . . . . . . .
>His retinue sit in a glittering line
>And empty their goblets of sparkling wine . . . .

With uncanny rapidity events rush forward. No ornamental epithets slow the impetus of the action or its tragic conclusion. At most, the singularity of the occurrences is suggested by the sound of the vowels.

>Belsazar ward aber in selbiger Nacht
>Von seinen Knechten umgebracht.
>
>Belshazzar was the same night
>Slain by his very own subjects.

No judgment is expressed, no reflection interjected. The ethical thought emerges spontaneously from the whole. In a sense the action carries itself along without the help of a narrator, like a scene from the Bible, a German-language Bible. The naïve poetic genius had intuited what reflective observation made clear to him much later: "In the Bible there is no trace of art. It is the style of a notebook in which the absolute spirit, as though without any human help, noted the day's occurrences with the same factual accuracy with which we write our blurbs. About this style it is impossible to pronounce judgment. One can only verify its effects on our being. Here all criteria fail. The Bible is the word of God."

*The Ballad of Belshazzar* is the first poetic document of the awakened Jewish heritage in the emerging poet. The conception of guilt and repentance expressed in it, of human arrogance and divine vengeance, will not always correspond to Heine's *Weltanschauung,* and a great deal of his life will have been spent before he humbly adopts once again, on his bed of pain, the Jewish teachings of an angry and punitive God, merciful, however, toward the repentant sinner. What lies in between is a unique struggle with the Jewish question, a continual resistance to his Jewish role, which seemed unbearable to him. He wanted to free himself of this spiritual inheritance as the Prophet Jonah did of his mission to the heathen city of Nineveh. Let us take another look at this drama of betrayal and return, the Jewish *leitmotiv* in Heine's life.

Heinrich Heine, the poet whose roots plunged deeply into the Jewish world of ideas, converted abruptly, at the age of twenty-eight, to the Protestant religion. Did this surprising step occur out of clear conviction, or was it a confused act, a break in his intellectual development?

Indeed, the change of faith was a tragedy in his life, no matter how incredible this may sound for this worldly knight of the Holy Ghost, this Storm-and-Stress fighter for progress and enlightenment. To be sure, Heine had never blindly embraced Judaism. Not only his nature, but also the spirit of the times and the attitude of his fellow Jews militated against this. For the Jews the French Revolution was more significant than for any other European people. For them it was a leap out of the Middle Ages into modern times. The gentile world reached the emancipation of reason through a lengthy evolution. Their religion and their religious feelings had had time to adapt to the transformation of Western consciousness. This transition occured in only one generation for the European Jews. Without preliminaries, they switched from talmudic scholasticism to the study of Hegel and Rousseau. Even their language had separated them from their milieu, since they had kept among themselves an archaic German dialect. As prominent a man as the respected banker Solomon Heine, who invited senators and generals to dinner, spoke in this colloquial idiom, and Betty van Geldern, admirer of Rousseau and Goethe, who dreamed of a career at the Imperial Court or in politics for her son Harry, wrote her letters most easily in Hebrew script, in a modern German in which dative and accusative were sometimes interchanged, a peculiarity that even her famous son did not entirely shake off.

The transition to modern times was painful and paid for with many sacrifices, desertions, and apostasies. These were the expression of the disproportion between social and cultural emancipation, the former of which did not keep pace with the more rapid intellectual adaptation, and as a result threw a whole generation into confusion. It was Heinrich Heine's generation.

His relation to Judaism is a reflection of this confusion. This relationship had long ceased to be religious, in spite of thorough Hebrew studies and in spite of a pious father, who considered atheism a great sin and extolled to the philosophy-minded gymnasium student the legitimacy of religious beliefs and the advantages of the Jewish customs, which were remunerative. He himself had in French class translated the word *faith* as *le crédit,* anticipating his later criticism of false piety. He conceived his Judaism, as did so many others subsequently, not as a religious, but as a social problem, with the typical inferiority complex of those who were taking their first hesitating steps in European society after leaving the ghetto. Thus, on June 28, 1825, Heine adopted the Protestant faith, between the two sections of his doctoral examination in law, as Christian Johann Heinrich Heine. For the rest of his life he never forgave himself this act, nor the people and circumstances that drove him to it: "The best become rascals. I do indeed understand the words of the psalmist: 'Lord, give me my daily bread, that I may not slander thy name!' "

After he had decisively turned his back on Judaism, Heine attempted to appease his conscience by giving his conversion a higher significance. The social banishment of the Jews seemed to him increasingly merely an aspect of the official policy of suppression. It is characteristic of great spirits that they are not circumscribed by their own fate, but out of personal experience and even defeats they find the impetus to creativity. Heine as a Jew had been restricted proressionally and socially, and so were many others. But he plunged into the essence of things, brought out their transcendent significance, transformed a failure into an idea, a rebuff into a contribution to the quality of life.

Thus, from his painful experience as German and Jew, from the bruises inflicted by rigid and outmoded institutions, arose his social, political, and religious world-view. The Jewish problem was also a German problem. The Jewish question was a question of democracy, of German democracy. Jewish subjugation was an aspect of German subjugation, the seduction of the Germans through the clever words of their leaders. Heine's conversion, not to Christianity but to Europe, with France as its intellectual capital, seemed to him a broadening of his battle for humanism. He may have found consolation in the thought of having transformed a defeat into a victory, of fighting for his beliefs on a higher level, of defending universal justice and freedom.

Nevertheless, in quiet moments he was often overcome by longing for the faith of his childhood. Melancholy invaded him at the most unexpected times, as, for example, in the situation he describes in the poem *Sea Spirit*. Far down in the sea he spies a maiden:

> Den Kopf auf den Arm gestützt,
> Wie ein armes vergessenes Kind—

> So tief, meertief also
> Verstecktest du dich vor mir
> Aus kindischer Laune,
> Und konntest nicht mehr herauf,
> Und sassest fremd unter fremden Leuten,
> Jahrhundertelang,
> Derweilen ich, die Seele voll Gram,
> Auf der ganzen Erde dich suchte,

> Du Immergeliebte,
> Du Laegstverlorene,
> Du Endlichgefundene—
>
> Her head resting on her arm,
> Like a poor forgotten child—
>
> So deep, so deep in the sea
> You hid yourself from me
> In a childish whim,
> And could not rise again,
> And sat, lost among strangers
> For centuries,
> While I, my soul full of sorrow
> Searched for you through the whole world.
>
> You eternally beloved
> You long-lost one
> You finally recovered.

Who does not recognize in this "sea spirit" the allegorical figure of "Daughter Zion," to which, during the Berlin days of enthusiasm for Jewish history, he had sworn eternal fealty.

An even clearer confession of his longing for the Jewish legacy that he still denied is found in the work *Atta Troll,* the last pure song of romanticism, in which, in a nocturnal vision, three figures appear to the poet: the Greek goddess Diana, symbol of classical harmony and beauty; the lightly-clad Celtic fairy Abunde, who symbolizes his love for carefree France; and Herodias, queen of Judea, who waves tenderly to him. For her is reserved his deepest affection:

> Denn ich liebe dich am meisten!
> Mehr als jene Griechengöttin,
> Mehr als jene Fee des Nordens,
> Lieb' ich dich, du tote Jüdin!
>
> For I love thee most of all!
> More than this Greek goddess,
> More than this fairy of the North,
> Do I love thee, deceased Jewish queen!

Again and again he pays homage to his Jewish inheritance as the most genuine, if not the most visible force in his soul. The promise he had made himself to continue to stand up for the rights of Jews, "to defend Carthage before the very gates of Rome," was kept. In the Damascus Affair—where with the complicity of the French consul several Jews were tortured because of an alleged ritual murder, and their French coreligionists, with the exception of the attorney Crémieux and Baron Rothschild, as well as all of official France, remained embarrassedly silent—Heine raised his voice with an indignant "J'accuse": "No, the descendants of Israel, of the pure, chosen, priestly race, do not eat pork, nor old Franciscans. They drink no blood, just as they would never drink their own urine. . . ."

Thus the Jewish *leitmotiv* runs through Heine's own life, even in his most heathen, his "Hellenistic" period, when he looked down philosophically on the "Nazarenes," the Jews as well as the Christians who were caught in earthly asceticism. Finally came that visit to the Louvre in which he broke down physically in front of the Venus de Milo, which struck him as a symbolic event.

His renunciation of the physically perfect, but armless (i.e., powerless) Venus meant the abandonment of the Hellenic *Weltanschauung,* of heaven on earth and the deification of man. It may also have been an echo of the Sinai commandment learned in his youth: "Thou shalt not make graven images nor worship false gods." This development culminates in the public admission during the last years of his life of his error in failing to recognize the validity of Jewish doctrine. In his last confession he says: "I did not see that Moses. . .himself was a great artist. . . .But he did not form his *objets d'art* like the Egyptians out of brick and granite. He built human pyramids, he sculpted human monuments, he took a tribe of poor shepherds and created a people which was also to defy the centuries, a great, eternal, holy people, a people of God. . . .

"Because of my Hellenic disposition, to which Jewish asceticism was repulsive, I failed to speak with adequate reverence not only of the craftsmen, but also of the work, the Jews. My preference for Hellas has since decreased. I see now that the Greeks were only beautiful youths, while the Jews have always been men, violent, unyielding men, not just in the past, but to the present day, in spite of eighteen centuries of persecution and misery. I have learned to honor them better since then, and if ever pride of birth were not a foolish contradiction to the champions of the Revolution and its principles, then the writer of these pages could be proud of the fact that his ancestors belonged to the noble house of Israel, that he is a descendant of those martyrs who gave the world a God and a moral code and have suffered and fought on all the battlefields of thought.''

These ringing words, written in his last years on his bed of pain, the ''mattress tomb,'' show clearly that Heine had returned to his beginnings after the great ellipse of his life. This was not an aberration, but a return. Like a new Faust, his life had been a relentless search for truth in every situation, through pleasure, suffering, exploration.

In the light of this development Heine's later works seem like an expression of his matured attitude toward his hereditary faith. Judaism now appeared to him as a noble achievement of the human spirit. When he spoke of Columbus, he added:

> Einer nur, ein einz'ger Held,
> Gab uns mehr und gab uns Bessres
> Als Kolumbus, das ist jener,
> Der uns einen Gott gegeben.

> Sein Herr Vater, der hiess Amram,
> SeineMutter hiess Jochebeth,
> Und er selber, Moses heisst er,
> Und er ist mein bester Heros.

> Just a single hero
> Gave us more, gave us better
> Things than Columbus. It is the one
> Who gave us a God.

> His father was called Amram,
> His mother Jochebeth,
> And he himself is named Moses.
> He is my greatest hero.

And to the work of art that Moses welded from an amorphous mass of slaves, Heine dedicated his *Hebrew Melodies*. They are the poetic expression of his renewed relationship with the Jewish religion and history. *Melodies* may be considered the appropriate word for the characterization of a people whose whole culture, learning, prayers, and gay and troubled moods are passed on in a peculiar chant from generation to generation. Heine himself had in his childhood studied the Bible, the Talmud, and even Hebrew grammar. He had also learned those wordless songs which complete the Jewish prayer text so affectingly. During his long illness he loved to have Alexander Weill, the Alsatian author (who, as the son of a cantor, knew all the liturgical melodies) sing all the traditional music to him, in which he detected the sobbing of the centuries. When Mathilde, his wife, burst into the room, wanting to know where the "barbaric" sounds were coming from, he calmed her with the assurance that they were old German folk songs. For the good woman knew hardly anything of Heine's background and had married him partly because she had heard that the Germans make better husbands than Frenchmen!

From this ringing inside him, this reawakening of youthful impressions, grew the *Hebrew Melodies,* romances with pictures and figures from Jewish folklore and history. His chastened attitude toward Israel is visible in the first poem, *Princess Sabbath.* In the Jews' day of rest Heine sees the secret of their spiritual rebirth from misery and humiliation. Israel is a bewitched prince, changed into a dog by a witch's sorcery. He, the outcast who wanders all week long through life's dregs, to the delight of street boys, throws off his rags on Friday at twilight, and becomes a human being again, with his head high. Now follows a uniquely moving description of the way the devout Jew receives his Sabbath, his princess, with prayer and song, accompanies her into his house, where a solemn, candle-lit atmosphere prevails, where *shalet* and other Jewish foods are eaten. This, claimed Heine thirty years earlier, had done more for the preservation of religion than all the sermons and theological journals.

But the day dies, the curse returns, the shudder of metamorphosis seizes the heart of the prince, the wax candles suddenly brighten —the last salute to the departing princess before the sordid battle for existence begins again.

After this idyll, woven of piety and heavenly gaiety, follow in the *Hebrew Melodies* the songs to the triumvirate of the Spanish-Jewish poetic school, Ibn Gabirol, Ibn Ezra, and Juda Halevi, the latter claiming Heine's special affection. His portrait of his medieval colleague is a description of his own, better self. Through the mouth of Juda Halevi, the Heine who had returned to his earliest beginnings expresses his Jewish confession of faith, which actually never completely disappeared during the years of estrangement, and which he expressed in so many forms:

> Lechzend klebe mir die Zunge
> An dem Gaumen, und es welke
> Meine rechte Hand, vergäss' ich
> Jemals dein, Jerusalem.

> May my languishing tongue cleave to
> My gums, and my right hand wither
> If ever I should
> Forget thee, O Jerusalem.

After such utterances in poetry and prose, is a closing confession in his will still necessary? "I don't need to return to Judaism, since I never left it."

Heinrich Heine, who wanted to escape his Jewish fate, later reassumed it in a higher sense, purified through suffering and sorrow. He recognized the emptiness of a simply abstract humanism, of a simply political liberalism. Judaism now meant for him the secret source of power that enabled him to raise his gaze to high human ideals, a concrete doctrine, a living art.

Hopefully I have succeeded in suggesting the three inextricably intertwined threads that form the fabric of Heine's thought. The matter of his identity cannot be given a categorical answer, since in science, particularly in the human sciences, there are no incontrovertible solutions, no generally applicable truths. One can only grope for light.

No matter how one evaluates subjectively the preponderance of this or that element in Heine's personality, the fact remains that he, whose spirit was fed by many sources, was in turn productive in many areas. Many nations have given him honorary citizenship; he has long been one of their intellectual possessions. His prose and poetry, even in translation, stimulate all literature and are part of the universal legacy of vital ideas. Heine is one of those figures of permanent importance given to the world by Judaism.

# 11

## The Dreyfus Case
## and Its Spiritual Repercussions
(A lecture delivered at the
University of Berlin, 1963,
after returning from emigration)

With deep emotion I appear before you today. For it is, after a "thousand-year" interruption, my first contact with the *alma mater* where, under distinguished teachers, I took my first steps into the world of literary scholarship and received an essential part of my humanistic education. Exactly thirty years have passed since the volcanic eruptions of barbarism that were ultimately to destroy German cities and cultural shrines and reduce Western civilization almost to rubble. The "Thousand-Year Reich" lasted only twelve years, and new life is blossiming from the ruins, but human devastation has something millennial about it. The bewildered exiles search in vain for the trusted faces of their college days.

> O wie liegt so weit, o wie liegt so weit,
> Was mein einst war,
> Als ich Abschied nahm, als ich Abschied nahm,

War das Herz mir bang und schwer,
Als ich wiederkam, als ich wiederkam,
War alles leer.

Oh! How far away, how far away lies
What once was mine!
When I went away, went away,
My heart was tense and heavy,
When I came back, came back,
All was empty.

My last memories of my Berlin student life are of my unforgetta-
ble teacher, Professor Max Herrmann, and his opening remarks in
the great auditorium Unter den Linden: "According to the ten theses
of The National Socialist Student Association, every Jew lies when
he speaks German. Well, whoever doesn't want to hear my lies,
please leave the room." Thunderous applause answered the courageous professor, who liked to think of the word *professor* as *confessor*,
interpreter not only of a science but also of a conscience. This memory, the last one I have of a free Germany, followed me abroad and
helped me take to heart Moses' warning to the children of Israel after
their flight from Egypt: "Hate not the Egyptians in spite of all they
have done to you, for you were sojourners in their land."

Since then, learning and teaching at many universities, I found that
God's spirit is present everywhere. I also carried the legacy of
Goethe and Kant deep in my heart like a sunken treasure, until the
time came to return to my past and help construct new life on its
ashes. I do this in the belief that the German people is increasingly
dedicated to true values after awakening from the Nazi nightmare,
and wants to perpetuate its best traditions. It is still spiritually divided and wrestling with its better self, and therefore a subject like
the one I shall talk about is not simply a chapter of irrelevent literary
history, but an attempt at contributing to a better understanding of
the problems of this nation by a portrayal of a similar situation in the
neighboring land of France. With this in mind I shall examine that
great crisis which has been recorded in the political and intellectual
history of France under the name of "The Dreyfus Case."

By crisis is not meant a symptom of disease. In the eyes of the poet Charles Péguy it was a process of recovery. He calls the Dreyfus Affair "an eminent crisis in three histories themselves eminent. . .in the history of Israel, in the history of France, in the history of Christianity."

This threefold division will serve as a guide for the examination of the subject. In looking at these various aspects, the fundamental significance of that trial will become clear for our generation.

We are used to trials of greater importance than this charge of espionage against an insignificant French officer of Jewish faith. Compared with some contemporary trials dealing with mass murder and unprecedented violence, including genocide, this trial seems an innocuous idyll. Actually, it contained the seed of what was to take bloody shape later on the stage of the world. In the few years from Dreyfus's conviction to his pardon, from 1894 until 1899, all the demonic forces that led to the recent world explosion were already manifest. The Nuremberg trials are momentous because of the magnitude of the crimes committed, but they are not morally crucial. They are concerned only with the question of guilt and repentance, and signify simply the liquidation of a criminal regime that came to power because the intellectual resistance evident in the Dreyfus trial did not take place this time.

Insignificant in its material content, the Dreyfus Affair is in its development and its effects an epochal example of the rebellion of the spirit agains the threat of an unjust state.

*"Tua res agitur,"* says Thomas Mann with respect to the Dreyfus Case. "At stake is the cause of your people, your land, your conscience." In a similar vein, François Mauriac remarks, on the occasion of the new edition of the *Devil's Island Diary,* that these events contain in miniature the problems of our time: "The Dreyfus Affair is only an episode, but the most significant one of a civil war that is still going on."

Before describing the course of that famous trial, as well as the forces at work in it, let us take a look at a war that had deeply wounded the pride of the people and made them waver between hope of revenge and fear of new military involvement with the redoubtable neighbor east of the Rhine. Understandably, this situation benefited the army, instrument of defense or revenge, the protector of national honor. It was easy for the military caste to assume an increasingly powerful position, to paint a halo around itself, and to set itself up as a state within a state. While the army had become democratized since its defeat of 1870, the professional officers who controlled it still came from a narrow layer of society: the conservative bourgeoisie and the nobility. In fact, the tradition has remained unbroken since 1789 to recruit the officer corps of the general staff from the descendants of the aristocracy, "le côté des Guermantes," as Proust describes them. Even today one meets many familiar names of the *ancien régime* in the ranks of the military command.

The perpetuation of this class system was effected through strict selection of the officer candidates from the Polytechnic Institute to which the "two hundred families" sent their children. This Polytechnical Institute in turn took its students from the Jesuit schools. For graduates of other schools, the path to the Polytechnic Institute was paved with endless difficulties. The nationalistic-monarchistic circles had their strongholds in feudal cavalry regiments, and especially in the General Staff. They preserved them as a conscious rebellion against the Third Republic, which had kept the upper bourgeoisie and the nobility from civil offices. Anti-Semitism, although contrary to the republican constitution, had found a refuge in these circles.

Nevertheless, Alfred Dreyfus, whose family had moved from Alsace to central France after the War of 1870, had overcome these obstacles through patriotism, industriousness, and tenacity. He had succeeded in rising to the General Staff as a "token Jew," helped by his constitutional rights. There were, to be sure, some Jewish generals in the army, but fewer in the General Staff, where they were considered particularly disturbing. Dreyfus remained an outsider socially and was tolerated only because of his professional ability. But he didn't let it bother him, for he believed, like all Jews emancipated by the Great Revolution, in the equality of rights as emanating directly from it, rather than in the Bible. He was a somewhat limited, but upright French patriot, much more than a tradition-conscious Jew. He believed in the France that had opened the doors of the ghetto in 1789. His "Vive la France" was honest. He considered the judicial procedure a regrettable error. According to Clemenceau, his defender at the review procedures in Rennes, he was the only one who did not understand the background of the Dreyfus Affair. Just before his death, Clemenceau said: "He seemed miles removed from the affair." Just once, relates Maurice Paléologue, counsel at the Quay d'Orsay, did the situation seem to dawn on him, when he mumbled after his verdict: "My only crime was being born a Jew." But he went no further, and participated in the battle raging around him only for his personal rehabilitation. His *Devil's Island Diary,* published recently, shows no sign that he realized the implication of his case, although it stirringly portrays the sufferings caused by his imprisonment.

No special enlightenment was needed to show the connection between the military tribunal's verdict and anti-Semitism, since this was so overwhelmingly obvious. A few years previously, Drumont had published a thick, two-volume book, *Jewish France,* a hodgepodge of the vilest medieval slander. This was, nevertheless, a gigantic success, a best seller, which overshadowed all other contemporary writings. The unexpected popularity of this trash led to the founding of the Anti-Semitic League in 1890 and the newspaper *La Libre Parole,* whose admitted goal was anti-Semitic propaganda. The first series of articles dealt with the subjects: "Jews in the Army" and "Jews in the Polytechnic Institute." This immediately preceded the indictment against Dreyfus.

The seed fell on fertile ground, since it had already been ploughed up by the fascist tactics of the Minister of War, General Boulanger, ploughed up also by the bank crash in the Panama scandal, where many people lost their money, and in which Jewish businessmen were implicated. Some politicians were compromised in this case of corruption and therefore welcomed the idea of diverting public indignation elsewhere. Republican constitutional guarantees prevented open discrimination against Jewish citizens, but these guarantees still had a precarious existence. France had an "aristocratic republic," which resulted from the merciless destruction of the Commune (with the benevolent armored help of the victorious Prussians). The unrestrained search for a universal scapegoat was therefore generously tolerated in the highest circles. Since there were not enough Jews in France to saddle them with total responsibility, the Protestants and Freemasons also came under attack, an attack with an understandably Catholic leadership, or more exactly a certain political trend within Catholicism, which, in general, is in no way identified with chauvinistic ideologies. Long afterward, Charles Maurras, the *spiritus rector* of *L'Action Française,* named four allied forces as enemies of French civilization: Jews, Protestants, Freemasons, and those of mixed blood. If we remember the role that Maurras played in the Hitler era, we see him as a link in the chain stretching from Drumont to Streicher.

Thus only a spark was missing to set the pile of tinder ablaze. That spark was the discovery by the secret service of a case of espionage, in the service of Germany, the archenemy at the time. The traitor could only be an officer of the General Staff. What a blow for the military, that the holiest element of the nation had compromised itself in such an ignominious fashion! A scandal had to be avoided at all costs. Thus began a series of events, a maelstrom of infernal intrigues, slander, falsifications, and acts of violence unparalleled in any work of fiction, even in Balzac's *Comédie humaine.* All that for the sake of the fetishes of national pride, war machinery, and racism, using the label of "highest national interest" as a disguise. Instead of attempting to describe the concatenation of events and passions, I will simply quote Anatole France, who gives the substance of the imbroglio in a few ironic lines. He tells of a case of espionage in the land of the Penguins in *Penguin Island,* a utopian and satirical depiction of world history:

A Jew of humble circumstances called Pyrot, eager to associate with the aristocracy and wishing to serve his country, joined the Penguin army. The Minister of War, who was then Greatauk, could not stand him: he criticized him for his zeal, his nose, his vanity, his love of learning, his thick lips, and his exemplary behavior. Everytime the perpetrator of a misdeeed was sought, Greatauk would say: "It must by Pyrot!"

One morning, General Panther, his chief of staff, informed him of a serious matter. Eighty thousand bundles of hay earmarked for the cavalry had disappeared. Greatauk exclaimed automatically: "Pyrot must have stolen them!" He looked thoughtfully a while and said: "The more I think about it, the more I am convinced that Pyrot stole the eighty thousand bundles of hay. I see his handiwork in the fact that he stole them to sell them at rock-bottom prices to the Marsouins, our implacable enemies." "There is no doubt about it," answered Panther. "All we have left to do is prove it."

The public, misled by the authorities, condemned the only Jewish member of the General Staff even before he was brought before his judges. And these judges, seven officers meeting behind closed doors "for reasons of national security," pronounced Captain Dreyfus guilty of high treason on the basis of very flimsy evidence. The nation breathed a sigh of relief, the army's honor was intact. "Thank God the traitor is a Jew and not a Frenchman." This newspaper quote expressed the general feeling. Even Jaurès and Clemenceau were convinced of the correctness of the verdict. They only wondered, and this shows the genius of their intution, at the relative mildness of the sentence for such a monstrous case of treason: life imprisonment on Devil's Island. Dreyfus was ignominiously cashiered amid the howls of the masses as a pathetic conclusion to the distasteful proceedings. But it was only the beginning.

The disgraced family did not rest. Bits of truth about errors in the hearings filtered out. Politicians began to become uneasy. All efforts, however, glanced off the iron wall of military and political solidarity. When serious proofs of Dreyfus's innocence appeared, they were dismissed with the argument: "Seven French officers cannot be completely mistaken," or, "It is possible that Dreyfus was condemned illegally, but it was done justly, and that suffices." Even when the new head of the secret service, Colonel Picquart, had the irrefutable proof in his hands that the only adverse document against Dreyfus did not incriminate him at all, but rather Major Esterhazy, the real traitor, he received the grotesque command to separate the two cases, that is, not to allow Esterhazy's guilt to result in Dreyfus's innocence. Maurice Paléologue tells of the conversation between Picquart and his superior, who implored him: "If you don't say anything, no one will know anything." "That is repulsive," answered Picquart; "I refuse to take this secret to the grave with me." And when Picquart, although of anti-Semitic background, but driven by his conscience, put his brilliant career on the line by notifying the proper authorities and demanding that justice be done, he was rebuffed, threatened, and thrown into prison. To all the remonstrances of his superiors this magnificent Don Quixote of justice could only reply with the gripping words: "But he is innocent!"

But this argument had already been bypassed. The public attitude toward Dreyfus had changed. Barrès had endowed it with an ideology: "The army is the honor of the nation, and the interest of the nation takes precedence over all else. Whoever opposes it is a traitor. Every utterance of an officer is sacred and needs no examination." In this context generals and ministers gave their explanations in frequent new trials, and the courts did not dare question their credibility, even though evidence against Dreyfus should subsequently prove to be forgeries.

Foreign affairs also played a role. The fact that the espionage turned out to be to the advantage of Germany served only to strengthen the resentment of the French public. To be sure, the German ambassador was not involved, but he was duped by his military attaché, Schwarzkoppen, who on higher orders did nothing for the release of the innocent Dreyfus (E. O. Czempiel, *Das deutsche Dreyfus-Geheimnis* [Munich, 1966]). The Imperial Chancellor at that time, von Bülow, advised his Emperor to undertake nothing in favor of Dreyfus, but to let the French stew in their own juice. In the *Diplomatic Acts of the Foreign Office,* published after the First World War, we read the following remark by von Bülow: "It is best for the affair to continue, to fester, to disintegrate the army and scandalize Europe." The Forgery Center of the French Secret Service, with Colonel Henry as instigator, exploited this silence to stir up public opinion through hints of diplomatic involvement and threats of war, and to brand any point of view favorable to Dreyfus as high treason. The traitor Esterhazy was defiantly set free and the judges wished him well. Again everything seemed to grind to a halt, and every attempt at bringing about a review through political, parliamentary, or legal means seemed doomed to failure.

But then Emile Zola, at that time France's most famous novelist, intervened. In Clemenceau's newspaper *L'Aurore,* he implored the young to remember the true ideals of the French nation. Unfortunately, he reaped only scorn, and was threatened with violence and death. He then decided to write a personal challenge to the president and all responsible ministers and generals: *J'accuse.* With fiery accusations he finally succeeded in rousing the conscience of the people and converting at least the undecided by his horrifying indictment:

> I accuse the minister of war of having made himself an accomplice, if only due to moral weakness, to one of the greatest injustices of the century. . . .
> I accuse the generals of having made themselves accomplices to the same crime, because of clerical passions or military *esprit de corps.*
> I accuse the first military court of a conscious miscarriage of justice. . . .
> I accuse the second military court of having covered up this illegality, of committing in its own right a crime against justice by knowingly setting a guilty man free.
> I have but one passion, that of the truth, in the name of humanity, which has suffered so much. They may take me to court. . . .I'm waiting.

He didn't have to wait long. He was attacked by the combined power of the political and military establishments. "One day France will thank me for helping it rescue its honor," he retorted defiantly. He was condemned and had to flee to England. In reality, however, the roles had been reversed with one stroke. Officialdom was on the defensive from then on. Courts, government, parliament, senate, every element allied by *raison d'état* had been shaken by an aroused public opinion.

The representatives of intellectualism rallied. Even Zola's literary opponents came over to his side—Anatole France, for instance, who called "J'accuse" a great moment in the conscience of mankind.

Charles Péguy organized his intellectual troops against Drumont's anti-Semitic bodyguards, the "butchers of Paris." Dreyfus became a legend. It was no longer a personal question, but one of principles and ideas against violence and inequity as foundations of the state. The nation divided into pro- and anti-Dreyfus camps, and these expanded to mean two different world-views. The division spread through the whole land, through families, and even through souls. There were conversions, as Marcel Proust describes them in his great panorama of French mores. The examples are the Prince and Princess of Guermantes and their moral struggle as they abandon their usual role and secretly have a mass read for Dreyfus. The Dreyfusards were numerically weaker, but their rallying cries were incomparably more eloquent, causing confusion, uncertainty, and sometimes turnabouts.

This was the atmosphere in which the review procedure was finally started in 1899. Once more the generals made their entrance, squared their shoulders, and challenged the judges to choose between a Jew and the French army. They shrewdly reminded them of Barrès's argument: It was not necessary to prove Dreyfus's guilt. It was sufficient to demonstrate that he was capable of treason with his disposition. Once more, they were successful in influencing the jury and at least in obtaining a formal verdict of guilty. But these were just the desperate measures of a morally defeated army.

The new Waldeck-Rousseau government was composed of men who brought with them new ideas and were firmly intent on decontaminating the atmosphere and liquidating the case. Dreyfus was again officially sentenced, to the indignation of the whole world. A few days later he and all the other people implicated in the affair were granted amnesty. The happy ending was not really satisfactory, but was effective in clearing the civil war atmosphere.

In the hearts of the Dreyfusards there remained a thorn. The main actor in the drama had settled for a pardon instead of demanding complete exoneration. His final rehabilitation occurred only much later, very privately and inconspicuously. Dreyfus was permitted to return to his family, but his supporters felt robbed, for he had been the symbol around which the partisans of freedom had gathered. Once again Dreyfus had shown that he was not up to the role intended for him by history and that he did not understand the significance of the whole affair. "So much the better," said Clemenceau in retrospect"; no one can reproach us for letting ourselves be swept away by the aura of his personality."

Politicians like Clemenceau and Jaurès were satisfied with the outcome of the struggle, and with good reason. A way had been paved for political freedom and the rise of new men and parties. The writers and intellectuals were disappointed because their ideas had not triumphantly prevailed. For uncompromising idealists like Charles Péguy, Dreyfus had only now committed treason—betrayal of the idea of which he *nolens volens* had become the symbol. The basis of politics is compromise, but the spirit is absolute and will remain, because of its very unattainability, the Socratic spur that drives the world forward. In practical terms the results were not so bad. Christian Sénéchal summarizes them in a few striking words: "The national crisis led within the army to a republicanization of the officers' corps and to its subordination to the authority of the state, although the temptation to self-glorification asserted itself repeatedly (most recently in the Algerian crisis). In religious life, it led to a reduction of overpowerful clerical influence in politics, and to non-denominational schools; socially, to a *rapprochement* of the proletariat and the intellectuals; in politics, to a strengthening of the left against the forces of reaction; in literature, to a fruitful self-examination, and to a new consciousness of responsibility on the part of intellectuals for governmental responsibility." Concepts such as patriotism and national honor were clarified and given new force because of the participation of intellectuals in the struggle. A writer like Maurice Barrès, ideologue of the reactionary sector, in his subsequent development submits the concepts *people* and *fatherland* to a reexamination. In the beginning he proclaimed a myth "du sang, de la volupté et de la mort" (1894) (of blood, sensual pleasure, death). He glorified the French character and preached opposition to everything "different," rejecting it as incompatible, and therefore harmful *(Les Déracinés)*. After the process of maturation that the Dreyfus Case meant to him, he discovered that the strength of a nation lay precisely in its multiplicity, in the emphasis on regional and historical peculiarities: "Be aware that you were made to react as Lorrainers, Alsatians, Bretons, Belgians, and Jews." He even went so far as to consider the Jewish population one of the spiritual families that, in the aggregate, make up the French people.

The ideological transformation of Maurice Barrès is symptomatic of the democratic development of France under the influence of, and as a consequence of the Dreyfus Case. The inflammatory chauvinism had crested, and had been followed by elucidation and purification of the seminal concept of democracy. Even though stubborn dogmatists such as Charles Maurras and Léon Daudet continued to attract unyielding fanatics, the people as a whole proved to be impervious to extremist impulses and reactionary experiments in the difficult times that followed—the two World Wars and the Algerian Crisis.

What then is the meaning of this prologue to the tragedy of our times? Is it anti-Semitism? Apparently not, since anti-Semitism had been around for a long time. To be sure, this pseudo-scientific term was coined in 1879 by William Marr in connection with Comte Gobineau's and Ernest Renan's theories about Aryan and Semitic people and was circulated at that time in deliberately false interpretations. But the matter itself was not new. Even without this pseudo-scientific analysis, which makes of anti-Semitism a spurious philosophy, there had been anti-Semitic excesses in Russia and Hungary, in connection with ritual murder trials. The specter of the ritual murder was also circulated in the Rhineland and in West Prussia, although without tragic consequences. Anti-Semitism expressed itself in Germany at first in a relatively harmless way by discriminating against Jewish citizens in certain professions. It also spread to France. Unlike Germany, it had no official sponsorship, since civil rights were guaranteed too clearly in the Constitution, and were the pride of a nation that had been founded on the Enlightenment. Rather it found an outlet in the exclusive salons, and in the conservative bourgeoisie, and then in an outpouring of anti-Semitic literature, because anything of any importance in France ultimately finds literary expression. This literary theme could not be called new, for Jews had been blamed for a long time for the Revolution and its sociopolitical consequences. The Dreyfus Affair cannot be explained in terms of anti-Semitism. It is only the mask that hid the true nature of the case.

Its significance was much vaster: the right and worth of the individual, his preservation against the anonymous juggernaut of the state. "Respect for human values, austere stake of Western civilization, whether filled with Christian humanism or rationalistic humanism, occupies the center of the drama" (Léon Metzler, *L'Affaire Dreyfus,* chronique publiée à Luxembourg, 1953). For its sake many took up the fight for Dreyfus without directly taking into account the person of the accused. Long afterward the Nobel Prize winner Roger Martin du Gard gives this thought eloquent expression in his great novel *Jean Barois.* The author summarizes in one lapidary sentence the problem of the relationship between the state and the individual: "There is no *raison d'état* that may prevent a court of law from being just."

There are, of course, situations where one must allow for the sacrifice of the individual for the sake of the people as a whole. This is the principle justifying every military action. But it is a case of voluntary agreement of the individual to the temporary sacrifice of his freedom in a case of national emergency. There are also human sacrifices in the fields of science and research for the sake of new knowledge. But these are the highest expression of human freedom for the welfare of the human race. Society does not have the right to demand such sacrifices, especially for a goal called *raison d'état.* A society that would make such a demand, even in a single case, would immediatley cease to be a civilized society. For the individual sacrificed represents all individuals, and in him all are threatened by the encroachments of an anonymous power. Besides, the *raison d'état* does not represent the interests of the people as a whole, or even a majority, but that of a minority that controls the machinery of government and therefore feels that it personifies the state.

Only in this context is the Dreyfus case an issue of particular questions, such as anti-Semitism, the republican form of government, nonsectarian schools, or the place of the Church within the state.

The young republic had to assert itself to curtail the tremendous influence of an ecclesiastic establishment left from the *ancien régime*. There were among the dedicated republicans sincere Catholics, such as Charles Péguy, Paul Claudel, and François Mauriac, who combined a deep faith with a progressive, liberal outlook. The struggle was not with Catholicism, but with that faction nurtured on political reaction, represented by Charles Maurras and his Action Française.

In the provinces positions revolved around local problems. Dreyfusism and anti-Dreyfusism were two standards under which innumerable positions were taken. At the highest level, however, the problem crystallized around basic questions of human society, about Judeo-Christian moral concepts introduced by the French Revolution.

The entrance of Zola, Péguy, Barrès, France, and other leading intellectuals and artists caused this sublimation of immediate problems into major ideological questions. We were now experiencing the revolt of the intellectuals in an even stronger measure than at the times of the *Encyclopédistes*. Like a young giant, the phalanx of intellectuals was astounded by its own strength. After the long sleep of an unworldly generation, French literature awoke from its aesthetic dreams and its love for formalistic ideas to resume its great historical role, that of a conscience taking a stand on public issues, "committing" itself, in Sartre's sense. Is this not the secret of its position in France as a quasi-official institution that must always be taken into account, and the prestige that French literature has always been able to maintain?

The intervention of literature transformed the Dreyfus Trial from a banal spy story with a background of anti-Semitism, an "anecdote misérable," as Charles Maurras puts it, into a forum of international scope. Literature simply stole the show from politics. It caused an avalanche and dragged everything with it. The courtroom became the scene in which, Shakespeare-like, an individual fate was played out in front of a metaphysical background. The five years from the verdict to the pardon resemble a five-act drama, a true world theater with antagonists from all levels of society, and with mass scenes acted out by a cast of forty million.

It is especially uplifting to our age, so used to political slogans, to see literature working as an active, life-giving force. There was in that generation and long afterwards hardly a writer who did not come to grips with the Dreyfus Affair. The boundaries between literature and life became blurred, one seeming to flow into the other. At a performance of Romain Rolland's play *Les Loups*, whose subject is a miscarriage of justice, Colonels Picquart and Henry were sitting in the loge, just as in medieval Passion plays.

Thus far I have traced French literature's influence on public life, but not the effect of the trial on French literature. Literature was going through a crisis at that time. It was part of the same crisis reflected in the Dreyfus Affair. "France is dying; don't disturb its agony." In these words Ernest Renan expresses the petrification and apparent exhaustion of the French nation. The war lost to the Prussians was just one aspect, not the cause of the situation that Paul Bourget describes as a fatal weariness, as an admission of the absurdity of existence *(Essais de psychologie contemporaine)*. Schopenhauer's philosophical pessimism had not fallen on fertile ground in Germany due to the unexpected military, political, and economic rise of the Bismarck Empire. It did fall on it, however, in humbled France where all the intellectual forces of the time converged to promote the mood of decadence.

Science seemed to have found its *non plus ultra* in the discovery of mechanistic determinism, that conception of a world dominated by blind forces and a race incapable of combating the processes of nature. There is nothing more depressing than the idea that we are tiny, insignificant cogs of a great universal machine.

This gloomy outlook is reflected in the novels of Emile Zola. His naturalism seems to be the unmasking of reality in all its inescapable ugliness. Others tried to flee from it by embracing a playful aestheticism or attempting to savor life's every pleasure. (This is called "desperate joy" by Prof. Max Herrmann.) Or, like Anatole France, they adopted an ironic and wry epicureanism.

The Dreyfus Affair, by its imperious call to action, worked like a thunderbolt. This reversal dominated not just for the duration of the Affair, but afterwards, and led to a new orientation in literature, to its rebirth in the spirit of humanism. Although many writers, disappointed by the unsatisfactory results, returned to their original skepticism, the shock had a permanent effect on others, and their changed attitude to contemporary problems made itself felt in the next generation of writers. Emile Zola changed from a resigned naturalist (Les Rougon-Macquart) to a flaming if somewhat awkward idealist (Quartre Evangiles). The development of Maurice Barrès has already been mentioned. With Romain Rolland the temptation to retire early "au dessus de la mêlée "(above the battle), as he expressed it in the title of one of his books, was checked from the beginning by the personality of Charles Péguy. For the latter, the Dreyfus Case was the starting point of a unique career as poet and prophet, molder of youth, and martyr, whose ecstatic existence ended with death in the Battle of the Marne. It is difficult to name any writer so characteristic of his generation, since they were all strong personalities and represent various aspects of the renewal of intellectual life. Zola and Péguy come closest because of the total commitment of their person and their art. The proud words of Emile Zola, uttered defiantly during his trial to hostile military judges, sum up the role of the writer who is *engagé*: "France can be served in different ways, with the sword or with the pen." To be sure, his later works do not equal what he wrote during the Dreyfus Trial. His four *Gospels,* written shortly before his death and left in a fragmentary state, *Fruitfulness, Work, Truth,* and *Justice* (these cardinal virtues are given as the foundation of mankind's future), deserve our interest more as an expression of Zola's new-found idealism than for their artistic merit. His abiding genius is crystallized in his manifesto, *J'accuse,* where deed and word become one, and of which Péguy said: "I know nothing that can compare with the overwhelming beauty and force of this powerful accusation." These lines of Zola made history. His work was carried on by Charles Péguy, direct heir and propagator of his militancy. As moving spirit of the rising generation of poets, he deserves close attention as an example of the literary consequences of the Dreyfus Affair.

For Péguy it was his whole life, his religious experience, so to speak; the starting point of his faith, a faith tending toward mystical ecstasy. His religious belligerence should not be taken only in the abstract. The "Dreyfus Fortress," built in the Quartier Latin by the young normal school students, served literally as headquarters for the student shock troops, from where they aided the prominent Dreyfusards threatened by the mob. Péguy saw the creative aspect in the difference of opinions during the crisis. In fact, when the Waldeck-Rousseau government made a compromise settlement and public tension was giving way to a general apathy, he deplored it as the real danger. "The Affair is dead; I am afraid it will no longer divide us!", he was heard to say. Claiming that the cause was being ruined by success, he separated himself from his comrades. Dreyfus's supporters were becoming discouraged with the latter's human failings and Dreyfusism was disintegrating. He then continued waging the war on his own. "France shall not lose its soul for the sake of temporal interests." In these words lies the substance of his creed. Without money and without help, he founded the *Cahiers de la Quinzaine,* a bi-weekly one-man publication like that of Karl Kraus in Vienna or Maximilian Harden in Germany, which he built into a bastion in the struggle for the highest ethical values of the nation. One of the issues (1910) called *Our Youth,* is dedicated to an interpretation of the Dreyfus Affair.

To Péguy, the whole affair was a symbol of the eternal struggle for truth, justice, and freedom. Gradually there formed in him that fundamental antinomy, spiritual versus temporal, intellectual versus material, according to which he measured all of life. Unlike politicians whose allegiance to moral values is only sporadic, Péguy could only deplore the pardon and amnesty of the guilty parties.

The fight for truth and justice is always a holy war, says Péguy. They are the main concerns of living religion. The struggle takes different forms according to the period involved. But the spirit is always the same. To seek truth and justice is to seek God, and to make compromises is to set up idols in God's place. The Dreyfus Affair brought to light a new form of heathenism. To sacrifice a person to the falsely understood interests of the fatherland would be the equivalent of bringing a human offering to a new Moloch, and Christian doctrine protested against this idol worship.

Péguy's concept of Christianity, somewhat akin to Schleiermacher's, was that of a spirit of constant change, a kind of creative idealism. Therefore Dreyfusism became a crusade led by enthusiastic knights of the cross, heroes and heroines, and not simply a political squabble between red and black, not the usual factionalism that runs through French history.

Péguy's ethical *élan* always strove to anchor itself in the absolute. He viewed all issues *sub specie aeternitatis*. This was even before his conversion to Catholicism. But he found in the Church a particularly eloquent expression of his yearnings. Thus he fought for a Catholic France, not in a material sense, but as the truest daughter of the Church. The battle for truth and justice in France was in his view, a battle of Christian ethics in general, with France as its standard-bearer. Only in France could an individual fate become a political scandal, and the scandal be raised to the sphere of the absolute. Decisive in the contest were the French national characteristics of quick reaction, cheerfulness, and stubborn courage. Therefore, explains Péguy, France is the soul of Christian civilization, the modern chosen people, not, however, replacing Israel as the first chosen people. While its mission has been transferred in part to the true Christians, the Christians in spirit, Israel remains a source of life-giving mysticism, as it has been since the time of the prophets. However, Israel is often unfaithful to its destiny by laying greater stress on political expediency than on moral values. Politicians, rabbis, the community in Dreyfus's time had become too accustomed to sacrificing one of their own to buy their freedom. They, whom Anatole France calls *"les grands Juifs"* (the big Jews), would also have gladly sacrificed Dreyfus just to calm the storm, as their priests once sent the scapegoat into the wilderness.

But this propitiatory offering to a false peace was always fought by some fanatic of truth, such as Bernard Lazare, the first advocate of a review procedure. Israel is still, Péguy continues, the race of prophets, but it is not willing to make use of them due to its bitter experiences. Israel's politics consists in not attracting attention. Yet Israel's mysticism forces the people to continue its painful and wonderful mission. That is its wondrous and inescapable fate.

Thus, this visionary poet sees the Dreyfus Affair as the intersection of three intellectual powers—France, Judaism, and Christianity. It was apparently with this ideological trinity in mind that the poet

Henri Franck considered it an unusual stroke of luck to be simultaneously a Frenchman, a Jew, and a professor; or that the author of the novel *Simler and Co.*, J. R. Bloch, defines, as remarked previously, the life mission of the Christian as a mathematical problem with two unknowns, and that of the Jewish citizen as one with three unknowns.

The most significant books of the affair are novels: Proust's *Remembrance of Things Past* and Roger Martin du Gard's *Jean Barois, The Story of a Free Conscience*. Du Gard's portrayal of the Dreyfus Affair is artistically sophisticated, and based on the ethos of a Péguy. The story of the book is the life of Jean Barois, who is in search of absolute truth untarnished by opportunism. He encounters many obstacles and is obliged to make many difficult decisions. The core and climax of the book is the fight against the injustice done Dreyfus. The narrator describes both the outward difficulties and the psychological barriers that the personality of the victim creates. So many had first to overcome their personal antipathy before joining the battle. "Reality did not correspond to our conception of it. Many of us haven't forgiven him, the accused, this one thing." But Martin du Gard defends him with the warm understanding of a true artist: "Dreyfus is a simple human being whose energy is directed entirely inward. Then he comes into public view, weakened by arrest and unprecedented agitation. He is sick, his is shivering with fever, he can hardly drink a glass of milk. How then should he be able to cope with such a public, three-fourths of which hates him as a public criminal while one-fourth venerates him as a symbol? Is not such a role beyond human resources? He simply does not have the strength to wildly proclaim his innocence as he had done in the courtyard of the Military School. The little energy that he has left has to be used against himself, not against others, to keep from being depressed, to remain a man. He must even fight to keep from weeping at times."

This heroic side of him was unsuspected. Perhaps he could have won over the public with a theatrical performance. But this self-control that he managed to maintain was taken as indifference by the masses, and those who had taken his side for four years held it against him.

His followers were, as I said, fighting more for an idea than for a person. This idea is formulated by Martin du Gard as follows: "An injustice, openly committed, even in the name of national security, if it is officially accepted by all, creates difficulties a thousand times more serious than the temporary troubles of a people. It compromises the only acquisition in which men can take some pride, those sacred liberties with which, in the past, French blood enriched the nations of the world. More precisely it compromises the right to justice of the whole civilized world."

From this idea, he concludes, the Dreyfus battle receives its historical significance. "Even if it represents, fifty years from now, only a small episode in the battle of reason against the passions which lead us astray; even if it is only a tiny step on the endless path of human progress, the task of each generation still consists in moving forward in the spirit of truth, as far as is humanly possible, to the extreme limits of knowledge, and to maintain its position as desperately as if it hoped to reach Absolute Truth. That is the way to man's progress."

Besides this short reference to the direct echoes of the Dreyfus Affair, I must also touch upon another of its consequences: the rediscovery of Judaism as a literary motif. (See chapter 12.) Through the main figure, attention was directed to the family and the *milieu* from which he had sprung. Numerous writers undertook to study and describe Jewish customs and rites, not always from the lofty standpoint of a Charles Péguy, but not from an anti-Semitic viewpoint either. Rather, it was with a sincere interest in the picturesque element in Jewish traditions and folklore. Thus, the brothers Tharaud, still under the influence of their "dear Péguy," and not of National Socialism, went into the ghettoes of Eastern Europe to describe to the French public the exotic atmosphere of these places. Others studied the phenomenon of Judaism in their immediate surroundings. Lacretelle, in a story of his schooldays, describes the unique fascination of his Jewish classmate Silbermann, who understood French Classicism and Gothic cathedrals better than his Christian companions, and also the tension resulting from his unusual superiority.

The unorthodox is now no longer challenged or condemned as in-

compatible, but seen as an enriching, although disturbing element
(e.g., André Gide, Duhamel, Sartre). If even Maurice Barrès praises
the heterogeneous character of French racial groups as a source of
strength, how much more so with other writers, who regard the right
to diversity as one of the basic human rights.

This aspect finds expression more clearly in Duhamel and Sartre
than in Lacretelle. In a book, *Chronique des Pasquier,* Duhamel
treats an episode very similar to the novel *Silbermann,* but with
much greater philosophical depth than Lacretelle. The action also
takes place at the time of the Dreyfus Affair, and describes the
Unanimistic experiment of an enthusiastic student group seeking
freedom and purity in an isolated country house *(Le Désert de
Bièvres).* The intellectual of the group is Justin Weill, the closest
friend of Laurent Pasquier, who represents the author. As long as all
goes well, Justin is accepted by everyone as an equal. But Justin is
practically killing himself trying to organize and finance the experiment, and they take his sacrifice for granted. "They were used to
seeing Justin row against wind and currents." When, after the
first blush of enthusiasm, the participants become tired and seek to
abandon the experiment, Justin is made the scapegoat. Remarks are
passed such as: "I don't like people who continually play the martyr," or even, "I'm a Dreyfusard by reason, but an anti-Semite by
inclination," or, "I'm all for Dreyfus, but on the condition that Jews
don't ruin our lives."

Finally this sordid hostility erupts openly against Justin, who now,
on top of everything else, has to assume the responsibility for the
negligence of all the others. In the face of this outburst of barbarism,
he breaks down and yearns only to return to his family to await with
them the great final pogrom. But then he pulls himself together
again: "You think you understand him, your Lord Jesus? Well, he
was one of us, a little Jew like me. Only I haven't accomplished
anything. I failed even at a small task." In spite of his humiliation,
he again starts hoping, believing, planning. "Our failure is no argument against the betterment of humanity. For who else is to hold
high the banner of a better future, if not those who have been defeated, conquered, abused? Blessed are those who suffer persecution

for the sake of righteousness, for theirs is the Kingdom of Heaven."
This faith of Justin's in humanity is the only bright spot after the
shameful evasion of a group of false idealists, each of whom took
everything from the others without giving anything in return. And
Duhamel concludes his symbolic tale with the words: "I began to
understand that Justin was not healed of his dream, and had not lost
courage."

Lacretelle's Silbermann and Duhamel's Justin are, as was Anatole
France's Clérembault, miniature reflections of the Dreyfus Affair.
With Anatole France everything ends in resigned helplessness. With
Lacretelle, one doesn't know whether he is thinking: "I am a
Dreyfusard by reason and an anti-Semite by inclination." At least the
honesty of his reason causes him to reject the mistrust of the unusual
and its inevitable prejudice: "Among the many races composing the
French nation, there are just as many differences as among the many
races of mankind."

With Duhamel, however, a new humanism is dawning, which
preaches peaceful cooperation among people, despite their differences, without illusions and in full awareness of their indestructible
barbaric instincts. Gide also preaches tolerance. "I admit that
minorities disturb our comfort. So much the better." The strange
element is no longer unacceptable. It has become worthwhile, "authentic" in Sartre's terminology.

To this writer, unique in his ability to express himself in many
literary genres, falls the task of leading French youth—a youth that
had lost its equilibrium because of the war—back to the sources of
humanism. His way of thinking is highly unorthodox and mirrors the
times, shaken by disturbing events. In the face of the apparent absurdity of the world he refuses to abdicate his moral commitment and
demands that every individual assume total responsibility for his actions.

Anti-Semitism is one of the current problems that Sartre examines
in the light of his philosophy. In a discerning, almost psychoanalyti-
cal study *(Thoughts on the Jewish Question* [1947]) he attempts to
get at the irrational roots of the problem. He doesn't believe in objective, rational causes of anti-Semitism. Here he agrees with Albert

Camus, who doesn't take seriously the pseudo-logical constructions of a Nazi ideologue such as Charles Maurras. "Anti-Semitism is a complex of passions, which incorporates, besides the joy of hating, an attempt at self-justification," says Camus. How this is to be understood is shown by Sartre in his short story *The Childhood of a Leader*, the development of a young Frenchman from these right-wing radical circles, who considered themselves the heads, even the masters of the French nation. Lucien Fleurier, a mediocrity, draws the attention of the other students in the class because he can't stand Jews (as Uncle Justin's prestige is due, in *Thoughts on the Jewish Question*, to his mysterious dislike for Englishmen). Lucien's ensuing rise results from his prestige as an anti-Semite, a rather slow process until he becomes the leader of a group sharing his feelings, called the *Camelots du Roi* (the Royalist Party). At the same time, Sartre concerns himself with the spiritual uncertainty of Jews in their modern *milieu*, with their guilt feelings, comparable to those of "K," the defendant in Kafka's novel *The Trial*, who struggles against a completely mysterious accusation. Captain Dreyfus found himself in an essentially similar situation when he was sentenced on the basis of documents he and his lawyers were never allowed to see. Dreyfus is symbolic of his fellow Jews. The Jews, according to Proust, are burdened with guilt feelings similar to those of the homosexual, who must continually try to hide his feelings from society. In Sartre, the *milieu* points an accusing finger at the Jew as soon as he wants to fit into it. His plans are frustrated by a wall of prejudices. Sartre collects all the accusations, all the demands made on the Jews, to explain: "If a Jew must possess so many qualities to be put on the same plane as a true Frenchman, how many Frenchmen are worthy of being called Jews?"

Sartre's own position on this question, in spite of his existentialistic crusade against traditional thinking, is based on the best classical tradition with its belief in reason and science. In *Thoughts* he says: "There is no French, no German, African or Jewish truth. There is only one truth, and the best finds it."

In his most recent play, *The Prisoner of Altona*, Sartre takes up this theme again, and comes to grips with the tragedy of our times,

National Socialism. The play becomes a trial not only of those directly guilty, but also of those implicated in mass murder by their passivity or their deals with the rising forces of injustice. He shows not only Germany's moral failure, but also that of other nations, in line with what he had proclaimed to his compatriots' fifteen years earlier: "The blood shed by the Nazis is on all our heads." Here, in this play, he points out how injustice, if not opposed in its beginnings or if tolerated as the lesser of two evils, grows into an all-devouring monster. This thought is a logical corollary to the idea that guided the Dreyfus supporters. Sartre goes further and emphasizes not only the right to individuality, but the duty to it, since the individual only attains worth and dignity in authenticity.

In addition to the interest of French literature in Jewish themes, there has developed in the twentieth century what might be called Jewish literature in the French language. Its ancestors are André Spire and Edmond Fleg, both nearly centenarians, who have been turning out works of Jewish inspiration for two generations.

This Franco-Jewish literature had its origins in the turbulent times around the turn of the century. At the Dreyfus Trial, a correspondent for the Viennese newspaper *Neue Freie Presse*, Theodor Herzl, was sitting among the spectators. He was a successful journalist and a favorite of polite Viennese society. The cries of "Down with the Jews" in the middle of Paris, the Jerusalem of emancipated Jewry, made him listen carefully with the ear of the prophet, taking note of the signals of a new era. If that is possible in Paris, he thought, then assimilation was a mistake, and emancipation a misunderstanding. Judaism must return to itself, to emancipation as a state. He went home and wrote a Utopian essay, *The Jewish State*. Fifty years later, the Jewish state was founded.

In the last ten years (1894-1904) of his short life Herzl fought for his cause as the head of the Zionist movement. It consisted of a group of utopians like himself, believers in Jewish mysticism. They were opposed or derided by the representatives of Jewish "politics," the "great Jews." In France, however, a young poet from Lorraine, André Spire, heeded the call of the Viennese prophet. His answer was a series of poems entitled *Et Vous Riez? (And You Can Still Laugh?)*.

He had begun as a follower of the Symbolist School, and his interests were directed toward the development of free verse, which was just as novel in France as Marcel Proust's unusual prose style. In his beginnings, André Spire reveled in the realm of poetry as a complacent aesthete; he felt completely French, assimilated, unrestrained. But then came the anti-Semitic outbursts in France, Germany, and Russia. Here also was this Zionistic Don Quixote from Vienna, who disturbed his artistic serenity, until finally the cry of his people was heard in his own lips:

> Tu voudras chanter la force, l'audace;
> Tu n'aimeras que les rêveurs désarmés contre la vie.
> Tu tenteras d'écouter les chants joyeux des paysans,
> Les marches brutales des soldats, les rondes gracieuses des fillettes;
> Tu n'auras l'oreille habile que pour les pleurs
> Qui tombent des quatre coins de l'univers.

> You will want to celebrate strength, daring;
> You will love only the dreamers helpless against life.
> You will try to listen to the happy songs of the peasants,
> The brutal marches of soldiers, the graceful dances of little girls;
> Your ear will be attuned only for the tears
> Shed at the four corners of the universe.

In his own way, Spire discovered the bridge from art to life and placed his talent in the service of real life. The mission he faced was not so universal as that confronting Zola's generation, but it was sufficiently important not to be neglected. In the poems that followed he tried repeatedly to rouse his coreligionists, to infuse them with pride in the past and zeal for the construction of a national future. One of the poems in the collection *Poèmes Juifs* is called *Exodus* and celebrates in biblical terms the departure from modern places of oppression:

Arrache de ton coeur ces sols de servitude;
Prends le pain sans levain et les herbes amères;
Ceins tes reins, prends ton bâton, chausse tes pieds,
L' océan se fendra de nouveau devant toi. . . .

Fais paître tes troupeaux, plante, greffe, ensemence
Et moissonne. Et parmi le miel de tes abeilles
Le lait de tes brebis, le raisin de tes vignes
Tu verras se dresser, convalescente et jeune,
Ta fierté, Israël!

Tear out of your heart these lands of slavery;
Take the unleavened bread and the bitter herbs;
Gird your loins, take your staff, put on your shoes,
The ocean will again open before you. . . .

Take your flock to pasture, plant, graft, sow,
And harvest. And in the midst of the honey of your bees,
The milk of your ewes, the grapes of your vineyard,
You will see, standing convalescent and young,
Your pride, Israel!

These lines by André Spire are an echo of the numerous works about the Jewish problem by both Jewish and non-Jewish authors inspired by the Dreyfus Affair. After the Second World War this genre experienced a revival, since Judaism had moved into the center of the conflict. The high point seems to be the four Goncourt Prizes awarded to Jewish authors of works dealing with the problems of modern Jewry. The authors are Romain Gary, André Schwarzbart, Roger Ikor, and Anna Langfus. Another high point seems to be Joseph Kessel's acceptance into the Académie Française. But in the opinion of many, it was another writer, Manès Sperber, who has interpreted the persecution of the Jews in the most gripping manner in his novel *Only a Tear in the Ocean,* for which André Malraux wrote the foreword.

Although this great conflict with all its moral implications took place on French soil, and constitutes a definite chapter of French history, the issues are much broader. The importance of the Dreyfus Case is universal. It is the triumphant affirmation of principle against expediency and national self-interest.

# 12

# Jewish Literature in France

French literature offers the appearance of a powerful tree resting on the solid trunk of classical culture, whose crown divides as it grows into ever more numerous ramifications.

It is one of these ramifications that I want to deal with here. I do not propose to study Jewish literature in France as a chapter of Jewish literary history, but as one of the elements making up French literature.

Throughout its history French literature was able to gather the disparate elements it found in its path, partake of all cultures, assimilate all influences. Unlike other civilizations, far from rejecting all that did not grow out of its own historical origins, it happily accepted and naturalized whatever it found in other nations that was compatible with its own genius.

The spiritual strength of a man or a people is not expressed by a haughty retreat within oneself, by the rejection of everything that emits a different sound. On the contrary, it consists in the ability to incorporate all that is precious, to develop one's nature and to enrich it with other spiritual values without losing one's identity.

In fact, it is this spiritual disposition peculiar to France that explains why its cultural and political evolution differed so markedly from that of Germany, with which it had formed one sole empire, and seemed destined to have a similar history. And it is this spiritual outlook that gave France its strength, its breadth of vision, and its universality, thanks to which it was always spiritually victorious even when physically defeated.

Historically, French literature went through several periods of foreign influence. From each of these phases it emerged enriched, aware of a new aspect of its own individuality. Thus, to the Italian influence it owes the aesthetic harmony, the formal balance that was to be so well understood by a nation whose genius is in great part moderation, balance, and harmony. From this contact that brought with it the classical heritage was to emerge the Renaissance and French Classicism. Then came a period of Spanish influence that gave to French writers a penchant for chivalrous adventures, then a British period that developed in the French the love of philosophy and romantic reveries.

It is therefore not surprising that the Jewish contribution also played a part, that French civilization, anxious to utilize what was useful to its development, found in Judaism a kindred spirit, capable of sprouting a new branch on its tree.

Semitic civilization, and Judaism in particular, was not the last to furnish spiritual nourishment to French culture. Let us remember that the most French of literary genres, born of the genius of the most French of poets, La Fontaine, was a fruit that ripened on French soil only after its importation from the distant East, and that it was Jews (Pierre Alphonse in the eleventh century, Rabbi Berachya in the twelfth) who were largely responsible for the dissemination of the genre in France.

Let us think more generally of the role of intermediary that the Jews played between the admirable Semitic civilization and the primitive world of the European Middle Ages. During the eleventh, twelfth, and thirteenth centuries, a very prosperous Jewish colony grew in the South of France, from which, thanks to their commercial and intellectual relations, the Jews directed the spiritual baggage from the Orient to the interior. The level of this Jewish colony was so high that the compilers of the *Literary History of France*, then under the direction of Ernest Renan, did not hesitate to devote several chapters to the literature of the French rabbis in the Middle Ages, although it had been written in Hebrew.

Its character, however, was radically different from the Jewish literature of the present, since developed in completely changed social, political, and moral conditions.

There was no organic transition between the French Judaism of the Middle Ages and today's. In the fourteenth century, a period of medieval decline, Europe relapsed into the most savage barbarism, into the intolerance and the persecution of everything that conflicted with its self-interest disguised as dogma. France also succumbed to this state of mind that eventually led to the expulsion of the Jews, stripped of all their belongings. The few centers of Judaism that survived vegetated in their ghettoes, too preoccupied with material concerns to dedicate themselves to culture.

It is only in the sixteenth and seventeenth centuries, with the conquest of lands inhabited by Jews, that they began to organize themselves into communities in various cities of France, enjoying the tacit tolerance of the authorities, while still excluded from national life.[1]

---

1. It is a curious fact that the period during which the Jews were banished from France was perhaps that of their most precious contribution. It was the time of the Reformation and the Renaissance, which brought the discovery not only of the Greco-Roman genius, but also of the biblical genius. The Reformation, a religious movement, and the Renaissance, a secular movement, have in common their desire to go back to the original sources. The Renaissance is the discovery of the sources of Greek civilization. The Reformation is the return to the Bible, whose text had been buried under the accumulation of commentaries and super-commentaries during the fifteen hundred years of Catholic absolutism. Those who reacted against the absolutism of Rome demanded the right to read the Bible. It was now translated into the modern tongues, and it inspired poets, scholars, and men of action: the apostles and martyrs of Protestantism, Coligny, Agrippa d'Aubigné, and the Huguenots spoke the language of the prophets of Israel, and evoked their memory by their austere and enthusiastic spirit. It was a kind of revenge or consolation for the descendents of the Jewish martyrs to see their Book, thus revived, inspire the Protestants in their controversies with the Catholics, and support a whole generation of Christians whose fathers may have been among those responsible for the *auto-da-fés* inflicted on the Jews. The influence of the Bible was felt even in the arts. French tragedy was inspired not only by the spirit of Greece, but also by that of Judea. The poets Robert Garnier and Jean de la Taille, who laid the groundwork for French Classicism, sought their subjects in the Old Testament as well as in Greek mythology. And when the classical era reached its apogee with Racine, he created his masterpiece *Athalie* by dramatizing an episode drawn from Jewish history. This work represents a masterful synthesis of the two conflicting currents of Judaism and Hellenism by borrowing the form from Greek tragedy

The inhabitants of these humiliating enclaves had become used to their living conditions and even found in them spiritual compensations, an inner dignity that contrasted strangely with their degrading existence. They were, in Heine's comparison mentioned above, like beaten dogs who every Friday night, thanks to the magic of the Sabbath, assumed the figure of princes, self-confident in their confined world. Finally the day came when they were told: "You are French citizens. The gentle land of France is your homeland; her cities, her fields and her rivers are now yours. In return, you will only be asked to forget the banks of the Jordan and to consider Paris your new Jerusalem."

Those who offered the Jews these alternatives acted in perfectly good faith. They asked of the Jews only what they asked of the inhabitants of the French provinces: to relinquish their individuality in order to become citizens of France. Raised on the spirit of the Age of Reason, they wanted to reorganize society on a completely new basis. They would, if they had had the power (and the Napoleonic wars were serving that purpose), have reorganized Europe by asking all its inhabitants to renounce their national differences to become citizens of Europe. The Jews, in the last analysis, were asked to break away from their past, to blend into French society. "To the Jews as individuals, everything; to the Jews as a nation,

and the spirit from the Bible. The idea of Providence found in the Bible displaced that of Fate, which had formed one of the major elements of the Greek world view, and had inspired the Greek theater. Cf. chapter 6 of this volume, also my *The Jewish Element in French Literature* (Cranbury, N.J.: Associated University Presses, 1971).

Here is how the eminent critic Brunetière expresses himself on the subject: "If we imagined that the sources of Hebrew inspiration had dried up, the Germans would not have Luther, the English *Paradise Lost,* the French Pascal, Bossuet, Hugo, the poets of the obscure and the inaccessible, those, so to speak, who gave us the thrill of the infinite, and those who, among men, have safeguarded the notion of the divine. The Greeks love life too much, their conception of it was too radiant. They could not imagine that it had a purpose other than itself. They lacked the sense of the otherwordly. This is where Israel ranks as unique in humanity. *(Nouveaux essais sur la littérature contemporaine* [Paris, 1897], p. 232.)

The spread of biblical influence, the "laicization" of the ideas of the Bible, is, perhaps, partly responsible for the movement toward the reconstruction of society on the foundation of The Rights of Man (an idea originating in England, where it was formulated by the Puritans inspired by the Bible). Even the atheistic philosophers of the eighteenth century were imbued with the social teachings of the Bible that they were fighting. The sacred book of the Jews thus contributed to the introduction of the spirit of tolerance that was to be instrumental in the emancipation of the Jews.

nothing,'' Clermont-Tonnerre had declared to the National Assembly, and that was the tenor of the process of assimilation in France, and to a more or less pronounced degree in all the countries where Napoleon had brought the principles of the French Revolution.

The Jews, filled with gratitude toward their new homeland, did not recognize the basic error of this type of emancipation. They did not see that, once deprived of its historic ties, Judaism would cease to be alive. Jewish thinkers such as Salvador and James Darmsteter, under the influence of the rationalistic concepts of their era, explained Judaism as the humanitarian teaching of the prophets carried out by the Great Revolution. These men admired the moral aspect of the doctrine of Moses, but they did not see that this doctrine had become the basis of a distinct culture, hallowed by three thousand years of history. They wanted to salvage from Judaism some fundamental notions, whereas it demands a total allegiance, affective and spiritual.

Saint-Simonism, strange synthesis of mysticism and dynamic socialism, was a movement whose followers considered the time ripe for the organization of a new humanitarian religion, erected on a few key principles of the law of Moses and the doctrine of Jesus. In this movement as elsewhere, Jews and non-Jews united in the same liberal aspirations, and the idealistic drive of the time certainly deserves the greatest respect.

Yet there was a serious error in these reconciliations that were too easy, too superficial—a fatal misconception about the Jewish religion, and one that failed to obtain the expected results in the political field.

As for the Jews, their anxious efforts to demonstrate their patriotic loyalty led them to forget the laws of simple humanity. Here is how a French poet evokes the Jewish situation toward the end of the nineteenth century:

> They felt united in body and soul with their country. They even came to lack in humanity out of patriotism. Sometimes they received very badly the wretched Jews of Poland and Russia, expelled by pogroms. . . .To argue that Israel scattered through the world was still one body was to insult them. (A. Spire, *Quelques Juifs,* 1:220)

The poet Edmond Fleg denounced this attitude in a delightful and significant scene in his play *Le Juif du pape (The Pope's Jew),* in which Mosé Latino, to show his patriotic loyalty, betrays his coreligionist Salomon Molco to the Inquisition and justifies his attitude by the following reasoning:

. . .Molco est-il mon frère?
D'où vient-il, par quels chemins?
Il a tant voyagé! Moi je suis Romain,
Chers seigneurs, Romain dont les ancêtres,
Romains avant César, eurent Rémus pour maître. . .
. . .Des Juifs de France, de Pologne, de l'Empire,
Mes frères?
Je m'appelle Mosé, mais Mosé Latino! Je suis Romain:
Conspirant contre vous, contre moi ils conspirent! . . .

Le Cardinal Inquisiteur fait un geste de lassitude. On emmène Latino qui se retire avec force révérences.

Oui, oui, seigneurs chrétiens, je suis Romain,
Romain comme seul un Hébreu peut l'être:
Car un Romain qui est Romain
Parce qu'il est Romain, est beaucoup moins Romain
Qu'un Romain qui l'est parce qu'il veut l'être. . . .

(act 2, scene 2)

. . .Is Molco my brother?
Where does he come from, by what roads?
He has traveled so much! I am a Roman,
Dear Lords, a Roman whose ancestors,
Roman before Caesar, had Remus as master. . .
. . .Jews of France, of Poland, of the Empire,
My brothers?
My name is Mosé, but Mosé Latino! I am Roman:
When they conspire against you, they conspire against me! . . .

The cardinal of the Inquisition makes a weary gesture. Latino is led away, and he retires with numerous bows.

Yes, Yes, Christian Lords, I am Roman,
Roman as only a Jew can be:
For a Roman who is Roman
Because he is Roman, is much less Roman
Than a Roman who is Roman because he wants to be. . . .

Thus civil equality, improvement of social conditions, but sweeping spiritual abdication—that was the position of French Judaism under the influence of the political and social climate that accompanied the liberal spirit of the French Revolution.

A hundred years after the Revolution there occurred another revolutionary event, which was to act like a cold shower on Jews intoxicated by a century of victories that were too easy and too unilateral, and to the French conscience slipping down the hill of the disintegration of revolutionary ideas. The Dreyfus Affair is the most decisive event in the spiritual history of the French people since the Revolution, more earthshaking than subsequent events because it had a more general impact. France has this unique fate, that what happens in her midst has repercussions in the whole Western world. The crisis provoked by the Dreyfus Affair was the crisis of the democratic idea in general. The manner in which it was resolved is, it seems to me, decisive for the progress of democracy. (See preceding chapter.)

France, beaten in 1870-71, underwent the same crisis that Germany would after its defeat in 1918. France, too, almost turned to a totalitarian ideology of pragmatic justice, of unconditional reason of state, and—strange as it may seem—precisely through the application of the humanitarian theories of the eighteenth century. The uniformizing that the states erect into a supreme principle in the name of a national mystique, France had demanded in the name of equality carried to its ultimate conclusion. In exchange for political equality it demanded conformity of mores and beliefs. The chauvinism of the Dreyfus period wanted to exclude the Jews because it questioned the possibility of their assimilation under the influence of new racist theories.

After the storm, French democracy emerged stronger, more spiritualized than ever. A new national ideal helped to support it: that of the right of the individual or ethnic groups to retain their distinctiveness, to go back to their roots, to draw from them their nourishment and in turn nourish the common trunk. This ideal was certainly not carried out integrally, but became implanted as a new orientation that won the allegiance of the elite. We have an example of this transformation in the person of Barrès. In his youth, Barrès professed a nationalism based on the idea of blood and race: "The difference in blood confirms my repugnance for Protestantism (secular education different from mine) and for Judaism (race opposed to mine).[2] Later, however, his nationalism would broaden. Instead of stifling differences, he demanded that everyone make of his individuality the best possible use.

Here was the new direction that French democracy was to take. This was finally the concept that formulated the Jewish problem in France in new terms. Public opinion realized that assimilation should not consist in repressing the past. It was understood that a nation is all the stronger for allowing its members, either as individuals or as groups, to cultivate their being. The First World War was the fire in which this democratic ideal proved its strength, where it became tempered. Maurice Barrès searched for the origin of this power that has invigorated France, and manifests itself particularly in case of danger, and he found it the voluntary union of the diverse families of France. He devotes a chapter to French Judaism, and he mentions, among others, the case of a Zionist, second lieutenant Rothstein, volunteer, who died for France, and whose last wish was to sleep under the Star of David. This patriotism is not an irrational, animal-like impulse, like the attachment of a child to his mother. It is a spiritual patriotism, an act of will, an intellectual choice. It is, as Anna de Noailles expressed it, "the great contribution of those, who, born in France and participating in it, rediscover through study and meditation the meaning of their origins, and offer it daily the gift of their own qualities."[3]

Such was the result of the Dreyfus Affair in relation to Judaism. But how active a role did Judaism play in the spiritual transformation that took place? The Dreyfus Affair was not a Jewish issue simply because the protagonist was a Jew. At the beginning of the trial even many Jews (the "big Jews," as Anatole France calls them in *Penguin Island*) turned against the accused. When the conflict evolved into a matter of simple justice, a struggle of expedient justice against absolute justice, a number of Jews, Bernard Lazare for instance, threw themselves into the fray, not to defend the Jew

2. M. Barrès, *Scènes et doctrines du nationalisme* (Paris, 1902), p. 67.
3. Henri Franck, *La Danse devant l'Arche*, préface d'Anna de Noailles, p. 14.

Dreyfus, but the principle of justice. As the anti-Semitic thrust took on momentum, an instinctive solidarity soon emerged in the scattered camp of Israel. First it was just a feeling of humiliation; then pride hardened under the attacks. Finally, there emerged among the Jews a new awareness of their origins, of their neglected traditions, a rebirth of Zionist ideas, a resurrection of the spiritual heritage abandoned for a superficial happiness.

We have an example of the first step in the reawakening of Jewish consciousness in Marcel Proust. Proust, the darling of the most exclusive salons of Paris, Proust, whose distant origins were overlooked by Parisian aristocracy and who was proud of his conquest of high society, felt the stirring of a new sympathetic interest in Judaism and gave expression to this interest even at the risk of compromising his brilliant social position. "Catholic through his father and raised as a Catholic," notes Cécile Delhorbe, "at this hour, the hour of persecution, he considered himself a member of his mother's race, this mother he adored and with whom he was proud to identify himself" (*L'Affaire Dreyfus et les écrivains français* [Lausanne, 1934], p. 262). Thus Marcel Proust offers an interesting example of the instinctive reaction of Jewish awareness strong even in a Jew as assimilated as he was.

Proust does not belong to Jewish literature, any more than do André Maurois, Henri Bergson, Julien Benda, and the like. They are writers of Jewish origin, of Jewish temperament, but not of Jewish consciousness. (See chapter 9.) Their subject falls outside of Judaism. It would no doubt be interesting to examine the distinct contribution to French cultural life of writers, art critics, and artists of Jewish origin, but removed from Jewish concerns and devoted exclusively to art, literature, or science. Lacretelle tells, in his admirable novel *Silbermann,* how the young Jew Silbermann reveals to his Christian friend certain nuances in Racine not ordinarily found on the stage; how he draws his attention to the beauty of cathedrals from a point of view that the other had not noticed up to then. It is also an incontrovertible fact that among the greatest interpreters of Wagner, Mozart, and Beethoven are found musicians such as Bruno Walter, Dobroven, Brailovsky, Stokowsky, Menuhin. It is unquestionably true that in any civilization a different temperament injects its own particular note, drawing out a new harmony that had remained unnoticed by its own members.

There is thus a very interesting unconscious contribution of the Jewish temperament to Western civilization. But I am only going to touch on this question in passing, for my subject is the conscious contribution of Judaism to the West, that is to say, of those who attempted to express their Jewish soul, discovered in France in the moral crisis caused by the Dreyfus Case.

Those who in the past had tried to hide their Jewishness now felt the need to proclaim it, to celebrate it. Poems, dramas, and comedies dealing with the whole range of Jewish life and Jewish problems appeared. All at once a Jewish literature in the French language was born. This literature was not possible as long as Jewish life did not exist, for each work of art draws its strength from the author's soul, and through him from his milieu. If the author and his spiritual family are in a false situation, his work of necessity sounds off-key. This discordant melody can be heard throughout the works of Heine, moving symbol of a generation that wanted to destroy its authenticity.

It was due to his false situation, the situation of all those who had just escaped from the ghetto but continued to carry it within themselves. It is only at the end of his life, during the seven years that he was shackled to his bed, that Heine noticed the great mistake of his life. As he examined himself, he discovered the true nature of his soul that he should have expressed to give his life true meaning.

This is when his *Hebrew Melodies* were born, thanks to which Heine gained immortality in Jewish and world poetry.

While Heine's tragic error ruined his life, it was not useless to the generation of Jewish writers who tried to find their way home. He is the hero of *Had Gadya*. If the famous prose poem by Israel Zangwill was able to stir such great emotions in French Judaism, so great that it was considered the godfather of the nascent Jewish literature, it is because its main figure was not the product of the author's imagination, but the poetic embodiment of a real tragedy. Zangwill paints in gripping colors the contrast between the dazzling civilization of Europe and the austere tradition of Judaism standing like granite in the midst of the waves.

The attempt to reconcile the dualism of those two worlds in a superior unity became the subject of a Jewish literature in France, an exciting but somewhat limited theme. The rub is that these writers did not draw their inspiration from below, from the people, from a picturesque and variegated folklore. Unlike Zangwill, they had no contact with the tumultuous life of the homogeneous masses of Whitechapel or the personal knowledge of Peretz and Shalom Asch of the typical quarters of Polish and American Jewry. They did not eat the Saturday chalet and gefilte fish with the humble people whose preoccupations they shared.

Only one French writer, Armand Lunel, undertook the task of evoking the peculiar atmosphere of the Jewish section of Comtat Venaissin, his native land. There, in this Roman enclave, and under the soothing influence of a gentle and serene landscape, the Jewish question never assumed the tragic proportions it had in the rest of France of the Middle Ages. The Jews were never expelled. Segregated from the Christian population, subjected to severe restrictions, they did, nevertheless, enjoy a certain freedom, and were allowed to retain their traditions. They kept them even after the French Revolution threw open the gates of the ghettos. The unreal, fairyland world that the Jews had constructed to forget their often degrading physical conditions cast its spell even when the need for spiritual compensations ceased to exist. It is this atmosphere, which filled Lunel's childhood, that he attempted to depict, just as Zangwill had done for the London ghetto, Shalom Asch for the New York ghetto, Shalom Aleichem for the Polish ghetto (if we interpret the word *ghetto* in the sense of a deliberate reversion to the habits and traditions consecrated by age-old customs).

However, the center of gravity of Judeo-French literature does not reside in the depiction of Jewish milieux. Its characteristic note is the painful search for a new position in the modern world.

In the next chapter, on the poet André Spire, I will examine the character of this spiritual dualism. The same problem could be studied in the works of Edmond Fleg, Gustave Kahn, Jean R. Bloch, H. Frank, H. Hertz, J. Milbauer, A. Cohen, a whole generation of Jewish writers (somewhat uneven in quality) who actively participated in the literary movement of their time, and who one day realized that they wanted to express a different feeling. A man can be unaware of himself during the periods of tranquility that level all characters. A crisis, however, individual or general, brings to light the soul's deepest yearnings. Oh! how they would like to celebrate the sky and the earth, the cities and the rivers of the gentle land of France. How they feel more than half captivated by the serene and warm atmosphere of this "adorable land." It would be so wonderful to listen to the happy songs of the peasants, to watch the graceful farandoles of the little girls, to admire strength and daring, to devote oneself to the joy of creation in the blessed kingdom where the Greek spirit reigns. But the ear attentive to songs suddenly hears the lamentations arising from the four corners of the universe, the cries of the outcast and the downtrodden. Does it matter? That is life. Let's pity the sufferers, let's write elegies on their tragic fate, and then "lead our vigorous lives," for you only live once! But, how can one live when in Kichinev there is a pogrom, in Morocco innocents have been massacred, or in Bagdad, or in China, or right here? How can one enjoy beauty when there is no justice in the world?

> Art, si je t'acceptais, ma vie serait charmante. . .
> Mais non coeur assouvi pourrait-il vivre encore
> Si tue l'avais châtré de son rêve splendide:
> Ce Demain éternel qui marche devant moi?

> Art, if I accepted you, my life would be charming. . .
> But could my sated heart still live
> If you had castrated it of its magnificent dream:
> This eternal Tomorrow that walks in front of me?

To prepare for Tomorrow is the quintessence of the Jewish ideal. The Jew does not live for today. He does not know the peaceful enjoyment of present happiness. This is how the Jewish ideal is essentially different from the Hellenic one.[4] The Greeks conceive of life as a harmonious present, the Jews as an eternal becoming. From the point of view of art, the Greek spirit unfolds in space, the Jewish spirit in time. Classical art aspires to circumscribed perfection and therefore restricts life through unities of time, place, and action, or

---

4. Phrynicos, a tragic poet, was fined because in his *Capture of Milet* he disturbed the Athenians too much by the description of misfortunes that they could have avoided.

by the immutable contours of a statue. Messianism, reminiscent in this respect of romanticism, aspires to unlimited perfectibility.

It is within this framework that Heine had established the conflict between the Hellenes, believers in a perfect harmony in the present, and the Nazarenes, dissociating themselves from an imperfect present to prepare for a better future. He brought Christianity and Judaism together under the name "Nazarene," opposing both to the Greek ideal. In reality, Christianity is closer to the Greek world than Judaism, and occupies an intermediary position between the two. If it resembles Judaism as to purpose, it disagrees with it as to means. While Judaism takes a fighting attitude toward evil, Christianity wants to defeat it by nonresistance. In this passive acceptance of the material world (summarized in the maxim: "Render unto Caesar what belongs to Caesar"), the Christian attitude corresponds to the Greek belief in Fate. Spiritual enemies, they are allied in practice, and form thus the basis of Western civilization. It is well, perhaps, that Judaism maintained its intransigence and fought actively against the flaws of the established order to balance a morality of philanthropic charity.

In his *Paroles juives (Jewish Words)* Albert Cohen contrasts the biblical ideal with that of Jesus in those words of the Prophet Jeremiah:

Ils voudraient à la légère guérir les plaies de mon peuple
Paix, paix! disent-ils;
Mais il n'y a pas de paix.

Casually would they like to heal the wounds of my people.
Peace, peace! They say.
But there is no peace.

The Jew is not satisfied with a peaceful life as long as he is aware of misfortune and injustice. From this renunciation of peace comes a characteristic anxiety that has often been criticized as a destructive element. In reality, Jewish anxiety, far from being negative, is, in fact, fruitful, for it helps to alert the conscience of the world, and to attract widespread attention to suffering and inequities. If it often seems disruptive because it introduces a discordant note in the harmonious life each of us wants to build, it is a beneficial dissonance, although thankless for those who assume the ancient prophets' role of goad. It is true that Jewish anxiety is not manifested in every Jew in its spiritual form. Among many it is a purely superficial instability. It is only among the elite, among scholars, thinkers, and poets, that it becomes the tireless quest for an ideal of universal peace and justice.

Thus, Jewish poetry not only bears the stamp of a naïve, unconscious anxiety, but also becomes the positive expression of the ideal of the prophets. The Wandering Jew is not the symbol of a curse, but of a vocation.[5] The conscious Jews are proud of the tragic duty that has befallen them: to march until the end of time, until the dream of a real peace has come to pass.

David Molco in the play *Le Juif du pape (The Pope's Jew)*, disappointed in his hopes for peace, once again assumes his mission with sorrowful determination.

> Qu'il est long le pèlerinage,
> De lieux en lieux, d'âge en âge,
> De travaux en travaux!
> On pense arriver: la fin du voyage
> Est un nouveau départ vers un départ nouveau.

> How long the pilgrimage,
> From place to place, from age to age,
> From labor to labor!
> We think we have arrived: the end of the journey
> Is a new departure towards a new departure.

It is not only through philosophical meditation that the Jews set out tirelessly to win justice, but because they have experienced injustice so often. The teachings of the prophets would perhaps not have endured, had not their deeper meaning been revealed anew to each generation through the lessons of suffering. It is in this context that André Spire calls anxiety and sadness his "ancient protectors." Thanks to its suffering, to its sadness, to the instability that was forced upon it for many centuries, Israel remained faithful to the role assigned to it by Providence—of awakening men's souls, of being, according to Juda Halevi, the heart and conscience of mankind.

5. "Ah! They know the blessings of exile, and their sadness has a radiance!" Henri Hertz, *Ceux de Job* in *Vers un monde volage* (Paris, n.d.).

External reverses do not explain how Israel was able to remain conscious of its thankless historic role. The memory and the hope of the Promised Land have always provided a spiritual counterweight against the material fate strong enough to transform it into a metaphysical duty.

Although the pioneers of the new Palestine were recruited for the most part among the Jewish youth of Poland and Germany, French soil played an important part in the spiritual renaissance of modern Zionism. It is in France that the most important spiritual battles were waged. It is in Paris that the Jewish thinker Moses Hess lived and meditated. He was a recluse who, under the influence of German and Italian unification, formulated around 1860 the first idea of a Jewish national life in Palestine. It is also in Paris, thirty years later, under the influence of the Dreyfus Case, that Theodor Herzl wrote *The Jewish State,* which was to become a kind of political program for the Zionist movement.

For French Judaism before World War II, Palestine represented not so much a political and geographic reality, or a homeland where one might want to live, as a spiritual center, in the meaning given to it by Achad Haam. According to him, the physical existence of a Jewish state was of no value except in support of prophetic ideals. This is the aspect of Zionism that appeared in Jewish literature in France. These writers were waiting for the historic atmosphere of Palestine to give birth to a center of Jewish culture through which they can reaffirm their Jewish identity. This is how I interpret the remark by Henri Franck, who found it so interesting to be simultaneously "professor, Jewish, and French."

This synthesis was expressed by a precursor of Jewish literature in France, Eugène Manuel, who wrote the following lines:

> Trois peuples m'ont donné ce qu'il me faut pour vivre:
> Les Romains, et les Grecs, et mon vieux peuple Hébreu.
> Rome m'apprit le droit, dont son code est le livre,
> Athènes, la beauté; Jérusalem, son Dieu.

> Three peoples gave me what I needed to live:
> The Romans, and the Greeks, and my old Hebrew people.
> Rome taught me law, whose code is the text,
> Athens, beauty; Jerusalem, her God.

Is this sentiment not an echo of the biblical promise that announced the reconciliation in the distant future of the ideals of Japheth and Shem?

This is the orientation of French Judaism in the first half of the twentieth century. It does not matter that a few, in spite of the lessons of contemporary history, remain outside this renewal of Jewish culture, this new awareness. It does not even matter that these indifferent Jews constitute the majority, for Jewish history has always been "the struggle of a minority against a majority, even in the midst of the Jewish people" (Hans Kohn, *L'Humanisme juif,* p. 175). It is this active minority that is responsible for the Jewish literature to which this essay is devoted.

In the process we are studying, it seems to me not only an aspect of modern Judaism, but of French literature. Judeo-French writers have also their roots in French soil. Their distinctive characteristics have not failed to have repercussions on the general tendencies of French literature. "In the intellectual realm," said the Comtesse de Noailles, "France is enriched by the devotion of those who choose her and serve her" (Introduction to H. Franck's *La Danse devant l'Arche,* p. 14.).

I believe that this attitude of the Republic of Letters will inspire the attitude of the French Republic and the democracies in general toward their Jewish population. A spiritual minority does not disturb the national equilibrium; on the contrary, it strengthens it. Democracy can only adopt the attitude formulated by André Gide: "It seems to me rather shortsighted to consider minorities in any society, any state, only as drawbacks. Unquestionably, they can be a disturbing element, but I feel that very often it is a good thing, and the disturbance can become salutary" *(Nouvelle Revue Française* [January 4, 1938], p. 635). This corresponds to Charles Morgan's idea of a permissive society, which gives a new meaning to the humanitarian ideal of the eighteenth century.[6]

Indeed, it is the free competition of ideas that enriches nations and people.

6. *Reflections in a Mirror* (London, 1946), 2:228. Such a society would be authoritarian neither in name nor in disguise, nor even tolerant in the old negative sense of not persecuting; it would be positively permissive, genuinely adult, with permissiveness and variety as the core of its political ideal. Still, the laws would preserve order, but an order designed not to produce uniformity or orthodoxy, but, on the contrary, to prevent any man or group of men from limiting the permissiveness of the state.

# 13

# *Philosopher of Duration and Freedom: Henri Bergson*

## (translated by Liseron Gibbon)

There exist three categories of thinkers. Some consider thought as a domain of its own, beyond or outside of social existence, like art for art's sake. They are capable of carrying their ideas to their ultimate consequences; of rendering them subtle even to the point of being paradoxical, in the conviction that this does not engage them to adopt any extreme attitude in their lives. They would not be ready, in any case, to run any personal risk for their opinions, and would be sorry to see them carried out to the letter by others. Nietzsche, the German philosopher, father of the notorious doctrine of the "will to power," seems to me an illustrious example of this, for he extolled a type of man above all morality, a violent contrast to the author's own personal nature; and he certainly would not have wished to see his dream realized, to the letter, by one of his own race.

A less tragic example of this attitude is that of the philosopher who taught an intractable skepticism with regard to all the values of life and to life itself. For all this, having one day fallen into the water, he made every effort to save himself. His disciples suggested that he might allow himself to drown, since life, according to his own doctrine, was not worth an effort. But he replied that his skepticism led him to doubt even his own opinions, and that he wished therefore, pending further information, to maintain the status quo of his existence like all other mortals.

These two examples illustrate the first category of thinkers.

The second category of philosophers, feeling more responsibility with regard to life, prudently regulate their conduct by their opinions, and they adapt these opinions to the necessities of life; they are the exponents of common sense, of gilded mediocrity, of maintaining order, even at the expense of progress and of absolute truth. Their opinion is based on their social position; they defend the existing order of things by means of a system patterned on that order, and rarely find themselves faced with a conflict between their lives and their ideas. Such thinkers undoubtedly also have their followers, to whom they offer the system that suits their interests. They enjoy a great popularity, for their ideas do not require any great effort, nor any great decision of their conscience, which finds itself in harmony with their interests; they are popular and respected, but they are not among those who greatly uplift humanity.

But, finally, there are philosophers with a great temerity of thought, like those of the first category; like those of the second category, they are desirous of bringing their thought into harmony with life. However, to accomplish this, they are not willing to sacrifice the consequences of their ideas, and thus to falsify them, but rather seek to raise life to the height of their conceptions, even though they may themselves be the first victims in the accomplishment of their ideal. It is these thinkers, whose words were deeds, who, by their doctrine and their example, have really elevated mankind to a higher dignity. Whether it be a Socrates, who set the seal on his teachings by the serenity of his death, in order to prove that a man must be capable of overcoming *all* his passions and emotions by means of reason and self-imposed discipline; or a Spinoza, who emphasized the autonomy of thought by a complete independence in his social existence, though it might be at the expense of his health and life and glory; to this category (to remain in the field of philosophy and not use examples furnished by religious or political leaders), belongs the man to whom I dedicate the present chapter—Henri Bergson.

Henri Bergson—the philosopher of liberty; the philosopher whose whole system represents a creative evolution, leading to a noble conception of moral and metaphysical liberty, of spiritual victory over matter—received the supreme grace of consecrating his glory by an end worthy of his captivating doctrine. He remained loyal to himself; to his native land and its ideal of liberty; to his religious origins and his race—to Judaism, toward which he turned all the more resolutely when external circumstances bade him turn away from them. Though tending toward Catholicism, which he believed to be the natural consummation of Judaism, he was unwilling that his profession of faith should be interpreted as a rejection of his origins. "I wished to remain among those who tomorrow will be the persecuted," he wrote in his will, dated February 8, 1937. And when the persecutions against those of his race reached their paroxysm, he made a supreme gesture to show his solidarity with them: when the Jews in Paris were being registered during the German occupation, the eighty-year-old paralytic, who could have invoked sufficient reasons to be exempted from this humiliating measure, had himself taken to the Town Hall to manifest the fact that he belonged to the most persecuted of the persecuted.

This magnificent act is not only a glorious rehabilitation of Judaism by one of its greatest sons, and of France at the moment of her deepest humiliation, but it is a living demonstration of the theories he taught all his life: the theory of duration as an organic continuity, where each moment of life is the result and spiritual consecration of the whole previous life; and the theory of freedom as the victory, in decisive moments, of the individual's own nature over the social and material constraints that have been superimposed upon the reality of a man's inmost being.

I have thus, starting from a simple action of this philosopher, seized a living expression of the two characteristic points of his doctrine, which I shall proceed to analyze in detail: duration and freedom.

Henri Bergson was not simply the exponent of a philosophical movement. He was neither a Neoplatonist, a Neo-Kantian, nor a Spinozist, but a completely original thinker, a creator of new concepts that have enriched our intellectual history. He is not a French or a Jewish philosopher, but a genuine guide of the human spirit. Judaism may nevertheless find satisfaction in having given the world another great thinker whose accomplishments surpass the most renowned representatives of modern philosophy, not a few of whom are Jewish.

It would be impossible to give, even in outline, Bergson's basic ideas, especially since his is not a carefully constructed philosophical system, but rather an almost prophetic vision, formulated in suggestive poetic language. All his works revolve around the intuitive viewpoint of organic evolution *(la durée)*. Each of his books is in a sense just the expression of some aspect of the world-view that revealed itself to him. His book *L'Evolution créatrice (Creative Evolution)*, published in 1907, may be considered his best work. Here Bergson treats the essential questions that have claimed mankind's interest since time immemorial. Problems such as the origin and evolution of the world, the essence of the body and the soul and their relationship, instinct and intelligence, determinism and free will, time and eternity are examined by this productive intellect in a completely original way, without his ever allowing the massive scientific material lying at the root of his speculations to detract from the verve and movement of his investigation.

Bergson's concept of a creative development of the life force *(élan vital),* issuing from the divine source, dividing into various living forms and roaring through the universe, sees its goal as the spiritualization of matter, or in other words, freedom. This concept is a decisive reaction, on the one hand, to the then-current materialistic theories of Darwin, and, on the other hand, to intellectualism. It leads to an affirmation of the religious forces that continue the work of creation in the realm of ethics *(Les Deux sources de la morale et de la religion,* 1932) *(The Two Sources of Morality and Religion).* This work is the consummation of a long series of philosophical labors and is, in a way, the sequel to his *Creative Evolution.* It is inspired by the same principles, transposing them from the biological to the sociological and religious domain.

By religion Bergson does not mean a definite confession, even

though an unmistakable sympathy for Christian mysticism finds expression in his last major work. This gave rise to various speculations, the result of which was the claim that Bergson had intended to
convert to Christianity, if he had not already done so. This is absolutely groundless. If Bergson discovered the characteristics of
"dynamic religion" that constitute the quintessence of his philosophy
of religion in Catholicism and not in his hereditary Jewish faith, it is
because he, in contrast with Spinoza, was not sufficiently acquainted
with Judaism.

Descending on his father's side from a respected Jewish family
from Poland (originally called Berson or Berekson), he grew up in
Paris in a purely French milieu and received the education of the
French elite. Some time after the appearance of a study on the
Jewish traces in his philosophy (Ch. Lehrmann, *Bergsonisme et
Judaisme* [Editions Union, Genève]), he confessed in a confidential
conversation that the Jewish religion was spoiled for him when he
was a child by the way it was taught. Does this not bring to mind a
parallel with Spinoza, who was banned in Amsterdam, and even with
Maimonides, whose *More Nebuchim (The Guide of the Perplexed)*
was suppressed in Montpellier?

According to Bergson, the courageous annexation of new territory
in the realm of thought, the eternally alert consciousness of responsibility to life, is dynamic religion, or religion in constant relationship
to the incessantly progressing life of the universe. If Bergson, alienated from the idea of Judaism by his education, did not consciously
make use of Jewish elements in his system of thought, his
*Weltanschauung* is nevertheless characterized by a Jewish orientation.
In him can be seen these dynamics that distinguish Jewish prophecy:
its high idealism and its belief in the moral progress of mankind, in
the victory of the spirit over technology, and in that lofty universal
mission "qui est une machine à faire des dieux (which is a machine
to produce gods). This is an echo of the Jewish messianic concept,
which runs through generations like an underground stream and
forms the inner bond among Jewish personalities who have worked
in various lands, languages, and branches of the arts and sciences.

A few years before World War II, the news spread that Bergson, granted the highest French honors, refused any special recognition in deference to the plight of his fellow Jews. It seems that destiny wanted to give him a final opportunity to express his bond with Judaism by a gesture more impressive than anything that could be said or written.

Society as a whole is for Bergson, in *The Two Sources of Morality and Religion,* the culminating point to which biological evolution has led. Animal communities, governed by instinct, do not need moral principles for their members. Human society, based on intelligence, elaborates a set of precepts, the regular functioning of which assures the existence of society itself. Taken separately, moral prescriptions may be arbitrary; together, they form a unit comparable to the biological entity of the animal community, fashioned by life itself. Society has the right to consider itself an organism willed by nature, and, as such, to assure its own conservation by imposing on its members useful laws; such is the origin of social morality.

Society is composed of a certain number of individuals whom geographical or historical conditions have brought together in the past and whom common interests unite in the present.

Respective interests therefore divide humanity into numerous societies, each being a law unto itself. (These are what Bergson calls "closed societies," each shut in upon itself and closed against outsiders.) Humanity as a biological unit does not exist; it is only the sum total of all the particular "closed societies," the ultimate degree of evolution. Divergences between these societies are natural, and the extermination of a neighboring society by war is, from the standpoint of social morality, as innocent a thing as for a wild beast to destroy its foe.

Morality ceases at the limits of a particular society.

The original impulsion has thus arrived at a blind alley, where it seems likely to remain bogged forever, the "closed society" being the maximum it has been able to extract from matter.

But alongside this marking of time, there continues to well up, in a thin stream, the source of life, which tends to fashion the material world in its image. It survives in a few of the elect, as the mouthpiece of a human morality going beyond the egoistical interests of "closed societies." Struggling against the stagnation of this relative morality, in spite of the unpopularity of such an undertaking, they awaken human conscience and draw a part of mankind into the movement that leads toward a new era, toward an absolute morality. Whence comes to them this gleam that causes them to break away from traditional paths, to scorn the quiet happiness of a passive life, which common sense offers them? It is because in them a spark of the creative impulse survives and their sentiment of the way yet to be traveled has a religious origin.

From this Bergson is led to state the problem of the origin of religion in a new way.

Religion has been explained by modern sociologists as a reaction of fear, born of the weakness of human beings before all-powerful nature. For Bergson religion (which is a characteristic only of intelligent beings) is the consequence of the substitution of intelligence for instinct, accomplished in mankind. It is destined to restore to man the assurance, the confidence in life, that the animal possesses by nature, but that in man is endangered by intelligence.

Intelligence, an instrument of the first order for opening up new fields of activity to life, carries within itself the germ that paralyzes all activity. For intelligence, apt at planning cleverly and aiming at a distant target, realizes at the same time the infinite number of circumstances that might intervene between the plan and its accomplishment, circumstances of which a single one would suffice to jeopardize all success. The effect of this foresight is a profound *discouragement,* which is altogether absent in the animal.

In the animal nothing is interposed between the action and its goal. It pounces upon its prey, and it does not think of tomorrow's prey as long as it is not hungry. If the goal is far off (as for the bee building its hive, for instance), the animal remains ignorant of the ultimate purpose and sees only the immediate end. It therefore carries out its daily work without a moment of discouragement. For man things are different. Between the plan elaborated by his intelligence and the goal, there is a great interval, during which all sorts of accidents may occur. The impossibility of foreseeing is so great that it would paralyze every impulsion in man. But life finds means to ward off this danger. It causes intelligence itself to produce representations that combat the harmful representations: man pictures to himself superhuman powers ready to intervene in his favor. This confidence in favorable powers gives him back that faith in life which had been seriously endangered by intelligence. This faith bridges the interval between the action and its goal; it is the defensive reaction of nature "against the representation, by intelligence, of a discouraging margin of the unforeseen between the initiative taken and the desired effect."

Religious representations vary according to the more or less developed mentality of human societies.

Primitive mentality personifies the forces favorable to man as benevolent spirits. The savage who shoots an arrow implores the gods to guide it aright. This is still a very primitive religiousness, which reduces the divinity to the image of man, but it already fills the need of restoring man's confidence in success. (We are, moreover, not so far removed from this primitive mentality, and notwithstanding the scientific explanations we are capable of giving about natural phenomena, we personify the cause that produces them, because our consciousness, in spite of having such a very scientific education, refuses to admit absolutely blind forces. People say of a particularly violent earthquake: "It was bent on destroying everything," as if there were a personified power endowed with a clear intention.)

Thus, in order to neutralize the fear of events that beings gifted with intelligence have—above all the fear of death, which threatens to paralyze all activity—in order to counteract this fear, the vital impulse has endowed man with a special function, the capacity for creating myths, produced by intelligence itself, which imagines a conscious power dominating the interval between our projects and their accomplishment. This is the religiousness studied by Durkheim and Lévy-Bruhl as a pure sociological phenomenon, but in only one aspect of religion, in its most materialistic function.

The forms taken by this pragmatic religiousness vary from magic to national religion. The religions of antiquity all have one characteristic in common, that of being limited to a "closed society," to one city or at most to one people. The religious impulse of these "closed societies" went no further than invoking the support of the local deity against enemy societies. It is the biological egoism of the species that survives in these religious systems. The role of these religions was to *maintain* the stagnant condition of the species that the vital impulse had reached; it was therefore merely *a static religion*. Durkheim's definitions of religion apply only to this primitive form of religion.

But there is a religion that springs from quite another source and tends toward quite another end than the jealous preservation of "closed" states. This is the religion that holds that the purpose of creation is not yet fulfilled, that man must rather complete creation by extending his love, which has stopped at the species, to the whole of mankind. The idea of creation was love. God, source of love (see chapter 5), created beings worthy of his love. For love has need of objects to love. All creation thus bears the stamp of the creator, and it is love that is the principle of every creative work on earth. But the current of love projected into matter, having run up against a desperate resistance from inert matter, withdrew into itself, and the impulsion forward was transformed into a circular movement. Mankind follows this circle, divided into "closed societies" with "closed" moralities. There are, however, individuals who, by a mystical impulse, rise toward the source of life, where the purpose of existence is revealed to them. The mystic, by reason of this revelation, breaks out of the mechanical orbit of life, frees himself from materiality, and prevails over it insofar as his own person is concerned; and he goes forth among men to teach them the ideal he has discovered. By the force of his personality he wakens their spirits, stirs the masses, and impels them toward a new goal. He replaces static religion with a dynamic religion.

Theology sets down in reasonable formulae some traces of the fire kindled by the founder of the religion. Every religious system is thus "a cristallization, effected by means of a skillful cooling of what mysticism had left, white-hot, in the soul of mankind." The mystics of all times come to stir up the smoldering fire, which, without them, would cool and die out. Organized religion, theology, is a means, albeit a very noble one, of rendering the mystical revelation accessible to future generations.

This then is how Bergson makes a distinction between two different moral codes and two different religions. The one is pragmatic, inspired by material causes, corresponding to the immediate needs of a closed group of individuals; the other is born of an impulse of the soul toward a spiritual principle, an impulse that outstrips the narrow outlook of the preservation of a closed society, and is transformed into a dynamic impulsion toward the love of all mankind.

Bergson designates Jesus as the founder of dynamic religion. Though indebted to the prophets of Israel, whose work he continued, Jesus immeasurably broadened the foundation of their moral code by opening up to it an immense field of activity. The justice of the prophets was applied only to the people of Israel, says Bergson; their religion was a closed system, their God a national God. This is why they cannot be classed as true mystics. Christianity, on the other hand, tended from its inception to become a universal religion, thus following the original direction of the vital impulse. The prophets of Israel had nevertheless, he admits, the merit of not having been content with contemplation, but of having been men of action. The mystics of Grecian antiquity, Plotinus for instance, considered action as impairing the powers of contemplation. The prophets, on the other hand, had a passion for applied justice. It was by virtue of this active element, inherited from Judaism, that Christianity conquered the world.

I admire the organic unity of Bergson's philosophy, the natural transition from biological research to philosophical speculation and to conclusions of a religious and moral order. While finding support in naturalism, he definitely broke its chains and in his system associated biology and ethics. Man is fitted into the framework of nature without the independence of conscience and moral values being jeopardized. These observations have already become self-evident in "creative evolution"; they are still more marked in Bergson's last work, where all pantheistic tendencies are definitely abandoned and whence emerges the idea of a God who is at once transcendant and immanent. We can observe in Bergson's system the unmistakable linking of philosophy to a positive religion. Not that it is a philosophy under theological tutelage; it is the natural conclusion of a philosophy without dogmatic premises leading to a positive religion.

Yet there remains a problem, from both the Jewish and the Christian points of view. Why did Bergson, the Jew, adhere entirely to the Catholic thesis, declaring it to be the only accomplishmnet of his religious theory? An external aspect of this problem is the fact that he devoted less than one page to discussing the religions of his ancestors. The parallels I have established between Bergsonism and Jewish thought render more likely a conscious approach toward Judaism than toward Catholicism. It is therefore indispensable to submit to a critique the application he makes of his theories to both religions by examining the Bergsonian conclusions in the light of the one and the other.

Bergson classed Judaism among the closed systems of religion and morality because he knew the history of a people that isolated itself from other peoples, that took pride in its God "who is stronger than other gods," a people that had withdrawn into itself while Christianity conquered the world and became a universal religion.

Bergson was mistaken as to the nature of both the universality of Christianity and the Jewish particularism; both are much less absolute than it would appear.

In fact, the millenary history of Judaism proves the presence of two tendencies, the one toward universalism, the other toward particularism, which have succeeded each other alternately. The rhythm of these changes was determined by exterior circumstances. The original tendancy was toward universalism. The father of Judaism adopted the name of Abraham, the father *of peoples,* which expresses the mission of Israel from its inception—to unite all peoples under the same ideal.

The Mosaic law, while tending to form a homogeneous national whole, nevertheless leaves broad prospects open to relations with the non-Jewish world. The later commentaries are expressly founded on the Mosaic text when they point out the universalist tendencies of Judaism. Here, for example, is a talmudic commentary (Mechilta on Exodus, 20-22): "He shall never perish, who brings about peace between men, between husband and wife, between one government and another, between one city and another, between *one people and another.*" They say further, that the particular social structure and the political situation in post-Mosaic times forced Israel to withdraw into itself, until the moment when the prophets restored the original tendency.

The Babylonian exile is the definite proof of the supranational character of the Jewish religion. For far from being bound to any given territory or political structure, it continues to exist through the dissolution of its national structure, though torn from the soil where it had flourished. It was like a confirmation of the intentions of Moses, who had promulgated his doctrine in the desert, in no man's land, as a sign that it was not bound to a certain country and a certain nation, but that it has a universal tendency.

Nevertheless, the impulsion toward expansion was restrained, after the return from Babylon, by Esdras and Nehemiah. History presents several more such reactions, conditioned by political circumstances, but the true direction can no longer be put in doubt.

"The Jew took pride in having something to say to the world, and in being able to bring it something which concerned the whole of mankind; the one God, pure spirit, creator of heaven and earth, and his holy moral law. And it was from the consciousness of this that he drew the sentiment of his mission" (Adolf v. Harnack, *Die Mission u. Ausbreitung des Christentums* [*The Mission and Expansion of Christianity)*] [Giessen, 1902], 1:14.)

At the moment of the appearance of Christianity, the pagan world in the Roman Empire had already drawn fairly close to the Mosaic religion. We learn from Flavius Josephus *(The War of the Jews,* VII, 3,3) that many Greeks regularly attended services in the synagogues. The case was the same in Rome, according to Horace (Satire I, 9, 67-72) and Juvenal (Satire I, 3, 296).

If Christianity was able to spread so easily, it was because it availed itself of the far-reaching network of synagogues, which already included active proselytism in their program. Appearing at first as a Jewish sect, it had only to develop the movement that was taking shape before its coming.

Historical data thus expressly contradict Bergson's affirmation when he attributes the success of Christianity to an innate universal character that was peculiar to it. The particular merit of Christianity lies perhaps in the rapidity with which it was able to spread its doctrines among the peoples. However, this rapid expansion was perhaps to the detriment of the depth of the prophetic ideal of a united humanity.

For two thousand years Christianity, spreading over the territories of the Roman Empire, has imposed itself as a supranational religion. But one cannot yet say that it has fulfilled the promise of Isaiah: "They shall beat their swords into ploughshares, and the lion and the lamb shall feed together." Christian Rome has not even succeeded in imitating pagan Rome, by imposing a "Pax Romana" on the world. The Christian peoples continued to tear each other to pieces while invoking the favor of the same God. Priests of the same religion blessed the weapons of armies destined to kill each other. Among Muslims, unity and solidarity is perhaps more fully accomplished than among Christians.

If one may judge by the result rather than by the program, one cannot frankly admit that the universalism of Christianity has succeeded any better than those of Islam or of Judaism.

Bergson makes the same fundamental mistake when he hesitates to class the Jewish prophets among the great mystics of antiquity.

The reasons upon which he bases his views, in order to incorporate Christian mysticism into his system, discovering in it only the characteristics that answer to his conception of true mysticism, are not conclusive.

If dynamic force is the essential characteristic of the true mystic, of the man who continues the creative work of the vital impulse, I cannot see how it agrees with the passive and contemplative mysticism of a Meister Eckhart, a Saint Francis, or a Saint Theresa.

Is there, on the other hand, a more dynamic movement than Jewish messianism, even up to its latest manifestation in Hassidism? Jewish messianism, as opposed to Christian messianism, projects its goal into the future, a goal to be realized only by a progressive effort. The idea that the summit of humanity's history was attained two thousand years ago was perhaps a serious obstacle to the birth of a moral dynamism worthy of the scientific dynamism that characterize the Occident.

Bergson appreciated the active impulsion of Jewish prophetism.

However, this seems to me to be just the current that is least followed by Christianity. This is even, contrary to Bergson's opinion, one of the most characteristic differences between the two systems. Christianity has distinctly separated material and spiritual life and has made it clear that its interest tends toward the latter, an attitude that has given it its character of an escape into the hereafter. Judaism, on the contrary, tries to realize the hereafter on earth. The most humble practical activity bears, in its eyes, the stamp of divinity.

"Higher than the pious man, is the one who lives by the labor of his hands" (Ber. 8a).

For work is a humble human contribution to the transformation of inorganic matter into an organized universe, and this is the first step toward the spiritualization of the world.

"Enoch was a cobbler, every movement of his needle linked God to the Shekhina" (transcendant to immanent divinity).

For God is present in all things; like the sleeping Beauty, He awaits only man's kiss of love to reveal Himself.

By giving himself to the whole of life, by devoting all his powers to it, man, whom the Talmud calls the collaborator of God, completes the creation of the world.

It is curious that Bergson himself should feel no kinship between his doctrines and those of Judaism, that he excludes the latter from participating in his ideas of vital and moral impulsion. He does so by what he says, but still more by what he does not say.

For it is more than surprising that in a work on the nature of religions, Judaism should occupy such an insignificant place, less than a page in a book that numbers 343. A religion that has given birth to Christianity and Islam would have deserved, in the eyes of any impartial critic, a more extensive study from such a penetrating philosopher, all the more as it was the religion of his ancestors.

All this shows merely his lack of familiarity with the Jewish religion.

Brought up far from any Jewish surroundings or influence, it was natural that he should lose the *conscious* comprehension of the thought of his race, which nevertheless lived on in him. For the dynamism and the idealism of his philosophy, and the very essence of most of his philosophycal ideas, show a close relationship to important aspects of Jewish thought. But it is none the less true that even an all-embracing mind may remain in ignorance of the roots of its own self. Or, to use Bergson's own terminology, it is only in decisive, dramatic moments that the inmost self breaks out in all its strength. That extraordinary situation was given in the tragic period of Germany's hegemony. In that moment the best elements of all peoples found themselves. And Bergson discovered his Jewish soul and affirmed in the face of the conqueror his solidarity with Israel, as a symbol of resistance against violence and barbarism.

By this act, Bergson emphasized the noblest points of his thought, and future generations always hear through his philosophy the voice of optimism, of confidence in moral progress, of hope of a united humanity, of the spirit's victory over matter—a voice that rang out in the darkest hours of mankind. The whole essence of biblical messianism thrills through these lines that terminate Bergson's work:

> Humanity groans, half-crushed, beneath the weight of the progress it has made. It does not yet know that its future depends upon itself. It is for humanity to see first whether it wishes to continue to live, and afterwards to ask itself whether it wishes merely to live, or to furnish as well the necessary effort, so that, even on our refractory planet, may be accomplished the essential function of the universe, which is a machine for the making of gods.

It might, however, be observed that these victories of humanity, this spiritual evolution of mankind, will not be accomplished merely by a return to the mysticism of which Bergson dreamed. He saw in it the only way to counterbalance the materialism that has arisen out of the rapid development of technology, due to the intellectualism in which mankind had become too much involved. Intellectualism created the technique and the implements by means of which man extends the influence of his body. Through technology man has inordinately expanded his body, without compensating for this by an increase of soul. From this lack of balance between the body and the soul of mankind springs the disquietude of our age. As Bergson himself says:

> Machines which run by gasoline, by coal, by electricity, and

which convert into movement potential energies accumulated during millions of years have come to give our organism an existence
so vast and a power so formidable, so disproportionate to its size
and strength, that surely nothing of the sort had been foreseen in
planning the structure of our species. . . .But in this inflated
body, the soul remains what it was, too small now to fill it, too
weak to direct it. . . .The overgrown body awaits a supplement of
soul, and mechanism demands a mystical conception. . . .It will
render services proportionate to its power only if mankind, which
it has bowed down still further toward the ground, succeeds
through it in standing erect again and looking toward heaven.

Thus Bergson expected that a new mystical conception would restore the disrupted equilibrium; that great prophetic leaders would
point the way for mankind to follow. Yet it has been justly noted
that a modern mysticism could not well have the same character as
the ancient, and it is not by having recourse to the old mystical conceptions that present problems can be solved. A. Baumgartner observes that, should the ancient prophets, who were at the base of biblical religions, be reincarnated in the great leaders we know today,
they would bear more resemblance to the figures of the great socialist
leaders.

This means that, in spite of the errors it commits in its effort to
succeed, the social idea is the one that contains the germ of that
progress dreamed of by the sublime figures of the Bible and by
Bergson himself.

As Bannung says: "To expect from parapsychology the great
transformation of social and international life is a yet more audacious
hope than to expect it from a mystical conception which would come
to found the kingdom of heaven on earth."

The idea of Socialism is the one most truly inherited from the biblical ideal, and if this ideal today bears the stamp of science, it is in
the same way as other prophetic inspirations were subsequently
elaborated into theologies, into logical and social systems. The
system that translates the ancient ideal into the language of our time
is Socialism. This trend was completely overlooked by Bergson, who
did not take it into account at any point in his doctrine.

It is possible that the material and political exigencies of Socialism made this movement appear to him as an expression of the materialism against which he waged war. Yet not to take into consideration so powerful a movement, which had been developing for a century, nevertheless betrays a weakness in a philosophical system that deals with all human phenomena. He might, for instance, have noted that a movement that spreads like a great river, both in breadth and depth, must, in spite of the material forms of social and political combat, be sustained by an idea that has its source in the creative impulse that animates the world.

The realization of certain democratic and socialistic postulates is perhaps an indispensable stage on the way toward the advent of that era of international solidarity, of unity and of love between men, which Bergson recognized as the terrestrial goal of creation.

Not that Socialism, in its materialistic interpretation and failures of today, is in itself the ultimate end; but perhaps, by creating certain conditions, it might contribute to the liberation of certain spiritual powers in mankind, powers that had hitherto been fettered and that would subsequently lead humanity toward new horizons, toward that spiritual aspiration which Bergson was never weary of proclaiming, and of which he remains, whatever may be found wanting in his system, one of the noblest incarnations in contemporary philosophy, postulating supplementary soul in a technical age.

# 14

# *Stefan Zweig*
# *and the European Tragedy*

The news of Stefan Zweig's suicide was announced at the very moment when the most inhuman of all wars was reaching its paroxysm, when human beings were being massacred, not only on the battlefield, but also before firing squads and in the sophisticated slaughterhouses of Poland. Yet his death did not go unnoticed. This isolated tragedy produced a profound shock. Everyone felt that the death of the famous writer had a historical significance transcending the individual. It symbolized the final destruction of a bygone era, that of the Europe of yesterday, that rich and contradictory flowering known as Western civilization. Zweig's tragedy, his self-destruction in spite of the possibility of living without care, for he was safe in a country that showered him with honors, reflected the tragedy of Europe's committing suicide without visible reasons in the midst of the greatest economic and spiritual expansion. The deeper reasons of his death can also give us some insights into the European catastrophe.

I could, of course, try to explain Stefan Zweig's case like so many other acts of desperation, by attributing it to a lack of courage before the necessity of rebuilding a career, to the exhaustion of his vital re-

252

sources on the threshold of salvation, a profound discouragement caused by the vicissitudes of emigration. In the biography that once again illuminates his triumphal journey before he disappeared into the eternal night, he complains of the humiliations with which the road to emigration is paved *(Die Welt von Gestern [The World of Yesterday]*, ed. Bermann-Fischer [Stockholm, 1943]). He whose words captivated millions of people had to keep quiet on the successive stations of his flight for fear of being expelled as an undesirable alien. As a refugee in England, during the critical prewar years, with the wisdom of his Austrian experience, he would have liked to expose the political mistakes of a government and a people who, with the exception of a few of Churchill's associates, were totally unaware of the true significance of the events on the Continent. How difficult it was to keep quiet in the presence of the irreparable mistakes whose consequences were going to be so disastrous! He who had met the most celebrated men in the world had to consider himself happy to know a minor official whose good will was more useful to his survival than the friendship of a Toscanini or a Romain Rolland. Upon his arrival in a city, his first step was to go to a consulate, to police headquarters, to sundry authorities, to obtain some kind of permit or other. And he discovered that the loss of his passport was to lose all right to existence. The kindliest asylum cannot replace the homeland, for at best one has only "zwei Fremden und keine Heimat" (you are a stranger in two lands, and at home in none). He thought of Gorki's remark: "In a foreign country we lose our strongest assets. None of us produced his best in exile."

Yet, this psychological misery of emigration would not have been sufficient to sap the resistance of a man possessing greater spiritual resources than the ordinary mortal. Did not Zweig have before his eyes the example of his friend Croce? This old man whose heart was young and enthusiastic, inspired by the contact with those whose *spiritus rector* (spiritual guide) he was, taught him that even solitude can become a source of strength, and that the struggle against material obstacles can be a fountain of youth for the spirit: "It is resistance that rejuvenated me. If I had remained a senator, I would have wound up becoming indolent and inconsistent." No, it was not external obstacles nor the endless wanderings that alone defeated a man who had expended such admirable energy to save his life and talent. His predicament was aggravated by another factor.

A Gorki, a Croce, living in a foreign country or in enforced seclusion equivalent to exile, are deprived only of an immediate, concrete activity. Their soul is not estranged, their ideals are not shaken, and they continue to defend them, although less directly. Zweig, on the other hand, could create for himself a new field of personal activities. He had lost, however, the solace of his intellectual home, of an idea in which he could believe. He had lost faith in the meaning of existence, and had even lost the language that embodied his ideas. Ten borrowed tongues are not the equivalent of one's mother tongue. Of course, his works had previously been translated into all the civilized languages, but it had been the translator's task to retain the rhythm of his language and the accent of his inspiration. Now Zweig had to adapt his thought to a climate for which it was not made. He could only be a tourist in a country and on a continent which, however glorious its future, was still infinitely inferior to the aristocratic civilization in which he had been thoroughly steeped. His nostalgia was not just a languid kind of sentimentality. It was spiritual in nature. For his homeland was not Vienna, his native city, nor Austria, nor Germany, but Europe as an idea: "Oh, Europe, our sacred fatherland and the Parthenon of our Western civilization!" *(Die Welt von Gestern,* p. 451). Vienna was precious to him because through the centuries it had been a nerve center of this old civilization that he and his generation hoped to perpetuate.

Now, among the men who in the twentieth century represent the Viennese tradition and carry its glory to its zenith, we find in classical music Gustav Mahler and Goldmarck, in the famous Viennese music Oscar Strauss, Leon Fall, and E. Kalman. Writers such as Hugo von Hofmannstal, Arthur Schnitzler, Richard Beer-Hofmann, and Peter Altenberg had almost as much renown in Europe as Grillparzer and Stifter. The Viennese theater attracted visitors from the entire world, thanks to such men as Sonnenthal or Max Reinhardt. As for Viennese science, its proverbial fame was increased by the prestige of names such as Freud and Adler. All the names mentioned are those of Jews, who, together with stars of lesser magnitude, contributed to making of the metropolis a unique center of art and science. On the other hand, they caused a great deal of hostility by the disproportionate number of Jewish artists, doctors, and architects. I will deal with this equivocal situation later. Let us note for the moment the drive of the Jewish milieu to increase the brilliance of the old metropolis which, otherwise, would have been living only on past glories. For the court, the nobility, the old brougeoisie were becoming intellectually lethargic, and were interested only in their "noble passions." It was the indolence of a blasé and tired country, whose consequence in the economic and political sphere was dependence on Germany. On the spiritual level, however, Vienna defended itself victoriously against Berlin and Munich, thanks to a Jewish bourgeoisie assimilated to the most indigenous Austrian tradition.

Stefan Zweig was a representative of this intellectual Austria that had the attention of Europe, and whose brutal extermination marked the end of the old humanist Europe. Jew, Austrian, intellectual —these were the triple roots of his soul, constituting his humanitarian ideal, summarized by the word *Europe,* whose agony and relapse into barbarism thus caused him a triple distress. Where is one to summon the strength to defend a hope three times destroyed?

Once, during the First World War, his ideal had almost collapsed. He assumed the role of defender of the cause of Europe. Of course, he did not do it openly, for direct attention was not his forte, not any more than it had been that of Erasmus, his spiritual brother (the book that Zweig devoted to him was the most intimate confession of an author whose unusual reticence kept him from talking candidly about himself). He did not frankly declare himself a conscientious objector, but his subtle weapon was nonetheless effective. His passionately pacifist play *Jeremiah* was an extraordinary success right under the nose of military censorship. To the masses still intoxicated with daily victory, he opposed the exhortations of the divine defeatist, Jeremiah: "War is great only in books. In reality it strangles and disgraces life. . . .People of Jerusalem, do not exalt war. It is a wild beast that gnaws at the flesh of the strong, and exhausts the marrow of the

powerful. . . .No war is holy; only life is holy! . . .Do not invoke
the help of God. It is not he who sends war. It is on his name that
men shunt the responsibility of everything they do not understand.
He gave us a life to live! . . .An unfortunate simpleton, he who is
wise among madmen, who calls for peace under the reign of the
sword." *Jeremiah* is a personal confession, like the book on Erasmus. The figure of the biblical moralist represents in the soul of the
poet the reverse of the tendency incarnated by the wise and prudent
humanist. But it is not simply as literary camouflage that Zweig put
his belief in the mouth of the old prophet. There is more. "Unconsciously, by choosing a subject from the Bible I had touched a chord
which until then had not sounded in me. It was the echo of my
Judaism, anchored in my blood or in tradition. Was that not my real
people, always beaten by every nation and yet outlasting them thanks
to an unexplainable strength, the strength to transform by the will to
live each defeat into victory?" (p. 291).

His Jewish vitality stimulated him to undertake, in the middle of
the war, the reconstruction of European humanism. Seeking refuge in
the Jewish component of his soul, he launched from there his attempt
to rebuild his ideal. His house in Salzburg that he had painstakingly
restored became an attraction in this already charming city. It came
to symbolize the restoration of Old Europe. But the first attack
against European values between 1914 and 1918 was still free from
the racist element.

This time, Zweig did not have this last refuge left. On the contrary, it was under the aegis of a crusade against Judaism that the
murderous assault against the foundation of Western civilization was
launched. Zweig now felt shaken to the very depths of his being, for
his European humanism and his pacifism were really rooted in his
Judaism, while the latter seemed to him to lead naturally to a spirit
of cosmopolitanism. The sociological law of "the circulation of the
elite," the drive toward the upper level of society, assumes a special
character among the Jews. Wealth is only a stepping stone to a
higher cultural level. Where the Jews lived in compact masses, as in
Eastern Europe, where they formed a closed society, the orientation
toward the spirit was expressed by the fact that the apex of the social

pyramid was represented by the rabbi. Wealthy bourgeois tried to marry off their daughters to poor Talmudic students, whose knowledge became the pride of the whole family. Among Western Jews the intellectual drive was expressed by a stampede toward university studies, resulting in academic brilliance along with increased social tensions due to the crowding of the liberal professions. Tragic paradox of the Jewish destiny!

Zweig recognized in this inclination for study his penchant for rising above the humble status of Judaism considered as a nation toward the wider horizons of Judaism as an idea. "Lost nation, immortal spirit"—these words from his play *Jeremiah* also summarized Zweig's opinion of the role of Judaism in the world. Judaism persisted in him as a creative urge, as the urge to act and to implant ideas in his European fatherland. When he was deprived of this fatherland in the name of an ideology that wanted to extirpate precisely the Jewish element from the human edifice, his mainspring broke and he died.

Perhaps Zweig's conception of Judaism, however noble, was erroneous. He categorically refused to grant Judaism the character of a community, and saw in their common destiny an intolerable and anti-natural constraint. "The Jews of the 20th century had long ceased to be a community. Now for the first time in hundreds of years, Jews were being pressured into organizing into a community, which they had not been since their exodus from Egypt" (p. 484). For while admitting the precious drive derived from his Jewish background, he did not recognize in Judaism a living reality, a concrete existence in which the Jew, isolated and disoriented, could steep himself to regain his equilibrium. Yet, on many occasions he had the opportunity to observe the maladjustment, the deep uncertainty of his type of Wandering Jew, freed of any tangible tie with his people and scattering his genius to every wind. He had known the profound tragedy of his friend Sigmund Freud, who had detached himself from his people to the point of trying to take away its greatest man, Moses *(Der Mann Moses* [1938]) and yet whose unorthodox theses were attacked as an expression of his race. He was on intimate terms with Rathenau, the greatest statesman of the Weimar Republic, and the most intelligent man of Zweig's acquaintance. "Verhaeren, Ellen Key, Bazalgette were not a tenth as smart, not a hundreth as universal, as sophisticated as he, but they had self-confidence. With Rathenau I always felt that he, with his immense intelligence had no ground under his feet" (p. 213). The lack of a stable base, of a solid support, made of Rathenau a contradictory figure. He felt Jewish, but confessed to a secret inclination for Jesus Christ. He was a millionaire who favored socialism, a businessman mad about the arts. This lack of consistency is the fate of many uprooted Jews, the fate of Stefan Zweig himself.

However, he also met coreligionists of a different temper, who exuded extraordinary serenity and self-assurance. Foremost among them was Theodor Herzl, the founder of the Zionist movement. Herzl had come from the same Viennese background as Zweig and had engaged in a career that held promise of being as brilliant. But the problems raised by the Dreyfus Affair gave his life a different twist, and he was dedicated to rallying the scattered forces of Judaism in order to weld them into a national synthesis that would capitalize on energies wasted in isolation. The Jewish spirit expressed itself in him in ways different from Zweig's generous but undirected drives. This elegant writer of the Viennese school grew in stature until he assumed the powerful image of a man chosen by destiny for its own designs. When Herzl died in his prime, consumed by the spark that he had cast into the world, Zweig was briefly excited by this farseeing idealist: "Suddenly Vienna realized that not just a writer or a mediocre poet had died, but rather one of those shapers of ideas, who triumphantly rise up in a people or nation only at very rare intervals.

When he met Herzl, Zweig met his destiny face to face. Herzl discovered Zweig thanklessly. Literary editor of the influential newspaper *Neue Freie Presse,* he accepted unreservedly the first essay of the young student Zweig, thus opening the door to a distinguished literary career. However, he did not succeed in drawing him to an ideal transcending literature. It was only at the end of his life that Zweig realized that the view of reality that Herzl was showing him was more important for him than literature (p. 211).

His confession resembles that of André Maurois when, after the French débâcle of 1940, he recalled his interview with Churchill a few years before the war. Churchill had begged him in vain to give up art for art's sake, and to write a daily page on the dangers that were threatening his country. Zweig, too, with few exceptions, confined himself to aesthetic contemplation. Otherwise, he would have understood Freud's warning that civilization was only a thin crust threatened by an eruption of destructive passions simmering under the surface; and that of Herzl, who insisted that Judaism, far from evaporating in historical memories and spiritual attitudes, existed as a burning issue calling for a rational solution, If every day he had written a page to explain Herzl's ideas to the vast audience whose attention he commanded, perhaps the Jewish question would not have taken the tragic proportions that we witnessed. At least, the Jewish homeland in Israel would have developed sufficiently to serve as a material and spiritual refuge to the shipwrecked existences of European Jews, where people like Zweig would not have felt alienated. He would not have been forced to abjure his European ideal, but as in Anteus's myth, would have found new strength in the contact with the land of the prophets.

Let this be said without any aspersions on Zweig's work and lofty spirit. He did not discover any new lands. He was a child of his own century, "die Welt von gestern" (the world of yesterday). He was its witness, chosen perhaps by fate to bring out the tragic error of a generation blinded by its pride and unaware of the numerous problems facing it. Unfortunate generation, lost at every crossroad, leaving us a heavy inheritance, but also the clear knowledge of our mission in the future.

Another writer understood better than Zweig the direction in which the Jew must proceed. The poet André Spire was able to formulate for the Jewish generation the ideal that will help it survive the collapse of the old Continent: "Ce demain éternel qui marche devant moi" (This eternal tomorrow that walks before me).

# 15

# From Symbolism to Zionism: The Spiritual Itinerary of André Spire

André Spire's literary initiation resembles that of Stefan Zweig. When he started to devote his *Essays* to the Jewish question, essays that were collected for the first time in 1913 *(Quelques juifs,* [Paris, 1913]; *Quelques juifs et demi-juifs,* 2 vols. [Paris, 1928]), he was a veteran writer. His name was better known in French literary circles than among Jews. It was rather belatedly that he began to study, to celebrate Jewish life, to take an active interest in the problems of Judaism. In other words, his identification with Judaism is the conclusion of a long evolution. At the beginning, we find a French poet of Jewish origin concerned mainly with poetic and technical problems that had occupied the first symbolist generation, and that the second generation, somewhat wearied by fifteen years of struggle, abandoned or left in abeyance. To maintain, to perfect, to give a solid rhythmical framework to free verse, this magnificent creation of the symbolist revolution that the supple, fluid aesthetic had left a little weak and spineless, was the core of his literary activity.

Eventually a new element was added to his personality, a new source opened up in him, invigorating the robust tree on which he had been a simple leaf.

Spire was born in Nancy in 1868. He was the descendant of one of those Jewish families that had settled there more than a century before 1789. We know that these privileged Jews had a tendency to identify with their French compatriots rather than with their fellow Jews. The atmosphere that prevailed in Jewish circles in Lorraine corresponded to André Spire's description in his essay on James Darmsteter: "They identified intimately with their country. Through patriotism they even came to lack in humanity. Sometimes they coldly received the wretched Jews from Poland and Russia, and even the Alsatian Jews, who requested asylum for a few days in Lorraine. To claim, as the opponents of the assimilation of the Jews were already doing, that the scattered elements of Israel were only one nation was an insult to them." (*Quelques juifs,* 1:220). Spire's Jewish education was about nonexistent. Without the Panama Affair, Boulangism, and the anti-Semitism of Drumont that resulted from it, he would have had no more Jewish interests than those of the Jewish writers he criticizes in his essays and his poetry. But his life was to take a different direction.

He was studying in Paris for his law doctorate and the competition for the *Conseil d'État,* which he passed at the end of 1893, when the working class decimated by the Communes of 1871 was beginning to stir. There did not yet exist any effective social legislation to protect it against the growing appetite of the industrial class to which André Spire belonged through his family ties. Demonstrations, riots, and anarchist attacks attracted public attention to the desperate plight of the proletariat. André Spire's eyes were opened. Like Britling's, they began to see clearly. Up until then, he had considered himself a liberal bourgeois. Now overwhelming facts showed him that he had to commit himself either for or against the working people. The philanthropy of previous generations seemed to the young generation a mere collection of worthless palliatives. The student refused to settle for peaceful work in a quite school atmosphere. He introduced passionate life in the impassive legal world and in the so-called eternal laws of this pseudo-science: political science. The thesis that earned him his doctorate of law bore the title *Responsibility of Municipalities in Case of Disorderly Assembly,* and it is devoted in part to the anarchist attacks of 1891-92.

Spire was now starting to lean toward socialism without, however, joining any organized party. He followed instead the social conscience that was so strong in French intellectual youth, strengthened in him by the tradition and the example of his family. This is when he produced the poems *Et Vous riez? (And You Are Laughing?).* It is a cry of anguish and pity for the suffering and the squalor of the people, as well as a reaction of disgust against the ''élite,'' oblivious to the misery that its privileges had brought to the world. He felt an intimate communion with the common people, but he wanted a strong and cultured people, participating in the life of the spirit. He hated the role of the patronizing intellectual who thinks he is serving the masses by lowering himself to their level, and adopting their manners and their tone, for the masses were inevitably backward, robbed of all energy for education, organization, and militancy by overwork and the loss of even the legal weekly day off. The poems in *Et Vous riez?* express Spire's disappointment in his socialist hopes and in his relationship with the socialist leaders (''En Mission'' [On a Mission], ''Au Peuple'' [To the People], ''Bataille'' [Fight], ''Paix Sociale'' [Social Peace]). In the poem ''Au Peuple'' is felt his sincere but helpless sympathy. Sincerity there was, but weakness too, in spite of the claim of leading a vigorous life:

> Non, je ne chanterai pas pour toi, Peuple,
> Grand peuple dépouillé, grand peuple malheureux,
> Nous n'irons plus troubler ta torpeur résignée.
> Sans remords de nous être arrachés de toi-même,
> Nous irons loin de toi mener nos fortes vies.
> Mais, n'oubliant jamais d'où nous sommes sortis,
> Nous irons nous grouper, parfois sur ton passage,
> Et tristement pleurer sur ton destin tragique,
> O fleuve infortuné de germes avortés.

> No, I will no longer sing for you, People,
> Great dispossessed people, great wretched people.
> We will no longer disturb your resigned lethargy.
> Without remorse for having torn ourselves from you,
> We are going to lead far from you our vigorous lives.

But, never forgetting where we came from,
We will sometimes gather as you pass,
And sadly cry over your tragic fate,
Oh, unfortunate river of aborted seeds.

Spire became a conventional member of his time. After his socialist inclinations had been rebuffed, he sought only to celebrate the sky and the earth, the cities and the rivers of the "adorable land" from which he drew his exuberant *joie de vivre*. René Lote is right in writing: "The Jew André Spire is also one of us. . . .He is a wealthy provincial bourgeois, from Lorraine, a province of the East, where the bourgeois is ceremonious and traditionalist as nowhere else in France." Yes, Spire had many old French characteristics. He felt, then, only as a Frenchman, a faithful son of France's rich earth, the land of golden wheat, of thrift, and easy living. He loved life in all its colors. His senses were open to all the beauty of the world. The delights and the pains of love were to remain his favorite subjects throughout his life. Other themes added only variations. Several collections of poems, from *La Cité présente (The Presence of the City)* to *Poèmes de la Loire (Poems of the Loire),* reflect this happy intimacy with the French landscape. Spire also felt bound with all the fibers of his being to the cultural life of France, the legitimate heir to Greek civilization. He read and reread the poets, first the Parnassians, and later the symbolists. But his poetic ambitions went beyond their aesthetic preoccupations, often precious and pseudo-archaic. He took from them only the technique of free verse, in which he wrote most of his poems, and of which he became, with Robert de Souza, the guardian, the perfecter, and the theoretician.

His conviction that he owed everything to France and nothing to the religious community of his ancestors did not last long. He was twenty-five years old when a series of extraordinary events took place that transfigured the social and moral character of France and gave a slap in the face to French Judaism, mesmerized by too long a string of successes, and too forgetful of its origins.

French Jews had thought that they had to pay for their emancipation by a hurried assimilation. They did not realize that France, unlike other nations, did not intend to impose uniformity on its children. The creativity of the French people comes precisely from the fact that many elements cooperated in its birth. France is a crucible in which the most diverse ingredients have blended into a superior unity. "A Montaigne, a Proust, a Bergson," writes Albert Thibaudet, "introduced in our complex and rich literary world what might be called the Franco-Semitic doublet, just as there are Franco-English, Franco-German, Franco-Italian doublets, just as France herself is a doublet of the North and the South" *(Nouvelle Revue Française* [January 1923], p. 138). I will return to this question later. Let us note meanwhile that it is not impossible that the anti-Semitic reaction was caused, in part, by the Jews' attempt to change their personality abruptly and completely. At any rate, the Dreyfus Affair had on the best circles in France, both Jewish and non-Jewish, the happy effect of a moral reawakening. Spire himself had no liking for a man who represented the super-assimilated Jew. Only after the Zola trial was he convinced of the innocence of Captain Dreyfus, and then his life underwent an upheaval. A literary event soon deepened the crisis.

Toward the end of 1894, Charles Péguy published in his famous *Cahiers de la Quinzaine* a translation of *Had Gadya* by Israel Zangwill. The hero of this prose poem is a Venetian Jew. After a long pleasure and study trip he comes back to his father's house. By chance, it happens to be Passover night. He comes into the big dining room of the Palazzo, where his father is in a dress suit, reclining, as his ancestors had done for three thousand years, on the ritual cushions, and celebrating the *seder* surrounded by his family. The contrast between the dazzling and skeptical world where he has lived as a dilettante, and the solemn calm of this ancient holiday, raises in him a multitude of questions, problems, and remorse. He feels that his soul is Jewish, can be only Jewish. And yet, will he have the strength to resume this Jewish life that he is sorry to have ignored and abandoned? He quietly leaves the room and descends the marble stairs to the wharf, where one by one the steps submerge by the canal. Just as he goes under for the last time, the words of the dying Jew rise to his mouth as it fills with water: "Listen, Israel, the Lord our God, the Lord is One."

Spire described the impression that the reading of this poem produced on him and a small number of other cultured Jews. *Had Gadya* played the role of a crystal in a supersaturated liquid, and in some particularly sensitive souls it brought on crying spells, emotional upheavals, conversions. Among the weak or the busy, the conversions were short-lived. Among others, they were permanent, changing the direction of their lives, giving birth to a vocation. French Jews who had lost all contact with Jewish life, who were almost completely ignorant of Jewish history, began to study them with enthusiasm. Gradually, instead of trying to disguise their Jewishness, they felt the need to express it, to celebrate it. Jewish poems, Jewish novels, and Jewish plays appeared. A Jewish literature in the French language was born (cf. chap. 8), and it was not confined to Jewish writers, but also attracted Christians, fascinated by the color of Jewish mores, and alarmed by the ominous problems raised by the existence of Jewish minorities amid Christian people in Eastern Europe and the Balkan Peninsula *(Quelques Juifs et demi-juifs,* Foreword, p. viii).

Zangwill's influence on André Spire would not have been so profound nor so permanent had his spirit not been predisposed to receive it. Education brings us nothing, says Lessing; it only helps us to attain what our nature would have attained anyway, but after many a detour. What predisposed André Spire to accept Zangwill as his master was his strong social conscience, and not what is strange and colorful in the ghetto. After his despair at not having been able to save a lethargic working class from itself, selfish in its resignation, he found, thanks to Zangwill, masses that, far from surrendering to a tragic destiny, had salvaged and carried with them in their migrations a passion for learning and for reading, and an obsession with eternal philosophical problems. He dedicated the first Jewish poems that he wrote from 1905 to 1908, during or soon after the first Russian revolution, to the Jewish proletariat, "the only proletariat for which there is still hope."

He did not fight for the Jewish cause condescendingly, removed from the wretches whose defense he undertook. He closely identified with them. He, the French bourgeois, empathized with the state of mind of the persecuted Jews in tzarist Russia. His past indignation against those who were still able to laugh in this imperfect world became more intense. The conflict that existed at the beginning of his career between his socialist leanings and his bourgeois environment reappeared, but sharper, transposed to another level; his personal conflict became symbolic. That is what makes a true poet.

A poetic vision that he had at his time in his life will indicate more clearly the nature of this dualism. One day around Easter, 1905, he saw on the southern portals of the Cathedral of Strasbourg two statues of pink sandstone that symbolized the Church and the Synagogue. The Church was standing wearing a crown, looking at the Synagogue without a crown, downcast, blindfolded, mournful, grasping in one hand her broken spear, while trying to hold on with the other the tablets of the Law slipping away from her. The young Law victorious, facing the old Law, defeated, dethroned. And suddenly he realized that he, who could continue to live in the kingdom of pleasure, also had to see the underside of things, where others saw only the radiant façade. Beauty seemed to him a luxury, luxury an abomination, and his diversions a theft.

These were his roots. His social conscience did not come from transitory feelings of generosity; it was the historical legacy of Judaism thirsting for justice that henceforth spoke consciously in him and opposed the naïve *joie de vivre* that we have encountered in his poems. It is the old conflict between Hellas and Judea that was reenacted in him under the modern form of the conflict between the Frenchman and the Jew. I must now elucidate the idea of "conflict," since it lends itself easily to misunderstanding.

There is a dualism that sooner or later must emerge in the European Jew when he realizes the polarity of his being. Those who do not experience this conflict are neither good Jews nor good Frenchmen. The abstraction "French citizen" does not belong to the ideology of France. Its people is composed of Normans, Provenceaux, and Gascons, each with its psychological idiosyncrasies, but all together forming a spiritual whole. The French Jew, even though he is a French citizen, retains his individuality. It is not by repudiating his origins that he becomes a better patriot. Such an assimilation remains superficial, according to Molière:

> Ce n'est point du tout la prendre pour modèle
> Que de tousser et de cracher comme elle.

> It is not at all taking her as a model
> To cough and spit like her.

Real assimilation consists in a synthesis of the two aspects of the soul of the French Jew. This synthesis is of necessity preceded by a conflict particularly acute in a superior intellect.

These two poles of Spire's soul are clearly reflected in his poem "A la France" (To France). He begins with a tribute to this land that has absorbed so many races, to the French spirit of reason, lightheartedness, balance, and serenity. And he feels half conquered by the kindly atmosphere that envelops him. Something in him, however, rebels against this superficial assimilation:

> Politesse, moi aussi, tu voudrais m'affadir!
> Blague, tu voudrais jouer à rétrécir mon âme!
> O chaleur, ô tristesse, ô violence, ô folie,
> Invincibles génies à qui je suis voué,
> Que serais-je sans vous? Venez donc me défendre
> Contre la raison sèche de cette terre heureuse.

> Courtliness, you would like to dull me also!
> Joke, you would like to play at shrinking my soul!
> Oh warmth, O sadness, O violence, O madness,
> Invincible genii to whom I am pledged,
> What would I be without you? Come and defend me
> Against the sterile reason of this happy land.

This other element that he notices in his soul ceases to paralyze him. He begins to feel his horizons broaden and his heart grow fuller as he becomes aware of the other component of his being. And, although he has not stopped yearning for stability, his anxiousness and melancholy become dear to him. Sometimes he speaks to the fertile soil of France:

> . . .Je t'aime. Je reste ici,
> Je vais découvrir une à une tes fermes;
> Les lignes de tes bois;
> Le secret de la noblesse de tes eaux.
> Je ne veux plus, comme un passant que l'on tolère,
> M'accouder, m'émerveiller, puis repartir.
> Je veux être ton maître, et dire de tes arbres,
> De tes fruits, de tes racines, de tes graines, de tes mottes,
> Et des fils d'araignée eux-mêmes qui se courbent
> Sous le poids brilliant du matin:
> C'est à moi.

> . . . .I love you. I remain here;
> One by one, I am going to discover your farms,
> The lines of your woods,
> The secret of the nobility of your waters.
> No more do I want, like a tolerated passer-by
> To lean, marvel, and leave.
> I want to be your master, and say about your trees,
> Your fruit, your roots, and your sod,
> And even your cobweb bending
> Under the brillant weight of the morning:
> They are mine.

This enjoyment and this possession are not made for men like him, however. Not yet! And his land answers him:

> J'aime à fixer les hommes,
> Mais j'ai peur des regrets de ton âme mobile.

> I like to settle men,
> But I am afraid of the regrets of your restless soul.

Yes, the Jew brings a disturbing element wherever he appears, even though he has been reassured by centuries of assimilation and calm, for he feels they are transitory. This fact, above all, makes him suspect, and creates an abyss between him and European society that makes it impossible for distinction to disappear. Perhaps it is not his religion, his race, his mores, that the world distrusts. No, he is held responsible for threatening the comfort of daily life. The little poem "Tu as raison" (You Are Right) illustrates his uniqueness in a rapid vision.

> . . .C'est pour ton thé; c'est pour ton bridge;
> Pour ton dîner; pour ton théâtre;
> Pour ta chère tranquillité.
> Et tu as raison, entre nous,
> D'avoir un peu peur, camarade!
> Car ils ne vivent que de fièvre,
> Mes deux antiques protecteurs:
> Mon inquiétude, ma tristesse.

> . . .It's for your tea; it's for your bridge;
> For your dinner; for your theater;
> For your cherished tranquillity.
> Just between us, you are right
> To be a little afraid.
> For they live only on fever,
> My two ancient protectors:
> My anxiousness, my sadness.

It is not lightly that the poet calls these distinctive traits of the Jewish people his ancient protectors. Indeed, they protect it against complacency, against satisfaction in an imperfect world. The anxiety of the Jew comes from the subconscious awareness of his mission, his messianism kept alive by external circumstances.

The Jewish Messiah is distinguished from the Christian Messiah by the fact that the former is an ideal yet to be accomplished, while the latter has already come to pass. For the Christian, God has already sent his heavenly messenger to earth; for the Jew, man must continuously rise and earn Heaven by his own powers, by the divine powers that exist potentially in him. In addition, Jewish messianism is distinguished from Hellenism in that the Greeks aspired to the complete possession of the present in the serenity of classical perfection, which implies the sacrifice of unlimited perfectibility. Jewish messianism is contemptuous of this smug, lethargic well-being that Nietzsche calls "Das erbaermliche Behagen" (that wretched comfort).

A better tomorrow is the hope of peace for all men, not merely an élite. But this peace is not exactly the one the Prophet Isaiah envisions, which André Spire describes not without a touch of irony:

> Le loup habitera avec l'agneau
> Et la panthère se couchera à côté de la chèvre,
> La vache et l'ours auront le même pâturage.
> Le lion comme le boeuf mangera de la paille,
> Et un petit enfant les conduira.
>
> Samael 3:5
>
> The wolf will live with the lamb,
> And the panther will lie down beside the goat,
> The cow and the bear will share the same pasture.
> Both the lion and the ox will eat straw,
> And a little child will lead them.

Above all, man must not settle for regretting and yearning for a mythical golden age located at the beginning of the world. Peace is a harmony to be achieved by a mighty struggle. Only this struggle will give the goal its dignity. The comfort of repose is measured only by the harshness of the struggle. A utopian paradise is but surfeit and the dulling of the appetite. The life that does not have to be conquered every day is not worth living. Thus, unlike the tradition that considers the disappearance of Eden the punishment for the sin of disobedience, André Spire maintains that the worst of sins, the original sin, is precisely regret for the golden age.

> Adam:
> Non, nous ne mourrons pas.
> La mort c'était hier, dans ce jardin fermé,
> Lorsque nos jours égaux passaient d'un pas égal,
> Lorsque nous nous quittions sans crainte l'un pour l'autre
> Et pouvions nous revoir sans défaillir de joie.
> Lorsque notre travail n'était qu'un geste vain;
> Quand nous étions sans soif, sans fatigue, et sans faim,
> Et sans faim l'un de l'autre.
>
> Samael 1:2
>
> Adam:
> No, we will not die.
> Death was yesterday in this closed garden,
> When our uniform days went by evenly,
> When we parted without fear for each other,
> When we could meet again without breathless joy.

When our work was only a vain gesture;
When we were without thirst, without weariness, without
  hunger,
And without hunger for each other.

Popular imagination created the figure of the Wandering Jew, whose instability is considered a punishment. A nature as dynamic as Spire's can only oppose such an attitude. Instead, he exalts Jewish restlessness. He who even in his youth had cried: "Do you think that I accept the established order," increasingly discovered in himself all that provokes in the complacent bourgeois cries of indignation and fear. He knew henceforth that his individual existence bore and nurtured a germ that had lived for thousands of years before him, that would live after him, and that linked him in time and space to a great mission: Israel. What he felt only instinctively at the beginning, now became a clear awareness: the awareness that he could not ignore his historical origin, that, on the contrary, by developing his distinctiveness, he would transform a paralyzing dualism into creative tension. Thus this poet, who will never stop loving France and celebrating its glories, acquired, nevertheless, feelings of brotherhood and loyalty to Israel that constitute a most beautiful confession of faith:

> . . .O mes frères, ô mes égaux, ô mes amis,
> Peuple sans droits, peuple sans terre;
> Nation, à qui les coups de toutes les nations
> Tinrent lieu de patrie,
> Nulle retraite ne peut me défendre de vous. . .
> Avec vous je suis fort, je suis sûr avec vous.
> Prenez-moi, rêvons ensemble, parlons ensemble
> De ce temple détruit que nous aimons toujours. . .


> . . .Oh! my brothers, oh! my equals, oh! my friends,
> People without rights, people without land;
> Nation for whom the blows of all nations
> Took the place of a homeland,
> No retreat can defend me from you. . .
> With you I am strong, I am secure with you,
> Take me, let us dream together, let us talk together
> Of that destroyed temple that we still love. . .

*Rêves juifs (Jewish Dreams)*

Spire did write a number of poems that on the surface had nothing to do with Judaism. These are poems that express his conception of the world, such as "Personnalisme," "Du Solide," "Immortalité," and many more scattered in all his collections, and in particular in *Vers les routes absurdes (Toward the Absurd Roads)* and *Le Secret.* His conception is not, however, that of a religious Jew. He takes an ironical view toward this God that men made in their own image. He despises the masses' tendency to anthropomorphize God and nature:

> Ah! ils vous donnent une pauvre âme humaine,
> A vous, et à leurs dieux!
>
> *Le Secret,* "Personnalisme"

> Ah! they give you a poor human soul,
> To you and to their gods!

His God is not the kind one prays to, questions, from whom one expects signs:

> Il leur faut des réponses!
> Il ne leur suffit pas d'avoir les yeux ouverts,
> Béants toutes choses;
> De chercher, de chercher toujours;
> D'aimer tout,
> Et la fleur, et l'agneau,
> Et le miel, et le boeuf, et l'azur, et les cimes,
> Et, derrière les soleils, les grandes forces secrètes.
> Il leur faut du palpable,
> Du carré, du solide. . . .
>
> "Du Solide"

> They need answers!
> They are not satisfied to have their eyes wide open,
> To marvel at all things;
> To seek, forever to seek;
> To love all things,
> The flower and the lamb,
> The honey and the ox, and the azure skies, and the mountain
> tops,

And beyond the suns, the great secret forces.
They need something palpable,
Something square, something solid. . . .

His God is greater. He does not conceptualize him, he does not imagine him. He sees him and touches him with all his senses, his whole body, his entire soul:

Les étoiles qui vont s'allumer tout à l'heure!
C'est à moi cette terre, et tous ces univers,
A moi, l'homme, l'unique, merveille des merveilles,
Pour aujourd'hui, ce soir, ces bruits, ce mouvement,
Et pour demain, toujours, d'autres béatitudes! . . .
Pour moi! Ah! jurez nuages bienfaisants,
Renaissantes lumières,
Et toi, mer immortelle, sur qui Platon, Philon, et saint Paul
    naviguèrent.

"Immortalité"

The stars that are soon going to light up!
It is to me that this earth, that these worlds belong,
To me, man, unique, the wonder of wonders,
For today, tonight, these sounds, this movement,
And for tomorrow, forever, other beatitudes! . . .
For me! Ah! swear comforting clouds,
Lights reborn,
And you, immortal sea, on which Plato, Philo, and Saint Paul
    sailed.

His passionate love of life:

Chante vie, ils te calomnient
Ceux qui cherchent plus loin que toi.

Sing life, they slander you
Those who seek beyond you

makes us think of the sensitivity of an André Gide, whose work is a hymn to life. In other words, Spire's religion is a Spinozist pantheism, in which the love of God consists of a love for all the "modes" of nature, for all the concrete expressions of the great unknowable secret.

> Foudre, chaleur, amour, lumière,
> Par où Dieu nous parle et nous mène
> Sans signes, sans ordres, sans visions. . . .

> Thunderbolt, heat, love, light,
> Through which God speaks to us
> Without signs, without orders, without visions.

And yet, even though these poems do not belong to the major currents of historical religions, they are not so foreign to the Jewish spirit as they seem, at least to some of the most religious aspects of the Jewish soul. They are Jewish not by the subject, but by the inspiration. Spire is not concerned with the concrete forms through which Judaism expressed its notion of the sublime. It is this notion itself that forms the basis of his religious sentiment. The first commandment, "Thou shalt not make unto thee any graven images or any likeness of anything that is in heaven above," implies Spire's struggle against anthropomorphism. The revelation on Mount Sinai had given the idea of an ultrapersonal God on which Maimonides and Spinoza erected their philosophical and scientific systems. Here is the origin of the attitude of our poet, as well as Zangwill's. We can't even speak of Zangwill's influence. It is more a case of affinity stemming from the same understanding of Judaism.

Thus André Spire's Jewish feeling is not contained only in his Jewish poems. It is scattered in all his works. There is not a single poem that does not express the instinctive reaction of a French Jew before the modern world. The boldness with which this French poet proclaimed his Jewishness at a time when more than one Jewish writer disguised his background or apologized for it was indicative of the direction that his evolution was to take. We have seen dim emotions transformed into a lucid awareness of his Jewish legacy, reaching finally the enthusiastic tribute, the expression of solidarity with the pariahs of European society. Once this attitude had become solidified, it was the starting point of an active program for the benefit of his coreligionists. Spire became a member of the executive committee of the Jewish Territorial Organization, founded by Zangwill to acquire land and administrative autonomy for those Jews who did not want to or could not live in the countries where they lived or had been born. In 1917 the Balfour Declaration transformed Spire into a militant Zionist. He founded the League of the Friends of Zionism, to which belonged eminent personalities, both Jewish and gentile. He published a magazine, *La Nouvelle Palestine,* gave propaganda lectures, and in 1919 played an important role in the Zionist delegation to the peace conference. His passionate words denounced those who continued to revere a dead past and those whose attitude was still that of the ghettos *("Pogromes"),* and celebrated a new dawn for a rejuvenated people.

This return to the ancient Jewish homeland was not for Spire a return to biblical history, He felt that Israel did not necesarily have to resume her history at the point where it had been interrupted 2,000 years before. Since then Israel had grown. It was only the servility that he wanted to eradicate, not the positive values that the Wandering Jew encountered among the nations of Europe. Israel had to become once more

> Un peuple saint, un peuple pur,
> Aux flancs féconds,
> Aux pensées chastes, au droit austère,
> Mais qui a tant appris sur les routes du monde
> Qu'il n'aura plus peur de son vieux péché,
> Et qu'il laissera ses yeux indulgents
> Jouir du mouvement, des lignes, des formes
> Que jadis il nommait une abomination;
> Un peuple où il y aura des pères et des mères,
> Mais aussi des garçons amoureux
> Et des jeunes filles dansantes,
> Des fronts tenaces, des mains vaillantes,
> Mais des mains caressantes aussi,
> Qui sauront disposer les soies et les laines,
> Qui broieront les couleurs, pétriront la glaise,
> Et glorifieront dans le marbre,
> Ta beauté, Israël.

> A holy people, a pure people,
> With a fruitful womb,

With chaste thoughts, with austere laws,
But that learned so much on the roads of the world
That it will no longer be afraid of its old sin,
That it will allow its indulgent eyes
To enjoy movement, line, form
That in the past it called an abomination;
A people where there will be fathers and mothers,
But also boys in love,
And dancing girls,
Stubborn foreheads, valiant hands,
But also caressing hands
That will know how to arrange silk and wool,
That will grind colors, knead clay,
And glorify in marble
Your beauty, Israel.

These beautiful lines extolling the ideal of the people of the prophets enriched by European civilization, Jewish ethics enriched by Greek aesthetics, also express the happy synthesis of the French poet and his Jewish origins. There is no dichotomy in his soul. The two poles of his personality are no longer hostile, but complementary. They no longer paralyze his creative impulses. By endorsing Zionism, he does not betray his French homeland. Nor does he betray the cause of Zionism by not living in Palestine because of his many cultural and personal ties in France. He found the solution that is incumbent on all Jews who cannot leave their native land or adopted country to go to Israel. The synthesis that Spire found as a French Jew must be adapted to their own conditions by the English and American Jews.

To his own conditions, for truth is not anodyne, easy, ready made. It must be willed, created, slowly conquered, in pain, in grief, at the cost of all our resources. But he who has found it, who has overcome obscurity and doubt, reaches a state of happiness far truer, greater, and nobler than the memory of the naïve, simplistic bliss of the Edenic legend.

The integration of the Jewish element into European thought and the enrichment of Judaism by European thought have been slow in the process of maturation, and at the cost of often painful tensions. May they result in a new harmony.

# 16

# The Disintegration of the German-Jewish Symbiosis

As I described in chapter 4 above, in the history of the Diaspora there is a period called the Golden Age. This was the time of the Jewish-Arabic symbiosis of the ninth to the twelfth century in Moorish Spain. Under enlightened caliphs, Arabs and Jews competed in all areas of political, social, and intellectual life, and developed that flourishing Semitic civilization that has been called a *Blütentraum* (Dream of Flowers) in the history of mankind.

This development seemed to be repeating itself in recent times when the doors of the ghettos opened and the emancipated Jews began to take part in the public life of their host countries to the full extent of their abilities, so long repressed. In Germany in particular in a period of 150 years, there grew a process of mutual influence, which had an undreamed-of effect on the intellectual life of the whole Diaspora. "Of all the relationships with other nations that Judaism has cultivated, none has been as fruitful as the German-Jewish one," said Martin Buber in 1933 on the occasion of the opening of the Frankfurt Jewish learning center. In that same year of earth-shaking upheavals, Karl Wolfskehl expressed the feelings of his

277

coreligionists about their homeland when he cried to the now de-
mented host nation:

> Euer Wandel war der meine,
> Eins mit Euch auf Hieb und Stich.
> Unverbrüchlich was uns eine,
> Eins das Grosse, eins das Kleine:
> Ich war Deutsch, und ich war Ich.

> Your life style was also mine.
> We were one through thick and thin.
> Indivisible that which united us,
> One in greatness, one in pettiness,
> I was German, and yet remained myself.

Franz Rosenzweig repeated this statement in simpler terms when he
said of himself, while reflecting on the German-Jewish problem:
"Being a Jew, far from making me a worse German, made me a
better one" (from his letters). In support of this claim, he mentions
that his main philosophical work, *The Star of Redemption,* will probably be regarded one day as a gift "that the German spirit owes to
its Jewish minority." He also maintains that the best book by the
philosopher Hermann Cohen sprang out "of the sources of
Judaism," that this great Neo-Kantian had developed a rational religion by the critical method, but based on the Jewish spirit.

Yes, they felt completely German and completely Jewish, these
heirs of Moses Mendelssohn. And just as the assimilation of Arabic
culture in the Golden Age had stimulated the development and flowering of Jewish disciplines, and reciprocally had led to an enrichment
of common cultural values, it was generally expected of the
Jewish-German symbiosis that it would result in a beneficial exchange for both partners, in an era of good feelings.

Nevertheless, in spite of this enthusiastic prognosis, there lingered
a certain uneasiness, which was progressively intensified until it became a concrete anxiety, even among those who had come nearest to
a rapprochement. "I see shadows appearing wherever I turn," laments Walter Rathenau, the Foreign Minister of the Weimar Republic; "I see them when I walk through the reverberating streets of Ber-

lin in the evening; when I experience the insolence of our now insane affluence. . .or when I hear of pseudo-German elitism.''

They all saw these ominous signs gradually appearing, the Jewish intellectuals, poets, and politicians. Even Hermann Cohen, a leading figure in German philosophy, felt compelled to make a melancholy ''confession about the Jewish question'': ''We younger people had indeed proudly felt that we would be successfully assimilated by the nation of Kant. . .that we could in time let the love of the fatherland speak through us without restraint, that we would be allowed to cooperate in the tasks of the nation with a sense of equality. This trust has been disappointed; the old oppressive anxiety has awakened again.''

Jakob Wassermann, the celebrated novelist, was ultimately discouraged about his fate as a German and as a Jew: ''It is useless to entreat 'the nation of thinkers and poets' in the name of these very thinkers and poets. Every prejudice presumably eliminated brings a thousand new ones to light, as carrion does worms. It is useless to turn the right cheek when the left one has been struck. . .they'll strike that one too. It is useless to live or to die for them. They say: 'He is a Jew.' '' Nelly Sachs, the Nobel prize winner, stood just as helpless against this German anti-Semitism as Wassermann:

> Warum die schwarze Antwort des Hasses
> auf dein Dasein, Israel?
> Im Chor der anderen
> hast du gesungen
> einen Ton höher
> oder einen Ton tiefer

> Why the dark answer of hate
> To your existence, Israel?
> In the chorus of the others
> You have sung
> One note higher
> Or one note lower.

Even the gentle, trusting Franz Rosenzweig limited his tenacious belief in the usefulness of intellectual collaboration to a resigned consolation: "Our work will be honored by Germany at very best posthumously," a statement that turned out to be, in the light of subsequent developments, a gruesome prophecy.

Visionary figures like the poetess Else Lasker-Schüler, who in her emotional outbursts seemed psychotic, gave unreserved expression to their *Weltuntergang* (doomsday) mood:

> Es ist ein Weinen in der Welt,
> Als ob der liebe Gott gestorben wär,
> Und der bleierne Schatten, der niederfällt,
> Lastet grabesschwer.

> There is a wailing in the world,
> As if the dear Lord Himself had died,
> And the leaden shadow descending,
> Feels as heavy as the grave.

Her people especially, for whose sufferings all measurement was missing on God's scales, was gripped by this sense of *Weltuntergang:*

> Und immer noch der Widerhall in mir,
> Wenn schauerlich gen Ost
> Das morsche Felsgebein,
> Mein Volk, zu Gott schreit!

> And still the reverberation in me,
> When toward the East, ghastly,
> That decaying skeleton of rock,
> My people, cries to God!

Thus the hopeful expectations of many generations of German Jews were clouded by tragic shadows even in moments of fulfillment. We therefore want to search for the reasons for the failure of a heroic effort that held so much promise.

From the beginning the Jewish situation in the midst of the German people was extremely schizophrenic because the Jewish people is composed of a perplexing combination of the intellectual aspirations of its elite and the unpredictable reactions of its easily influenced masses. There is a flagrant contradiction between lofty ideals and prosaic reality. This cleavage can best be exemplified from the early history of the Jews. The very origin of the Jewish people offers a graphic illustration of the sublimation of base appetites into spiritual goals, without which a people, just like an individual, does not reach maturity. It will be instructive to examine this process of maturation in the Jewish people and contrast it with the Germans' failure to find a *modus vivendi,* which failure proved so costly.

The revelation on Mount Sinai signifies the appointment of Israel as the bearer of God's highest ethical message to mankind. The proclamation of the Ten Commandments is not simply the beginning of ethical monotheism, it is also the zenith of religious ecstasy in the history of the nation of Israel. The power of religious fervor, to a certain extent the idealistic rise of a whole people to a God-inspired humanism, culminated in the sacred role of *Priestervolk,* priestly nation, for the present and all future generations.

How amazing then is the sudden fall of this people in worshiping the Golden Calf, in sinking into the depths of moral degeneration, in unrestrained debasement, in the reeling frenzy of an oriental *Walpurgisnacht.*

Everyday life stood in gross contradiction to spiritual revelation, to religious expression. In the light of such an abysmal fall, God was about to abandon this nation, recently called to the highest priesthood, to its destruction, to let it sink into historical insignificance. However, Moses the Liberator did not forsake his people. He had led it out of slavery to the summit of Sinai, but recognized that the greatest enthusiasm or the highest ideals offer no security from the powers of Satan, from the dark regions of human nature. And thus he undertook the endlessly difficult task of anchoring his doctrine in the soul of the people by exact prescriptions about daily life.

After announcing his goal on Sinai, he cleared the way to its achievement. The greatest of all prophets, who had raised an amorphous mass to the loftiest revelations, now became the humble guide and educator. That is his immortal monument in Israel. "Our teacher Moses" is his honorary title, rather than "Our prophet Moses," although his prophecies are of a more exalted nature, according to Maimonides, than those of all other prophets. In contrast with them, he measured the gap between ideal and real, and built a bridge from one bank to the other. Israel has been marching over the bridge through the centuries. Generations of teachers have worked to transform the essence of the revelations into the direct possession of the people. To carry out this mission is the noblest calling of the rabbi, regardless of his affiliation or orientation. "Tout le reste est littérature" (Everything else is irrelevant.)

The problem of the painful conciliation of idea and reality, of theory and practice, did not always encounter a solution among other people. They did not always find a formula like the Law of Moses to strike the proper balance between ethereal ideals and the oppressive pull of the earth. That applies especially to Germany. "Das Ideal und das Leben" (The Ideal and Life) is a famous poem by Friedrich Schiller in which the subject is those "happy regions where pure form alone dwells" beyond all the boundaries of human necessity. Schiller praises the flight "from this narrow, stifling life into the realm of the ideal," and the German people justly venerates him as the poetic advocate of the categorical imperative, of moral demands. He, the exponent of pure culture, was only the most popular figure in a series of scholars and intellectuals who put their stamp on the nineteenth century and earned for Germany the reputation of being "the nation of poets and thinkers." German science, philosophy, and technology led the whole world. And for the Jews who had settled in Germany generations earlier, indeed as early as the time of the wandering among nations, it was a noble challenge to test their own tradition, their own intellectual heritage against new methods and ideas and to reconcile both; thus, on the one hand, to become pace-setters in the intellectual expansion of their fatherland and, on the other, to found the science of Judaism by the application of modern scientific methods. This development was furthered by the influx from the Talmudic centers of Eastern Europe. The fusion of various types of minds resulted in dynamic stimulation and increased fecundity in all areas of knowledge.

Thus German-Jewish culture traveled an ascending road that led from Moses Mendelssohn, Lessing's friend and model of humanism, via Salomon Maimon, the first interpreter of Kant, and Hermann Cohen, his most original one, to Martin Buber, the exponent of Chassidism, and Leo Baek, the spokesman for modern Judaism. The movement set in motion by Moses Mendelssohn to combine the timeless ethos of Jewish tradition with the epoch-making ideas of his time and country infiltrated the most conservative Jewish circles. Even the Frankfurt Orthodox community, founded by S. R. Hirsch, with its uncompromising attitude in matters of religion and law, looked with possessive pride on the most famous citizen of its city, whose quotations from *Faust* thundered from the pulpit, an echo of the Goethe cult as it had existed even during the lifetime of that prince of poets, revived in the Jewish salons of Berlin.

If Goethe was the idol of the Jewish bourgeoisie, Schiller, on the other hand, became the inspiration of the Jewish proletariat. His advocacy of human rights reached even the textile workers in Lodz and the Talmudic scholars in Wilna. It quickened their hearts with its sound of Western ideas. The German language was indeed the only medium through which the Eastern Jewish masses became acquainted with the culture of Western Europe, since their colloquial tongue, "Yiddish" (a South German dialect pre-dating the origin of the German literary language), gave them access to German literature, and therefore to European culture in general. Thus Germany possessed, without realizing or paying attention to it, not to mention appreciating it, millions of good-will ambassadors, voluntary messengers of its own culture, first in the Slavic regions, and later in all parts of the world, wherever the Jews fled from czarism.

But was this the real Germany? The division of Germany into two zones did not originate after the Second World War. There had always been, in an intellectual sense, a region of thinkers and poets, of art and sciences, and another of the military and the Junkers, which dominated the government apparatus and therefore thought of itself as the sole embodiment of the state. "In what authority does Germany believe," asks Walter Rathenau; "in the authority of truth? No, in the authority of blood and legal power."

This cleavage between intellectual aspirations and sword-rattling militarism made it hard for the Jews living in the sector of German culture to find a harmonious balance between assimilation and self-assertion. Indeed, there were no defenders, followers, or interpreters of German thought and poetry more enthusiastic than the Jews. And how many German intellectuals of Jewish descent, how many German-speaking Jewish poets contributed to the worldwide prestige of their homeland? Without the "Thousand Year Reich" it would have been unthinkable that the library donated to a postwar American president by a group of publishers could contain only one work of world significance by a German author, for the number of famous German-Jewish writers was extensive: Max Brod, Stefan Zweig, Leon Feuchtwanger, Jakob Wassermann, Hugo von Hofmannstal, Arthur Schnitzler, Richard Beer-Hoffman, Joseph Roth, Else Lasker-Schueler, Nelly Sachs . . .

But at the same time they stood helpless before the sinister side of the German character, as I have observed in the utterances of the most convinced partisans of assimilation. In their dismay they were led to identify the German people with the symbolic concept *Amalek,* that is, according to biblical tradition, the implacable enemy of the Jews.

Thus the German people's spiritual dichotomy created in the Jews a tragic conflict, so stirringly expressed by Heinrich Heine at the beginning of Jewish emancipation. This enthusiastic interpreter of German Romanticism, a "thesaurus of German feelings," the greatest German lyric poet since Goethe, fled into Parisian exile, sick of unrequited love for his homeland, forced to warn the world against the dark recesses of the German national character, about its demonic powers, about "the Teutonic barbarism that would unquestionably break out and seek to destroy the world."

Heine's Cassandra-like cries died unheard, unheeded, or misunderstood. Only among a few of the great did they find a terrified echo. The bulk of Jewish citizens remained untouched by them, and sang with enthusiasm *Die Wacht am Rhein (The Watch on the Rhine).* That alone explains their surprise, their complete astonishment in the face of a development that led, first, to a Jewish, then soon after to a worldwide catastrophe. I do not use the word *catastrophe* lightly, for under Himmler and Freisler the nation of "Dichter und Denker" (poets and thinkers) was transformed into a nation of "Richter und Henker" (judges and hangmen), whose shocking deeds threaten to obliterate every other memory, just as in Pharoah's dream the thin cattle devoured the fat, without leaving behind the faintest vestige of it. Germany's national poet, Schiller, gives an ominous description in *Das Lied von der Glocke (The Song of the Bell)* of what was to become a gruesome reality under Nazi domination.

> Nichts Heiliges ist mehr, es lösen
> sich alle Bande frommer Scheu;
> Der Gute räumt den Platz dem Bösen,
> und alle Laster werden frei.
> Gefährlich ist's den Leu zu wecken,
> Verderblich ist des Tigers Zahn,
> Jedoch der schrecklichste der Schrecken,
> Das is der Mensch in seinem Wahn.
> Weh denen, die dem Ewigblinden
> Des Lichtes Himmelsfackel leihn!
> Sie strahlt ihm nicht, sie kann nur zünden,
> Und äschert Städt' und Länder ein.

> There is nothing holy anymore.
> All bonds of pious reverence are loosening;
> The good man surrenders his place to the bad,
> And all vices are set loose.
> It is dangerous to wake the lion,
> Destructive is the tiger's tooth,
> Yet the most dreadful of scourges
> Is man in his insanity.
> Woe unto them who lend
> The eternally blind the heavenly torch of light!
> It won't glow for him, it can only ignite,
> And reduce to ashes cities and nations.

Where were the great deeds of German culture in those critical times? Where, above all, were her pillars, the intellectuals, philosophers, and poets? The whole tragedy is based, alas, on this very fact—that they dwelt in higher regions, that German culture remained estranged from its people and academic in its greatest representatives, as did no other culture in the world; that it thrived in the isolation of a greenhouse, without taking root in the people and nourishing it. Intellectuals imagined that they served the absolute spirit if they meditated and wrote, removed from reality. They sought the blue flower of romanticism, the magical night, the "lunar luster which holds the senses captive," and gladly lingered in Utopia. Schiller was not unique in contrasting the Ideal and Life as irreconcilable opposites and giving the former his preference. The famous philosophers of German Idealism (Kant, Fichte, Hegel) also built glorious castles in the air, without translating their theoretical humanism into the language of practical reality, without even daring to tackle political and social problems, without protesting, enlightening, solving. The individual exceptions, like Jaspers, were deprived of university chairs, or, like Thomas Mann, were outlawed by the power structure. Art and science flourished in an ivory tower, and scorned those who concerned themselves with immediate questions, in contrast to France, for example, where the leading thinkers have their own column in the newspapers in order to comment regularly on current events and thus translate their *Weltanschauung* into everyday terms.

Yes, that was Germany's collision course. The thinkers emphatically chose otherworldliness and asceticism, soared to Olympic heights, indifferent to the political dance the false priests and prophets were performing around the Golden Calf, seducing a people waiting in vain for guidance from its intellectual leaders. It is no accident that the professors of philosophy, that is of true wisdom, with Martin Heidegger at their head, were the first to adapt in 1933. And thus the world witnessed to its boundless amazement, on the one hand a Germany of highly developed science, technology, philosophy, literature, and music, and on the other a country of primitive lust for military conquest, martial glory, and the intoxication of victory with its ugly accompaniments. Two souls coexisted, alas, in Germany, and split it into hostile camps. And in light of the misfortunes that were wreaked, in light of the unprecedented genocide, the survivors are left only with the eternal lament of Jeremiah, uttered anew in our time by Nelly Sachs:

Wer von uns darf trösten?
In der Tiefe des Hohlwegs
Zwischen Gestern und Morgen
Steht der Cherub
Mahlt mit seinen Flügeln die Blitze der Trauer
Seine Hände aber halten die Felsen auseinander
Von Gestern und Morgen
Wie die Ränder einer Wunde
Die offenbleiben soll
Die noch nicht heilen darf.
Nicht einschlafen lassen die Biltze der Trauer
Das Feld des Vergessens.
Gärtner sind wir,
Und stehen auf einem Stern, der strahlt
und weinen.


Which of us may furnish solace?
In the depth of the chasm
Between yesterday and tomorrow stands the cherub,
Painting with his wings the flashes of sadness.
His hands, though, hold the cliffs apart
Which are yesterday and tomorrow
Like the edges of a wound
Which will remain open
Which may not yet heal.
No, do not let the flashes of sadness fall into
The sleep of forgetfulness.
Which of us may furnish solace?
Caretakers are we,
And stand on a star that shines, and weep.


And we are still standing on the rubble of a ravaged world, even though the rubble of stone has long since been cleared away and has made way for magnificent, imposing palaces. For let no one succumb to deception. The worldwide prosperity and revelry, the rampages of angry youth, the general frenzy, are dances over graves, to drown out Hamlet's lament:

> The time is out of joint; O cursed spite
> That ever I was born to set it right.

But the world will be cursed much more severely if we do not succeed in setting it right, in reconstructing it humanely. The Jewish people is doing this in its own way, and the state of Israel, born of sweat, blood, and tears, is the visible sign of it. Its customary word of greeting, *Shalom,* is an expression of its innermost longing for peace with its immediate neighbors and Germany, for today all nations are neighbors.

The prerequisite is, of course, that Germany draw lasting and proper conclusions from its disastrous experience. The Jewish people, to be sure, is only a small pawn on the chessboard of world politics, but the purification of Germany's relations with even this small state will be a clear indication of Germany's true reconstruction.

"Overcome the past." The political intentions of the postwar German generation, now transformed into a slogan, must not be limited to the idea of financial compensation. Above all, Germans must not sun themselves in the self-righteous feeling of canceled debts and expiated guilt. The restitution of stolen goods is no gift, and we would all have gladly renounced all material reparations if we could have recovered our relatives, so senselessly sacrificed. But we dare not demand that the Germans of good will go around in sackcloth and ashes. The words of Ben-Gurion when he met Adenauer are still valid today: "The men who took over the inheritance of the Nazi Regime and rule postwar Germany are of good will, and their efforts to pay for the Nazi crimes are sincere."

It is extremely important, however, that the new spirit be not assumed by only a small circle of men of good will, without being firmly rooted in the people. The past to be overcome must not just refer to the "millennial calamity" of the twelve-year Reich, or be regarded as just a deeply regrettable historical accident over which the cloak of oblivion will be spread as quickly as possible. This past must extend over the whole evolution that led to the Third Reich. The whole nation must repudiate its whole history with a shudder. The Weimar Republic was a well-meant reaction to a recent catastrophe. But it collapsed unceremoniously because this reaction happened only outwardly, on a political plane rather than on that of ethics and a sound world-view, and therefore remained without influence on the people.

There is another graphic illustration of this situation, that of Spain, on whose territory the Jewish-Arabic symbiosis had taken place. Why did it have no continuation, why did it appear like a fairy tale from *The Arabian Nights?* Because the Spanish people, in the succeeding Christian era, failed to recognize the significance of the Jewish population for the economic and intellectual development of the nation, and by driving out the Jews robbed itself of a dynamic and socially equalizing element. The Spanish people is suffering to this day from this iniquity, since they could not overcome the medieval structure of their society, namely, the repression of the masses by a feudal class of barons and aristocrats who simply answer to other names today. The stifling influence of the feudal relationship prevented the full development of that great emancipation movement, the Renaissance, in spite of numerous geniuses from El Greco to Goya, from Cervantes to Unamuno, and aborted the democratic movement. Spain, once a leader in all areas, has become the most backward country in the Western hemisphere. And I do not hesitate to see in the expulsion of the Jews a cause of this stagnation. In like manner France was crucially weakened by the expulsion of the intellectually and economically active Huguenots.

This danger still threatens Germany through the loss of its Jewish element, through the disappearance of a highly developed segment of its population, even if the temporary economic boom disguises that fact. Indeed, Spain was also inundated by an abundance of gold in which it smothered its national conscience. It is therefore vital that the German people grasp this problem in its full historical scope as its own existential problem, and that it recognize the genocide of the Jews as its own and not just as a Jewish tragedy, as a loss to its own substance. To the perceptive observer, this is noticeable in many areas of intellectual creation. A Jewish settlement is even more important for that nation than for the Jews themselves, as a reminder to its own national conscience. Germany must not forget. Even the Berlin Wall should be recognized as a symbol not just of persecution but of guilt, not just as an accusation against oppressors, but as a wailing wall against which to bemoan collective acts of atrocity. If it signifies a tacit yet continual exhortation to self-criticism, then the incorruptible judgments and exposures of national abuses by thinkers and journalists should no longer be dismissed as "fouling one's own nest." The capacity for self-criticism would be a criterion of a mature democracy, a sign of the recovery of the German people, of the healing of its crippled soul, a start toward the construction of a new future, not only through their proverbial diligence and efficiency, but also through their poets and thinkers, from Kant to Jaspers, from Lessing to Heinrich Böll, from Moses Mendelssohn to Martin Buber.

This does not mean a revival of the ruined German-Jewish symbiosis. Too much has been destroyed that is simply irreplaceable, not only in terms of human lives, but of spiritual and intellectual affinities as well. It was in reference to these invisible ruins that Leo Baeck, an ardent supporter of that symbiosis, said wearily after his return from Theresienstadt: "For us Jews from Germany an era has ended. It was our belief that the German and Jewish spirits could meet on German ground and become a mutual blessing. That was an illusion. The Jewish period is irrevocably ended in Germany."

A historical epoch once ended cannot be revived. Those forces which helped to shape it have disappeared. What little remains has been transplanted to other shores on the Mediterranean, there to write a new page of Jewish history.

But given the new situation, the search for another form of understanding is imperative. History never stands still, and whoever clings to the past out of bitterness will be simply passed over by history. This is well known in Israel. It is aware that it must overcome understandable feelings of hate. Hate produces ugliness and destroys the spiritual equilibrium, so laboriously reconquered. The Jewish people is seeking peace of mind and soul though it is quite disturbed by all that happened to it, and forgiveness is just as painful a feeling as the moral development that is a prerequisite for a new Germany. Just how contradictory the Jewish position on this issue is can be seen by the Eichmann trial. On the one hand, when the atrocities were brought up, all the pain and bitterness dormant in the Jewish soul were revived. On the other hand, however, the Germans reporting the trial mentioned the openness and hospitality of Jewish circles. Similar things can be said of the assumption of his functions by the first German ambassador. After the first surge of pain, the will wrestled its way through to dialogue. Is it not written at the very beginning of history: "Thy name shall be no longer Jacob, but Israel, for thou hast wrestled with God, with thy better self, and hast been victorious."

This self-conquest in the spirit of the Bible was recognized by the worldly Lessing as a characteristic trait of the true believer, of the genuinely wise man, the spiritually wise man. He personified it in the figure of Nathan the Jew, who after a pogrom to which his whole family fell victim finds his way to a God-inspired humanism after the first wild rebellion against his gruesome fate:

> Doch nun kam die Vernunft allmählich wieder.
> Sie sprach mit sanfter Stimm: Und doch ist Gott!
> Doch war auch Gottes Ratschluss das! Wohlan!
> Komm! übe, was du längst begriffen hast;
> Was sicherlich zu üben schwerer nicht,
> Als zu begreifen ist, wenn du nur willst.
> Steh auf!"—Ich stand und rief zu Gott: Ich will!
> Willst du nur, dass ich will!

> Yet reason was gradually returning.
> It spoke in a gentle voice: "God exists after all!
> But this was also God's decree! So be it!
> Come! Practice what you have long realized.
> It is certainly no harder to practice
> Than to conceive, if only you are willing.
> Arise!" I arose and called to God: "I am willing!
> If that is your wish.

In daily practice this self-conquest expresses itself in hospitality toward the German youth, for instance, who come in growing numbers, be it through attempts at reconciliation or in organized study trips, to visit the land of the Bible and to meet the Israeli population. They discover that Jews neither can nor want to hate, for in every human contact Jewish bitterness dissolves into quiet pain, free of vengeful thoughts. The teachings of the prophets that children should not die for the sins of their fathers, that the innocent must not suffer for the guilty, is too ingrained in our people. This feeling for justice, inculcated in the Jews through a long process of development, explains our spontaneous rejection of collective German guilt. Only, to be sure, if the children free themselves of the sins of their fathers, turn away from them in disgust, and take upon themselves the crimes of the past as a national obligation of moral vigilance—vigilance toward the subterranean embers of neo-Nazi activities that continue to smoulder. Otherwise these words of the Scriptures will prevail: "I will visit the iniquity of the fathers upon the children unto the third and fourth generation of them that hate me."

In this new, laborious, but vitally necessary task of reconciliation, the present Jewish settlement in Germany must take the lead. In no way does it represent a continuation of the previous colony of German Jews. But as has often been the case in Jewish history, there has settled again, after all the expulsions in Europe, England, France, a Jewish community on German soil. For the spiritual leaders, it is irrelevant whether this development is sound or unhealthy. The Jewish settlement is a bastion of Judaism at large. It is our duty to organize and lead Jewish groups, wherever they form, whatever the circumstances, to feed, or at least awaken, their intellectual hunger, remembering the promise: "Wherever my name is honored I will come to thee and bless thee."

# 17

# Zeitgeist versus Eternal Values in Jewish Perspective

(A speech given at the German Protestant Church Convention in Düsseldorf under the motto: "Where did we come from?")

> Know where you come from and where you are going and to whom you must give account.
>
> —*Mishna,* "Awot" III, 1

We are guided in our thinking today by the question: "Where did we come from?" In order to know ourselves better, we must investigate our origins, the roots that nourished us.

This realization may have caused this church convention to direct its thoughts to the origin of Christianity, not looking back, like Lot's wife, but measuring the road already traveled and attempting to bring the new into harmony with the old. (The new is not always good just because it is new, and the good is not always new, albeit never old.) Even the dove in the story of the Flood had to keep returning to the Ark, its point of departure, which contained the life substance of a lost world and carried it over to a new era. Christianity, confronted with the turbulent events of our day, reexamines, as during the Reformation, the Old Testament, in order to draw vital strength from this source of ancient truth and religious revelation and resume with renewed energy the struggle with current problems.

Perhaps it was a serious mistake on the part of the Church to have neglected this, its most important foundation, or even to have risen against its immediate ancestor, like a child against its progenitor (and not only during the Middle Ages). Jesus and the Apostles lived and died as Jews; the first Christian congregations consisted of Jewish Christians. The Church is the legitimate descendant of the Synagogue. While daughters, delighting in their health and vigor, are often inconsiderate of their old mother, she, on the other hand, does not cease to boast of her children, who in spite of all differences, are still flesh of her flesh and spirit of her spirit, and perpetuate her teachings.

This was the view of Moses Maimonides, the greatest postbiblical authority of the Synagogue, to whom Thomas Aquinas often referred. May such mutual candor and tolerance guide this church convention as it plumbs its own depths, and lead it to a deeper understanding of the mission of Christianity. Judaism and Christianity are, willy-nilly, allies in a continuous, ruthless confrontation with the *zeitgeist* in its changing manifestations. The questions: *"What is the zeitgeist?"* and "What are the eternal values?" bring us to the subject of our discussion.

Every epoch faces new problems. Some arise through political and social developments, some through the birth of new concepts, some through scientific discoveries and technological inventions that deeply permeate public and private life. More difficult to handle than the practical aspects of the problems, however, are their ideological and moral implications. These can lead to extreme tensions. Goethe said:

> Was ihr den Geist der Zeiten heisst,
> Das ist am Ende nur der Herren eigener Geist.

> What you call the spirit of the times
> Is really just the spirit of the men in power.

Traditional values are to be opposed to the *zeitgeist.* I am referring to that treasure of wisdom and humane thought which is not subject to ideological fashions, but has an eternal validity. Traditional values are quickly regarded as anti-progressive and are discarded. The Church and Synagogue, by their very definition protectors of tradition, bearers of an ethical message derived from divine revelation or human experience going back to the dawn of history, find themselves in a seemingly hopeless position. And this applies even more now than it did in the Enlightenment, where biblical authority and authenticity were being universally challenged. In a century like ours, when so many empires have gone down to inglorious ruin, should not religion also be regarded as a decaying empire, ripe for destruction? Thus speaks the *zeitgeist,* a new generation convinced of the soundness of its views, and proud of its perceptions and its radical emancipation from tradition. Nevertheless, we should not scornfully reject these restlessly progressive forces, just as we do not condemn the Enlightenment out of hand and ignore its great achievements.

Judaism, especially under normal circumstances, does not disdain the demands of a new era. "Normal circumstances" means periods when it is not forced into the isolation of the ghetto, where, of necessity, it has to limit itself to maintaining the *status quo,* and therefore appears anti-progressive and otherworldly. Judaism is inherently open to progress. Indeed, it is not only accustomed to repeated changes in its long history, but many times has been instrumental in bringing them about. The world has always profoundly altered itself, as all life must. Only the dead remain immutable. Now, however, with the universal cultural revolution, the wheels of history are whirring at an accelerated tempo. Religion, to maintain its validity, must neither move backwards nor stand passively on the shore and watch the passing stream of events. Martin Buber's words apply to Judaism in every phase of its history:

> A religion only remains fruitful as long as it permeates its dogmas with new, fervent meaning, so that each generation feels that the revelation it receives is new and directed only to its particular problem.

That the Jewish people and its religion are still a vital force after almost four thousand years of existence is shown by the latest and most remarkable resurrection of Israel. This event can be traced directly to that impulse to creative renewal which has characterized Jewish dogma from the beginning. Judaism has always contributed to changing the constitution of the world and creating new and fruitful life-styles.

On the other hand, the bearers of Jewish doctrine have often had to stand against false, deceptive "progress." They have vehemently resisted these epidemic, fashionable ideologies, which do their best to contaminate the *zeitgeist*. I would like to illustrate this with some examples of Jewish contributions to the betterment of the world, taken from ancient and modern times.

The actual beginnings of Judaism are found in Abraham's ethical monotheism, that is, the derivation of social morality from the belief in a single Creator and a rejection of the widespread practice of human sacrifice, which the rest of the world continued to tolerate for a long time. This lonely revelation in the midst of universal idolatry was the beginning of a religious tradition carried on by Christianity and Islam, and destined to conquer heathenism. It contrasted dramatically with the pagan fear of unknown powers, of which human sacrifice was a dismal expression.

After the establishment of the Abrahamitic and patriarchal tradition in the twelve tribes, Moses the Lawgiver appeared. His protest against the Pharaohs' despotism, his liberation of an enslaved people, proclaiming the right to freedom for all people, and the giving of the Ten Commandments as a basis for social organization led to a new way of thinking, unprecedented in ancient times. It represented a revolutionary attitude toward human rights and duties, perpetuated by Christianity. Its humanistic standards were much more sweeping than those formulated by Greek philosophy, which ignored the enslaved masses.

Judaism continued to participate in all the developments in the history of ideas, and consequently in the formation of succeeding *zeitgeists*.

As Leo Baeck says in his famous *Essence of Judaism:* "It proves the creative force of the Jewish genius, how many cultural elements of foreign origin it could, during its long history, adopt and adapt to its own tradition. . . . Judaism always maintained its own character when assimilating outside ideas.''

This happened during the Babylonian captivity, and when prophetic doctrine changed to rabbinical, Talmudic Judaism. It was also true during the Judeo-Arabic Golden Age of Spain, and later when Jews were the initiators of modern socialism and our contemporary concepts of the universe—the outer one of space and the inner one of the mind—through pioneers such as Einstein and Freud. It is obvious that the Jews' relationship to the progressive manifestations of the *zeitgeist* is a thoroughly positive one of creative cooperation.

At times, however, Judaism adopted a conservative role. It had to resist new movements and their enticements in order to defend the eternal values of religion. In its embattled position, it has had to stand alone since time immemorial. The Old Testament is the epic story of spiritual resistance to false gods in every form. Even after the canonization of the Holy Scriptures about 150 B.C., the situation had not changed much. Seductive Hellenism had become a world force in the wake of Alexander's conquests. He himself was magnanimous and tolerant. But the frivolous materialism of Epicurus spread among his successors. It was opposed to the ethical teachings of Judaism as well as of Christianity and tried to destroy them. The struggle and martyrdom of a heroic minority (the Maccabees) fully conscious of its own tradition were the only resistance to the prevailing Hellenistic *zeitgeist,* enthusiastically adopted by the whole Eurasian world. Admittedly, even among the Jews there were blind disciples of Epicurean Neo-atheism, but the core of the people rejected the worldwide *zeitgeist.* They regained possession of the desecrated temple, this symbol of faithfulness to their unique creed.

Without this apparently absurd resistance by a people whom the Bible calls "stiff-necked," without this stubborn self-assertion, there would be no Christianity, for the preservation of the Old Testament made the New Testament possible.

However, adamant opposition to Greek thought was not characteristic of Judaism. In neighboring Egypt, the Jewish Platonist Philo of Alexandria sought and found a bridge to classical Greek philosophy, a bridge between the prophets and the world of Platonic ideas. A millennium later, the Aristotelian Moses Maimonides took on the task of introducing his Greek teacher into the Judaic tradition. Judaism reacts negatively only when foreign ideas threaten to debase its concepts.

Two hundred years after the Maccabees, the Apostles, also unbending Jews, spread the biblical doctrine of faith, love, and messianic hope in a cruel empire of violent and bloodthirsty masses. They were triumphant beyond belief and in some measure vindicated the Maccabees.

To be sure, in spite of its spiritual kinship with Christianity, Judaism separated itself from its first-born, divorcing itself from Christian Rome just as it had once done from the heathens. While recognizing Christianity's redemptive message to the pagans, it held fast to its own doctrine of an all-encompassing justice in the messianic future; of a kingdom of God that can be attained, not through the undeserved grace of a Heavenly Redeemer, but only through the redemptive act of every worshipper. Judaism also teaches salvation through grace, but only as God's response to the human struggle for redemption and happiness.

This historical sketch should make it clear that our religion for thousands of years has not hesitated to take a position on the *zeitgeist* in its various manifestations. And that will continue to be the case, since the thirst for knowledge is unquenchable and continually evokes new problems.

Since Adam tasted of the tree of knowledge, and even forfeited a life of undisturbed bliss as a consequence, man has been filled with a creative, but often destructive restlessness, which can make him the most sublime or the most gruesome of God's creations. Religion's mission is to come to grips with the continually changing expressions of the times, to create order, to purify man's drive for knowledge in a critical but not negative spirit. What a crucial task in the turbulent twentieth century! Experiences and discoveries of every kind tumble over each other, upsetting the equilibrium of modern man. What would happen in such a storm-tossed universe if nothing stood firm, if all the ethical values so doggedly gained and preserved through the ages were suddenly abandoned so they would not seem old-fashioned? Shall all past socioethical knowledge now be jettisoned as so much useless ballast? Goethe warned:

> Wer in schwankender Zeit schwankend gesinnt ist,
> Der vermehret das Übel und breitet es weiter und weiter.

> He who in unsteady times is also unsteady
> Only increases the malady and spreads it further.

The mass psychoses we have witnessed in this century could make out of the earth a vast insane asylum if every expression of the *zeitgeist* received approval. First there was an explosion of exacerbated nationalism within and outside German borders, which led to the internecine slaughter of Christians, these same Christians who had for centuries taught the biblical admonition: "Love thy neighbor," and even the more emphatic exhortation: "Love thine enemy." If the First World War betrayed the Ten Commandments, then the Second World War totally repudiated them, as German citizens substituted an idol for God under the indifferent gaze of the rest of the world. The Führer cult was a mockery of the First Commandment, the abrogation of all the other ones, and was generally evil, as in every dictatorship, where one man is the measure of all things.

Every year Judaism continues to celebrate the revelation on Mount Sinai, the commitment to the Ten Commandments, which begin with the admonition: "I alone am your God, you shall worship no others!" All the misfortunes and abuses of public life have come from the neglect of this commandment. The Ten Commandments are not only the statutes of the Jewish people; they are also the Magna Carta of civilization.

The currently raging sex inferno, fanned into flames in the Hitler youth movement and since then increasingly uncontrolled, is another manifestation of the *zeitgeist*. It has taken on fantastic proportions, as if it were the only gate to eternal bliss. This criticism is not meant as a Puritanical condemnation of private sensual pleasures. But Freud's discoveries, so important for guidance in sexual matters, led to a pansexualism in the masses, to a rejection of all inhibitions, as if decency were only an ancient taboo. As a consequence of the commercial exploitation of the *zeitgeist* now in vogue, the "naked" truth is the only truth.

But the Old Testament demands: "Thou shalt not commit adultery!", and warns why not, with reference to unnatural unions and sexual perversions:

> so that the land will not spew you out, as it has spewn out the Canaanites because of such atrocities.
>
> (Leviticus 20)

I would like to return to Nazi Germany as another example of the terrible excesses that the *zeitgeist* might engender. It is bad enough when a nation launches open warfare against another, except in self-defense or when its legitimate interests are being threatened. But the situation that arose in the Nazi period was infinitely worse, the most terrible perversion of this century. Laws were created declaring the cold-blooded murder of defenseless people a national duty. Enough minions were found to carry out this infamy. Worse, eminent judges, baptized Christians all, rendered judgments that heaped contumely on every traditional concept of justice. Even today many judges in the Federal Republic accept the argument of national emergency as extenuating circumstances for these horrible crimes. Physicians were similarly guilty of accepting Nazi racist propaganda after taking the Hippocratic Oath.

Thus many millions were tortured and killed, one million of them children. Everyone claimed to have carried out orders and was therefore not responsible, since he was duty-bound to obey under penalty of death. It is true that many men of the cloth refused to comply and traveled the bitter road to martyrdom. Their actions are a shining page in the annals of Christianity. Unfortunately, no guidelines were issued by the ecclesiastical authorities to disturb the conscience of the upper military and intellectual circles.

We must consider the question as to whether the Church, relying on the Sermon on the Mount, did not content itself with accepting the Ten Commandments only in a general sense, as merely a part of the Old Testament, without appropriately stressing their central significance.

Rabbinical Judaism, continuing the inherent thought of the Ten Commandments, teaches that in times of emergency one may, to save his life, transgress all religious laws, since *Pikuach Nefesch* (mortal danger) cancels all commandments and prohibitions except three. These are the summary of the Ten Commandments, namely, blasphemy, lechery, and murder. Such deeds are prohibited even in spite of orders from above. *Jehareg welo jaawor.* One should submit to execution rather than transgress these fundamental moral precepts.

The Old Testament has fulfilled its role by giving clear ethical norms, here in Talmudic elucidations. It is the churches' mission to build dams, to swim against the current if necessary, to defend its own traditional values against the *zeitgeist,* in other words, to state it clearly: "so far and no farther!" They must stand like lighthouses in the maelstrom of social and ideological change.

Similar situations might be repeated in future conflicts. This, however, does not imply that we must greet every manifestation of the *zeitgeist* with suspicion. Even in the worldwide revolt of youth, for instance, there is hope despite regrettable excesses. This revolt signifies disengagement from a generation that has achieved miraculous technological advances but has suffered moral shipwreck, a prosperous generation steering all the accomplishments of the human spirit toward a dangerous future.

"Overcoming the past" would be an empty phrase if it did not mean learning from past mistakes in order to avoid them in the future. Happy the people who commit not merely the glamorous chapters of their history to memory! Pascal characterized the Old Testament as a document of divine truth because it portrays the offenses and oversights along with the accomplishments of the Children of Israel.

It is not Germany alone who must overcome a painful past, but all nations who have yielded to violence without the justification of self-defense. An international armament boom is already changing the world into a gigantic powder keg. The search for the good life resembles the arrogance of Sodom and Gomorrah before their destruction. The race to the stars resembles the building of the Tower of Babel, when power-hungry men tried to storm heaven. Billions are squandered on space research and armaments instead of meeting the needs of the hungry with the surpluses of an unprecedented prosperity.

Thus youth rebels, out of contradictory motives to be sure, but in the final analysis against a repetition of the past and against a complacent society without ideals. The fact that they fall prey to a false god, a Ché or a Mao, is one of the pitfalls of a directionless age.

This radical generational conflict is not new. Consider Goethe's bit of wisdom spoken by the overconfident Baccalaureus in the second part of Faust:

> Das Alter ist ein kaltes Fieber,
> Im Frost von grillenhafter Not;
> Hat einer dreissig Jahr vorüber,
> So ist er schon so gut wie tot.
>
> Am besten wärs, euch zeitig totzuschlagen.
>
> Old age indeed is a cold fever spent
> In a capricious frost of discontent
> Once past the age of thirty, men
> Already are as good as dead;
>
> It would be best to shoot you then.
>           *(Faust,* 11. 6785-89; English by Charles E. Passage)

But Goethe did not settle for this "trust no one over thirty" attitude. He gives a vision of hope that may be valid today:

> In wenig Jahren wird es anders sein:
> Wenn sich der Most auch ganz absurd gebärdet,
> Es gibt zuletzt doch noch'n Wein.
>
> But we are in no danger from this fellow;
> In just a few years he will mellow;
> Let grape juice act as silly as it will,
> There is wine to be made from it still.
>           *(Faust,* 11. 6811-14; speaker, Mephistopheles)

My sincere wish is that the Church may be successful in filling its demanding youth with a new spirit. May I also mention that this revolutionary fever has bypassed one nation: Israel. Its youth is engaged in meeting an enormous challenge: rebuilding a devastated land, making room for future returnees from all over the globe, and protecting from destruction a people suffering six million dead.

Where youth has goals to accomplish, it finds fulfillment and is not bent on destruction. If you will permit a person of a different faith but who stands close to the Christian ethic to make this comment: I believe that the World Church should recognize in the revolt of the young, without condoning its destructive aspects, some promising aspirations. After all, the Church's founder, Jesus of Nazareth, was an agitator, and undermined the foundations of Roman military might.

And the Synagogue's task in the secular life of Israel, in the struggle against so many social and educational problems, should be to recognize the workings of God's spirit and teach the people to see it.

Those responsible for the composition of the Bible were to a great extent shepherds, farmers, and artisans who earned their bread by the sweat of their brow and earnestly sought to do right. The prophets set the religious emphasis, guiding the work and efforts of the people and condemning transgressions. The religious spirit is also at work in modern Israel's daily life in spite of secularization, desertion of houses of worship, and similar manifestations of the times. As long as the Bible remains the folk epic, the history book, the national reader of Israel, its people will be able to renew itself through this source of eternal values.

We thus return to our starting point, the question we are all asking: "Where did we come from?" Jews and Christians have their origins in the homeland of the Bible, in the region where Moses and the prophets, Jesus, and the Apostles performed their labors. A return to the Bible means for both a special kind of renewal, a better understanding of themselves and one another by respecting their biblical brethren. Christianity no longer needs Jewish pioneers. But if it does not need more Jews, it will gain in depth by accepting more Judaism. This concludes my modest contribution to this impressive event.

It would, however, be discourteous to our host city, Düsseldorf, if

I did not leave you with some words of a great son of this city, Heinrich Heine. He was neither a good Jew nor an exemplary Christian, but a great sinner in God's sight. Yet his whole life he fought with his own weapons on all the battlefields of progress and truth, and he fought without hope of victory. At the end of a tortured life he pondered his origins and recognized them as the source of his power. To be sure, he did not return to the Church's bosom, nor to Abraham's, but unreservedly to the Bible itself, which he simply called "the word of God." He makes a gripping confession, which may be a guide to many truth seekers who have deviated from the prescribed path.

In his last *Confessions* he reflects on Judaism, of which he had once said it was not a religion but a misfortune. He talks of his weakness for Hellenistic and pagan *joie de vivre,* which undermined his vitality. He refers to Judaism as the real source of his ideals, the cradle of his spirit, and in misfortune his only support. He continues:

> I did not see that Moses. . .was a great artist. . . .He did not create works of art like the Egyptians out of brick and granite, but he built human pyramids; he took a tribe of poor shepherds and made of them a great nation which was, like the pyramids, to defy the centuries, a great, eternal, holy people, a people of God.
> Neither have I spoken with sufficient report of the Jews, the work of art of this master craftsman. This is certainly due to my pagan disposition, always at odds with Jewish asceticism. But my Hellenism has diminished.
> I see now that the Greeks were just beautiful youths, but the Jews were always men, powerful, unyielding men, not just in the past, but to the present day, in spite of eighteen centuries of persecutions and misery. I have since then learned to appreciate them, and if pride of birth were not a contradiction of democratic principles, I could be proud that my ancestors belonged to the noble House of Israel; that I am a descendant of those martyrs who gave the world a God and a moral code and have suffered and fought on all the battlefields of thought.

Is not this return of the baptized Heine to his origins a message to Christians, who in search of self-understanding have assembled today to ask: "Where did we come from?"

# 18

## Conclusion

## The Election of Israel
## from a Jewish Point of View

The term *chosen people* belongs to the biblical vocabulary, and long ago it found its way into the language of various people. In this apparent claim of the Jewish faith to be exclusively valid, we seem to find the expression of a religious and national arrogance that stands in diametrical opposition to the universalism of the Catholic Church, for instance. The conception of a chosen people also seems to exclude the attitude that has rightly been considered the highest achievement of the Western world, namely, religious tolerance, the pillar of democratic society. Judaism, by calling attention to its privileged position in the Bible, apparently represents the principle of a religious-national particularism conflicting with the universalism of Western origin, which justifies the anger and mistrust of various people. Unfortunately, this deeply rooted mistrust belongs to the regrettable misunderstandings that have unnecessarily clouded the relationship of the Jewish people with the surrounding nations over such a long period of time, and have led to such tragic consequences.

For, in reality, Judaism contains a wealth of teachings and revelations that not only explain its historical significance as the mother religion of such universal confessions as Christianity and Islam, but also legitimize its continuation as a unique religion. These teachings are not theological abstractions of a tangential nature, but the central concern of the Jewish religion, though at times not even recognized even in its own camp.

One should examine the total life of the Jewish community as it was organized by rabbinical decrees, and look back to the time when rabbis were still able to make such decrees and were not demoted to obedient religious officials. The calendar of the religious year should also be examined as it attempts, with its festivals, rituals, prayers, and customs to form, lead, and educate the Jewish soul. The ideal that the teachers of Judaism had in mind in their educational effort then becomes clear. The lesson of the Jewish year, the liturgy of the holidays, is the repository of all the experiences undergone by Judaism in its endless wanderings, raised into the religious sphere and transformed into enduring values. The High Holy Days in particular, celebrated as a prelude to the religious year, express the most important teachings of Judaism, its deepest perceptions and highest revelations. In the middle of these days of reverence, the New Year and Day of Atonement, stands a prayer that belongs to the liturgy of the whole year but is given added solemnity at this time through special rituals and stirring music:

> Therefore we trust in Thee, Our Eternal God! That we may soon see the glory of Thy omnipotence, that Thou shalt remove idols from the earth, so that all sons of men may call upon Thy name, so that all the earth's inhabitants may see and realize that every knee must bend to Thee, every tongue must swear. They shall sink down before Thee, O Eternal One, and give praise to Thy name. All shall take upon themselves the yoke of Thy dominion, so that Thou shalt rule over them soon, forever and ever.

The belief in the rule of God over the earth, not just over the people of Israel, is central to other prayers, which express the yearning for the messianic era when all men shall be reconciled through one faith:

Let the fear of Thee, Our Eternal God, come over all Thy creatures and reverence before Thee over all that Thou hast created,
so that all Thy creatures shall hear Thee, and all beings shall bow
down before Thee so that *they shall become as one* to do Thy will
with their whole heart.

These prayers clearly show what the greatest concern of the Jewish
faith is: the uniting of the whole human race, not through forced rites
and customs, but with the retention of their own historical traditions
and dogmas, through a confession of the heart directed at the Creator
of the universe as the Father of all his creatures. Such universal
humanism is a basic dogma that pervades all stages of Jewish history. Around it are grouped the Mosaic commandments. It inspired
the prophets of Israel to their most exalted prophecies and the wise
men of the Talmud to their most fervent admonitions. Thus we see
why the Jewish New Year in all its other rituals continues those por-
tions of the Holy Scriptures which make the concept of the God-
ordained brotherhood of all mankind the starting point of the Bible,
in form and content. The Bible begins with the idea of one world
ruler, Creator of heaven and earth, and of one original man, Adam
*(homo)*, the one created out of the humus. The most authoritative interpreters of the Holy Scriptures, the scholars of the Talmud, emphatically point out the equal worth of all mankind. Adam is the father of all
men created in the image of God, not only of one race or class.
To him is given the first, basic revelation of the tree of knowledge,
that is, the differentiation between good and evil. This moral awareness, in contrast to man's impulsive vital drives, is the material from
which all subsequent religions are formed. Right at the beginning of
human history, with the first brothers, Cain and Abel, the essential
aspect of all religions comes to light, according to the Jewish view.
Although the very different brothers served God each in his own
way, biblically speaking, bringing him offerings of different nature,
their mutual responsibility remain undiminished: "Cain, where is thy
brother Abel?"

The schism running through subsequent world history has not then
arisen, according to the Bible, because of differences of expression
of belief, but from the rejection of loving responsibility for brothers

of a different nature or a different creed. This disastrous fratricide led to the first fall, until the Great Flood washed the contaminated earth clean of a decadent race of men. A new era began with Noah, the righteous, and his three sons, Shem, Ham, and Japheth. With him God made a new covenant, which was to extend to all his descendents and to all races. Only seven ethical commandments are to be observed in order to receive the blessings of the divine covenant. These are the laws of Noah, which according to rabbinical decree are to be applied to the non-Jewish races to assure them equality. They consist in acknowledgment of the principle of justice as the basis of society, in acknowledgment of a Supreme Being, in rejecting idols, and in forbidding murder, stealing, incest, and brutality to animals. The observers of Noah's laws are recognized as righteous, to whom salvation is promised on a par with the righteous of Israel with their 613 commandments and prohibitions.

Thus, human history from Adam to Noah, which introduces the Old Testament, embodies the philosophical basis of Judaism as it is impressed upon the soul of the people during the High Holy Days. For this reason Noah, his descendents, and the "Covenant of the Rainbow" are dramatically commemorated through prayers and the sound of trumpets, and the blessing is pronounced for them. For the same reason, the story of the Prophet Jonah is a high point in the ceremony of Yom Kippur, the Day of Atonement. There it is told how Jonah only reluctantly followed his divine calling, which consisted in preaching repentance to the foreign city of Nineveh, and how he returned as soon as possible to the shade of his tree to meditate. When he complained about the wilting of his tree, God said to him: "You complain about the tree and I should not complain about Nineveh?" For the concern of Judaism is the well-being of all people—not only in its biblical phase, but in its postbiblical phase as well.

This scriptural humanism was subsequently adopted and lovingly transformed by Jewish theology and religious philosophy of all shades, by Philo, Maimonides, Hermann Cohen, and Martin Buber. Philo, the Jewish Platonist, great both as a philosopher and as an exegete of the Scriptures, explains the meaning of Judaism to his coreligionists in Alexandria in this manner: "The priests of the heathen are in the habit of bringing offerings and prayers only for their relatives, friends, and fellow citizens. The Jewish high priest, on the other hand, says his prayers of supplication and thanksgiving not only for all mankind, but even for the components of nature: earth, air, fire, and water."

A thousand years after Philo, Maimonides, the greatest religious philosopher and teacher of the Law in postbiblical history, attempted to explain the relationship of Judaism to its milieu, to be a guide to the Jews of the Diaspora in their dealings with Christian or Moslem neighbors. In one of his open letters he warns: "With respect to your question about races, know that God demands the heart, that things are to be judged according to the disposition of the heart, and therefore our wise teachers say: 'The righteous among the people will have a share in the hereafter if they have a sincere awareness of God and live virtuous lives" *(Iggarot, Letters with Halakhic decisions)*. In this Maimonidic candor Hermann Cohen sees the secret of the fruitful cooperation of Judeo-Arabic and scholastic religious philosophy.

Martin Buber's interpretation of the Prophet's words: "Open the gates, that the righteous nation which keeps faith may enter," also stems from this point of view. It is not stated that only Israelite may enter, but that a *goy zaddik* (virtuous gentile) may enter also. The gates of Heaven are open for all. The Christian does not need to go through Judaism, nor the Jew through Christianity to come to God. Such a fundamental tolerance in all Jewish writings immediately clears up the question of the absence of missionary impulse in Judaism. The would-be convert should be turned away three times before acceding to his petition and accepting him into the covenant of Abraham. But this coolness does not grow out of conceit (as even many Jews, in their ignorance of the Law, believe), but out of tolerance in the best sense of the word, namely, out of the ability to honor and respect a different belief while loving one's own.

The great thinkers of Israel, therefore, strive for a historical understanding of the phenomena of Christianity and of Islam, since they conceive these religions to be pioneers of ethical monotheism. The man who has worked out this thought most unequivocally is Moses Maimonides, who writes in his now classic compendium of the religious laws laid down in the Talmud (Mishna Torah, Hilchot Melachim, chap. 2): ". . .God's ways are not ours, and his purposes are different from ours. Thus it happened that the first (Christian) as well as the later (Islamic) religious founders contributed to paving the way for the real Messiah, who shall found a single creed for all people. Indeed, in the meantime, thanks to these religions the whole world has become full of the thought of the Messianic Redeemer and the spirit of the teachings and commandments."

The Jewish religion is strict in formulating its own dogmas about God, but lenient in judging the faithful of the daughter-religions. The reason that the attitude limits itself historically to Christianity and Islam lies in the fact that Judaism never came in contact with the Hindu or Chinese civilizations.

It seems appropriate to study the links and divergent elements of the two religions to which Judaism is so closely related.

Judaism realizes that it shares with its daughter-religions the rejection of idolatry and heathenism, including its modern version, materialistic morality. With Christianity it has in addition all the essential prayers in common, the Psalms of David for instance, and Biblical ethics with its doctrine of reward and punishment, faith in God, love of one's fellow men, and belief in an afterlife. A Christianity without Judaism would be, as Leo Baeck said in one of his last speeches "rootless and without basis." A Judaism without Christianity would mean giving up its God-ordained message to all people. Therefore Christianity has, as Maimonides indicated, a historical mission that justifies its existence in the eye of the mother-religion.

While there exist essential contrasts of a dogmatic kind between the two religions just examined, they are small compared to the differences between Judaism and Islam, which goes much further than Christianity in the defense of an abstract monotheism. It sets up the postulate, unacceptable to Judaism, of Mohammed as the personification of highest prophecy. But just as Christianity has civilized the heathen Occident, Islam has raised the standard of culture in Africa and the Middle East.

Judaism fully appreciates the cultural accomplishments of its daughter-religions, an appreciation that is hardly reciprocated. Daughters, in the flush of their youthful strength and beauty, are often thoughtless toward their old mother. The mother, however, never stops boasting about her children, who, in spite of their differences, are nevertheless her flesh and spirit, and carry on her teachings.

But, if Judaism acknowledges so thoroughly the intellectual values of other religions, and recognizes itself in them, why then has it from time immemorial surrounded itself with such a thick barrier, and lived in a splendid isolation which can easily be interpreted as aristocratic conceit or petrification? Even though the refusal to proselytize is ideologically founded, as has been shown, there nevertheless exist many consecrated expressions that seem to indicate a claim to superiority and exclusiveness. Does it not say in these same New Year's prayers: "Thou hast chosen us from all other people?" Does not Moses promise the twelve tribes: "You shall become a kingdom of priests, a holy people"? Does there not lie in such words, combined with ritual laws aimed at a biological separation from the outside world, the clear belief in a privileged position in God's scheme? And does this not contradict the prophets' emphatic message of universal salvation?

In reality, there is no conflict between nationalism and humanism. The two ideas complement and enrich each other. The Jewish religion is indeed closely bound to the belief in a chosen people, but the election of Israel, far from being a privilege, was the heaviest burden a people ever took upon itself. The formation of the Jewish religion goes hand in hand with the stubborn will of the tribe, wherever it may be, to incarnate the faith in universal salvation in its purest form, to protect it from all ambiguity, to become its uncompromising bearer, to separate itself, not for its own sake, but for the sake of all people.

This ideal developed also out of the early history of Judaism. It emerged first from the deeds of the patriarchs and is the logical complement to the antedeluvian history of man from Adam to Noah, which I interpreted as the teaching of human brotherhood. The Covenant of the Rainbow made with Noah, father of races, is in no way abolished by the new covenant of Abraham, which distinguished the Jew through circumcision. The figure of the first patriarch means rather the historical beginning of the transformation of the Noachian ideal into reality by a devoted priesthood. Therefore Abraham, who seized God's standard after Noah's sons and their descendants relapsed into depravity, became a "father of nations," and the progenitor of a race to which he entrusted his majestic legacy. "Through thee shall all families on the earth be blessed," is what the revelations tell him. But from its inception to its fulfillment, the path is long and arduous, and to keep the goal from disappearing from the conscience of his descendants, it is impressed upon each generation. Those who are unworthy are refused their separateness. Not Ishmael, but Isaac is the appointed bearer of the testament, although they are both children of the patriarch. The principle is laid down here for all time that in Judaism racial origin shall be no privilege. Not blood and soil, but spirit and heart shall determine membership in Judaism. Whoever is a traitor to this spirit through national or social pride is not considered a descendant of Abraham, Isaac, and Jacob. This thought is prefigured and symbolized not only in Ishmael and Isaac, but also in the twins Jacob and Esau. Not Esau, the first-born, but Jacob, who wrestled with and conquered his demon, is given the name of Israel ("fighter for God") and the spiritual inheritance. His children recite to him on his deathbed the solemn credo that, through auto-da-fés and gas chambers, was to become a battle-cry through the ages: "Hear, O Israel, the Eternal, our God, is one!" Moses, the Lawgiver, undertakes to anchor this solemn cry in the Law, to transform enthusiasm into deeds, to educate a people of priests and prophets, and to call them to lead mankind to the knowledge of God.

Thus Israel chose its God and its fate. It became a "chosen people," the first-born of God, the historical first herald of monotheism, alone through almost two thousand years in a desert of heathen immorality. But even in this enforced isolation for the sake of its mission, it retained the eldest son's awareness of his duty to set an unswerving example for his brothers. The Torah itself, the national book of laws that welded the twelve tribes into a people, is at the same time the most universal book of mankind. Again and again, attention is drawn to the fact that the Torah belongs to all people. "Not for the sake of your greatness have I chosen you, for you are the smallest of all people. Which people is great? A people that has wise, just laws such as those which this book contains." In this manner Moses admonishes Israel before his departure. And the rabbinical commentators refer constantly to the fact that the Torah was revealed in the desert, that is, a neutral land, a place that belongs to no one. "If the Torah had been given in the land of Israel, this would have indicated to the heathen that they had no part in it. Therefore it was given on neutral land, and whoever accepts it may come and take it" (Mechilta to 2nd Moses 19).

Therefore, propitiatory offerings were made in the Temple of Solomon for the seventy peoples of the earth. The prophets spoke to other nations also, and recognized in their history the hand of the Creator. Thus they prophesied the conversion of all idol worshipers. "The Eternal shall be King over the whole earth. In that day shall the Eternal be One and His Name One." This utterance by the Prophet Zechariah, which even today closes the daily prayer, expresses the great messianic hope of the Jewish people, a hope that extends to all men and strives for no privilege or preferences for Israel. Its only distinction consists in the historical accomplishment of having first recognized the true God, and of having lived as a witness to all people, true to Abraham's promise: "Through thee shall the families of the earth be blessed." Faithfulness to one's religion is not, therefore, to lead to a moral ghetto, but is to become the root of all humanitarian virtues.

In this sense the eloquent vision of the Prophet Isaiah is another fruit of the tree of Judaism, the vision of the ultimate brotherhood of mankind and its communion in a great family of nations.

> In the days to come. . .peoples without number will come to it (the Temple of God); and they will say: "Come, let us go up to the Temple of the God of Jacob that he may teach us his ways so that we may walk in his paths; since the Laws will go out from Zion and the oracle of God from Jerusalem."
> He will wield authority over the nations and adjudicate between

many nations; these will hammer their swords into ploughshares, their spears into sickles. There will be no more training for war.

This prophecy of Isaiah remains to the present the great certainty of the Jewish faith. Even in its most modern aspects Judaism cannot stray from its messianic mission if it does not want to become untrue to itself. The most recent episode in the Jewish existential drive, the return to Zion, far from contradicting the ideal of human brotherhood in the spirit of the Bible, is a step in its direction. Zion must again become a place from which the word of God issues. The political emancipation that culminated in the formation of the state of Israel does not mean Israel's isolation from the world. It means facing up to the moral duty of setting an example of freedom on its own soil, of taking part in unfettered intellectual activities, of attacking the creeping poison of material saturation. It means resisting social and political selfishness, moral cowardliness, indifference to a persecuted neighbor, disguised as pacifism. The nominal love of freedom and misguided moderation is denounced by the Prophet Jeremiah when he indignantly cries out: "They speak of freedom where there is no freedom!"

Thus we see ourselves transported to the arena of our own responsibility. For God, to quote Goethe, has "in no way gone to rest after the six days of creation, but is still as active as on the first day." This applies also to the warnings of the prophets, these builders of Judaism's ethical imperatives. Thus the antinomy between universalism and election is not simply a theological consideration. The prophets of Israel were not theologians. They saw life in all its manifestations. Religion is an effective force only when it sharpens the conscience and strengthens our sense of responsibility for all things to which we are witnesses.

A key role in this responsibility lies with the men of science, who literally hold the fate of mankind in their hands. The myth of the tree of knowledge and the tree of life has taken on a new, frightening actuality. The election of Israel, in our sense of a heightened, tragic commitment, has found expression nowadays in the attitude of the leading Jewish intellectuals, of an Einstein or an Oppenheimer, who set themselves against the chauvinistic "atomic psychosis," and accepted opprobrium for their unpatriotic ways of thinking because their conscience was plagued by concern about the future of the human race. But were not the prophets also accused of defeatism and treason against their people because they placed the brotherhood of man not in a vacuum but in a concrete political situation fraught with tragic decisions? Today as well, religion dares not be just an abstract confession of faith, but must commit itself where decisions that affect our future are being made. What had been for two thousand years the religious practices of the ghetto must now face the storms of life. Judaism must take a position on all human questions, drawing strength from the religious and national renaissance in Israel.

The whole plight of mankind concerns us. We must respond to it, if not through immediate action, then by a continuous revival, reorientation, and expression of our Jewish conscience. For Judaism is commitment, *engagement* in the existentialistic sense. Prophetic literature achieved its world reputation not by cautious opportunism, but by its uncompromising involvement on the battlefields of the mind.

In this highest sense Judaism is found in all the people of the earth, insofar as they utilize the same dynamic biblical ethic. The Christian nations have indeed spoken of themselves symbolically as "the new people of Israel," which says nothing more than that they consider themselves the heirs of the biblical legacy. All nations are "chosen" if their self-imposed moral goal is lofty and humane enough. Judaism does not begrudge them their claim in any way, since it signifies not the disinheritance of the historical bearer of the biblical revelation, but a broadening of the field of moral responsibility (or, in Bergson's terminology, a transformation of "private tribal ethics" into a worldwide responsibility of the elite of all people).

A political expression of this moral attitude came to light in the Oppenheimer trial, when the director of the Carnegie Institute, Dr. Busch, set himself against the tendency to create an "official science," where a narrow-minded administration measures a scholar's research and directs it. Such a development was to him not only against the spirit of democracy and an insult to free research, but paradoxically undermined its very purpose and actually harmed the nation. And Dr. Busch put Oppenheimer's attitude in the following words: "Do you know why Hitler's technology failed? First, because Hitler drove out the Jewish intellectuals. Secondly, because he replaced them with compliant workers who obeyed only political commands instead of their own initiative. Science and technology conscious of their responsibility imply free research, the exact antithesis of state control."

But the responsibility for the dignity and freedom of mankind does not rest only on the shoulders of the luminaries of science. To delegate it to them would be as cowardly as it is convenient. It is the way of the amorphous masses. Wherever men have been appointed to lead or teach even a small circle of their fellow men, as politicians, priests, physicians, or intellectuals, they are confronted by the alternatives of comfortable timidity and painful integrity, between the gilded cage and freedom, elusive and difficult. In all circumstances, not only in international politics or momentous scientific decisions but also in our professional spheres of activity, there are delicate situations where the dignity of man is at stake. The Oppenheimer and the Dreyfus cases are not unique. There are also affairs of more modest scope that equal them in substance and in moral importance. Every land, people, segment of society, and community of any kind must continually be alert, continually willing to defend its values, continually striving to keep its own camp clean. Thus in Judaism too, however strong its allegiance to ethical principles, there is a struggle between the spirit and materialism.

Even such a warm friend of the Jews as the poet Charles Péguy, who called the Dreyfus Affair a "divine affair" because it gave the powers of good the opportunity to fight the powers of bigotry and to conquer them, speaks openly of the two powers warring against each other in Judaism: "The mysticism of Israel and the politics of Israel." By that he does not mean the modern state of Israel—although politics are certainly born of mysticism—but rather the contrast between the representatives of the great intellectual tradition of Israel and those who want to make of the Jewish communities an instrument of politics, a springboard for recognition, the theater of their passions.

In all areas the spirit of Judaism has had to fight against such all too human tendencies, and to stand fast, often against great odds. An ethical principle remains in operation, which is, in simple terms: no one is a good Jew who disdains the laws and customs of the host country. No one is a good citizen who violates the ethics of the Jewish religion. That is the tacit code of honor of Judaism in the Diaspora, and those who live according to it and want to impress it upon the masses are the true representatives of Judaism, even though the others control the offical apparatus. Judaism signifies exactly this: the struggle between spirit and power, in which power wins many battles, but the spirit emerges victorious in the end. The name *Israel* (God's fighter) is a hint of this fateful struggle, not only against heathen antiquity, but also within its own ranks. Jacob, the progenitor, who came forth limping but victorious from wrestling with the angel, is the archetype of all the prophets and preachers, rabbis and spiritual leaders who were able to oppose usurpers, and their mercenaries and henchmen, with their words and their faith alone. Their idealism prevailed, even though the law of power was temporarily triumphant.

Nowadays, in the beginning of the atomic age, unbounded materialism is seeking to put its stamp on all forms of human existence. In an epoch where the discovery of unheard-of riches is threatening to lead only to the stronger enslavement of the human spirit, it is time for men of good will of all camps to clasp hands. Mankind finds itself once more before the Tree of Knowledge and the Tree of Life. This confrontation could lead again to a great flood, to the destruction of all life through the misdirection and ruthless exploitation of scientific knowledge. Only when science becomes conscience, when power becomes humanity, when dogma becomes kindness will the disaster be avoided.

The knowledge gained from Jewish history in general and from individual experience in particular justifies faith in the future of mankind in spite of inevitable crises. God is walking the Garden of Eden and calling to us: "Adam, where art thou?" The call goes out to us all, Jews, gentiles, children of God from all nations, and each is chosen according to the scope of his ethical commitment.

# Index